Brothers in Blue

The Cardwell Men Who Fought for the Union

Rand Cardwell

This book series is dedicated to my son.

Corporal William T. Cardwell (1986-2020) - *Scout/Sniper, 1st Battalion, 2nd Marine Regiment, 2nd Marine Division ▪ Combat Veteran of Persian Gulf, Afghanistan, and Iraq*

Contents

Brothers in Blue: The Cardwell Men Who Fought for the Union

First Edition

Copyright © 2025 by Rand Cardwell

First published: October 2025

Imprint: Published by Rand Cardwell

Editing: Bhavana Patel

Cover Design: B-RAD, LLC

Photographs and images: Sourced from family archives, Ancestry.com, FindAGrave.com, and public records. Some images edited and enhanced by the author.

ISBN: 979-8-9933293-2-1 (paperback)

Preface

This two-volume set is the culmination of over four decades of research into the Cardwell family of America. As a young man, I was always fascinated by history, which led me to begin investigating my own genealogy. Back in the 1980s, the internet didn't exist, and if you wanted to discover anything about your ancestry, it required spending long hours at local archives. I vividly recall sitting at microfilm readers, scrolling through endless reels, spending hard-earned dollars making copies, and anxiously awaiting brown envelopes—hopefully stuffed with answers—from the National Archives.

I was fortunate to receive guidance from some of the best researchers of the Cardwell surname. From my earliest correspondence, one lesson was drilled into me: **Document! Document! Document!** Thinking back on those days brings many fond memories of sharing discoveries with my mentors as we collectively attempted to piece together the story of this remarkable family.

One of those mentors was the late Helen E. Hart Peyton, author of *Some Early Pioneers of Western Kentucky*. In the late 1990s, she invited me to visit her in Charleston, South Carolina. Helen was battling cancer at the time, but we sat for hours going over her files. She gifted me several boxes of her research—material far beyond the scope of her published work—including three notebooks of correspondence dating back to the 1960s. It was a treasure trove of family histories. Some of the material contained incorrect assumptions, as we now know, but it provided a valuable foundation. Before I left, she acknowledged that her time was limited and asked me to do my best to "figure it all out." I've carried that promise with me ever since and hope she would be pleased with what has come of it.

The past two decades have brought an explosion in the availability of records online. What once took weeks to obtain from the National Archives can now be found with a few keystrokes. This digital revolution has transformed family history research in ways that earlier generations could scarcely imagine. But it has also introduced new problems. Websites like Ancestry.com provide access to millions of records, yet many users haven't learned the discipline of verifying facts or distinguishing between individuals with common names—especially when researching among the many Jameses, Johns, Thomases, and Williams. Erroneous information gets posted, then repeated by others, and the cycle continues.

This issue is compounded when early written sources, often published with good intentions, are treated as infallible. Some of these works presented assumptions as fact. I cringe when I see them cited uncritically today. My hope is that this work will stand the test of time through its careful sourcing, documentation, and dedication to accuracy.

In 2004, I launched the Cardwell Family DNA Project and served as its administrator for many years. The use of DNA in genealogy has been a game-changer, offering definitive proof in many cases. As of this writing, we have identified **four distinct genetic lines** within the Cardwell family in America. While we all share a common ancestor about 600 years ago, slight genetic mutations allow us to track specific lineages. Y-DNA, which is passed from father to son, creates a direct and reliable line for analysis.

At the end of each biography in these volumes, you will find a note identifying the individual's predicted or confirmed genetic line (e.g., *Cardwell Line I – Predicted*). A "confirmed" designation indicates that a living male descendant has tested and matches others within that line. A "predicted" designation means that the individual has been genealogically connected to a confirmed line, though no descendant has yet tested.

In the course of this research, I also encountered individuals whose paper trail did not align with their genetic profile. Through traditional documentation and DNA testing, we have identified several **Non-Paternal Events (NPEs)**—cases where a man carried the Cardwell surname but did not match any of the known genetic lines. Often, these are instances where a child was born out of wedlock and raised by a Cardwell mother, inheriting the surname but not the Y-DNA. While cataloging all of these events is beyond the scope of this series, several of the veterans included here are NPEs. They and their descendants still carry the Cardwell name, and they are rightfully part of this history.

The Cardwell Family DNA Project is hosted by FamilyTreeDNA.com, which offers detailed Y-DNA marker testing essential for identifying genetic lineage matches. Unfortunately, other commercial DNA services do not provide the specific marker data we need for inclusion in the project. I'm occasionally contacted by people who've tested with those companies, but their results cannot be compared or grouped with ours. I hope that future descendants will understand the importance of this research and choose FamilyTreeDNA when testing.

One of the most disheartening things I've come across in old correspondence is the mention of ancestor photographs—images that once existed but can no longer be found. Often, the researcher has passed away, and surviving family members have discarded their files. A painful example involves a series of letters from descendants of Anderson Huffman Cardwell, a sergeant in the 5th Missouri State Militia Cavalry (Union). In those letters, they describe a photograph of Anderson in uniform. But after the researcher's passing, the photograph and supporting documents appear to have been lost. It's a common tragedy—too often, people don't realize the historical value of what they possess until it's gone.

That's why I urge everyone with old family photographs to make digital copies and share them widely with other descendants and researchers. We cannot assume that what we have today will survive tomorrow. Every shared image is a preserved piece of our collective history.

Sadly, there are also individuals who possess heirloom photographs but refuse to share them with others. Please consider this: while you may be the fortunate caretaker of an image passed down through generations, there are dozens—perhaps hundreds—of other descendants who would treasure that same photo. Hoarding such items only deprives others of their history. If you have old family photos, **please share them**.

I fully admit to being a family history nerd. This work is the product of forty years of effort, made in the margins of life. My goal has always been to create a lasting and reliable resource for present and future researchers. If you've found value in these pages, then the effort has been worth it.

I can be reached at **cardwellhistory@yahoo.com**.

—Rand Cardwell

Introduction

A LEGACY OF SERVICE: CARDWELL MEN IN THE UNION ARMY

The men documented in this volume represent a vital part of American history: those who fought for the preservation of the United States during the Civil War. The Cardwell soldiers who served in the Union Army stood in defense of national unity at a time when the country faced its gravest internal threat. Their service was shaped by a range of motivations—patriotism, duty, opportunity, or circumstance—but all shared in the hardship and sacrifice of war. This book offers a comprehensive record of their lives and service, structured to serve both researchers and descendants seeking to understand their family's place in the national narrative.

This volume organizes each Union Cardwell veteran by the state from which he served. Within these chapters, individual biographies include their military service, pre- and postwar lives, and—where available—photographs that put faces to their names. The accompanying alphabetical index allows readers to quickly locate specific individuals. The Union Cardwells came from diverse states such as Illinois, Indiana, Kentucky, Missouri, Ohio, Pennsylvania, Tennessee, and even parts of Virginia. Some were early volunteers; others were conscripted. Some served on the front lines at battles like Antietam and Gettysburg; others guarded railways, managed logistics, or labored in support roles critical to Union victory.

The story of these men is also inseparable from the broader geographic and political complexities of the era. Border states like Kentucky, Missouri, and Tennessee saw deeply divided loyalties. Families were split, and communities fractured. In such regions, the decision to fight for the Union was not merely ideological—it was often personal, and dangerous. These dynamics shaped the lives and fates of many Cardwell men.

Documenting Service and Analyzing Legacy

Unlike Confederate records, which were often incomplete or destroyed, Union military documentation was more thoroughly preserved. This allowed for detailed reconstructions of many soldiers' lives using a mix of official service and pension records, census data, and oral traditions. Some challenges remain—misspellings, inconsistencies, and missing files—but every reasonable effort has been made to verify the identity and service of each Cardwell man included in this book.

Beyond the biographies, readers will find an **Appendix** that includes four important statistical analyses. The first two, *Union and Confederate Cardwell Combat Outcomes*, provide a breakdown of how these men fared in terms of battlefield wounds, deaths from disease, imprisonment, and other wartime experiences. The second, *Branch and Unit Service Comparison*, charts the number of Cardwell men who served in infantry, cavalry, and artillery units, offering insight into enlistment patterns and battlefield exposure. Both analyses serve as a quantitative complement to the individual stories presented throughout the volume. Additionally, it shows an interesting trend for all the Cardwell men in their choice of service that is outside the norm of overall statistics for that conflict.

Also included in the Appendix are **brief histories of both Union and Confederate prisoner-of-war camps**, shedding light on the conditions faced by captured Cardwell soldiers. The section outlines the harsh realities of both Union and Confederate prisoner of war camps, where overcrowding, disease, and lack of resources often led to suffering and death—conditions tragically exemplified by notorious sites such as Andersonville and Elmira.

Battle Case Studies: The Cardwells in Action

To offer a closer look at how these men experienced some of the Civil War's most important engagements, a dedicated section titled *Battle Case*

Studies presents focused narratives on five major battles where Cardwell men were present: **Shiloh, Stones River, Chickamauga, the Wilderness, and Morgan's Raid**. Each case study explores the specific units involved, the strategic context of the engagement, and how individual Cardwells participated. These accounts bring history alive by combining regimental movements with personal stories, illuminating the dangers these men faced and the roles they played in shaping critical moments of the war.

The Cardwell Union Experience

Whether they enlisted from patriotic fervor or were drafted later in the war, the Union Cardwells joined an army facing long marches, poor rations, and ever-present disease. Letters from the front were rare among surviving materials, but where available, oral family traditions have filled some gaps, preserving memories passed down through generations. In camp and in battle, these men forged bonds with comrades and endured the brutality of 19th-century warfare—from massed infantry charges to primitive field medicine. Some came home changed but resilient; others never returned.

In capturing their stories, this volume does not seek to glorify war but to preserve truth. The men profiled here were sons, fathers, immigrants, and laborers. Their legacy is one of endurance and service to a cause greater than themselves.

Preserving the Past for the Future

As generations pass, the urgency of preserving individual stories becomes greater. The Cardwell men who served in the Civil War were part of a defining chapter in American history. Their contributions deserve not only remembrance but also understanding. By combining detailed biographies, statistical overviews, and in-depth battle studies, this book aims to offer a full portrait of their service.

This project, like the military record analysis that supports it, is ultimately about connection—between past and present, between soldier and descendant, and between pure data and humanity. It is my hope that the stories within this volume will endure as a testament to the sacrifice, resilience, and lasting impact of the Cardwell men who fought in that war.

Cardwell Union Veterans
Listed by State

Delaware
Cardwell Union Soldier

Delaware was a border state with divided loyalties, but it remained in the Union throughout the Civil War. While some residents supported the Confederacy, Delaware provided several regiments to the Union Army, primarily for garrison and defensive duties. Due to its location along key supply and communication routes, Delaware played an important role in protecting Washington, D.C., and the mid-Atlantic region from Confederate incursions.

Only one Cardwell man, Thomas Cardwell, served in a Delaware regiment during the Civil War. Although Thomas Cardwell did not serve in a frontline combat role, his regiment was essential to protecting Union logistics and infrastructure along the mid-Atlantic. His service in the 5th Delaware Infantry reflects the broader role that Delaware troops played in securing the Union war effort.

This chapter honors the Cardwell soldier of Delaware, preserving his contributions to the Civil War's history.

* * *

Photo 1.1: *Thomas Cardwell (1831-1912) Headstone.*
Wilmington and Brandywine Cemetery, Wilmington, New Castle
County, Delaware

Thomas Cardwell (1831-1912) - Private - *Company F, 5th Delaware Infantry, USA*

Thomas Cardwell was born on 30 August 1831 in Manchester, Lancashire, England. He was the son of Thomas Cardwell and Martha (Gorton) Cardwell.[1] He immigrated to the United States on 23 July 1843, likely with members of his extended family. By 1850, he was living in the household of William Cardwell—probably his brother—in Philadelphia, Pennsylvania.[2]

On 15 September 1856, Thomas was naturalized as a U.S. citizen. Two years earlier, he had married Ann Adamson in 1854. The couple went on to raise a large family, including: Robert Cardwell (1855-1920), Anna Cardwell (1856-), Emma Cardwell (1857-), Barbara Cardwell (1858-), Ida Cardwell (1860-1930), Roland Cardwell (1862-), Charles Cardwell (1864-1951), Thomas Cardwell (1867-1869), and Infant Male Cardwell (1870-1870). The family was residing in Wilmington, New Castle County, Delaware, by the time of the 1860 census.[3] According to the states of birth of their children, Thomas moved from Pennsylvania to Delaware around 1856.

Thomas enlisted in the Union Army on 26 November 1862 in Wilmington, Delaware, as a Private in Company F of the 5th Delaware Infantry. The 5th Delaware was a short-term regiment organized for the defense of the Delaware and Maryland peninsula, with its companies assigned to guard railroads, bridges, and other infrastructure crucial to the Union war effort. Though the regiment was not engaged in major battles, its presence helped deter Confederate raids and ensured the safe movement of troops and supplies along vital Mid-Atlantic corridors.

While his exact discharge date remains unknown, Thomas returned to civilian life in Wilmington after his military service. He is listed in the 1870, 1880, 1900 and 1910 Wilmington, New Castle County, Delaware census records.[4,5,6,7] Throughout his postwar life, he continued working as a painter and raising his family in the city.

Thomas Cardwell died on 21 February 1912 in Wilmington, New Castle County, Delaware. He was buried at Wilmington and Brandywine Cemetery, where many veterans of the Civil War are laid to rest.[8] Cardwell Line III - Confirmed.[9] Photo Credit[10]

Illinois
Cardwell Union Soldiers

ILLINOIS PLAYED A SIGNIFICANT ROLE IN THE CIVIL WAR, PROVIDING over 250,000 soldiers to the Union Army—one of the largest troop contributions of any Northern state. The state was a center of logistical and military training, with cities like Chicago, Springfield, and Cairo serving as key supply and recruitment hubs. Illinois regiments fought in nearly every major campaign in the Western Theater, helping to secure critical victories for the Union.

The Cardwell men from Illinois served in both frontline combat and security operations, contributing to Union victories across the Western Theater. Their involvement in infantry and cavalry regiments reflects Illinois' critical role in maintaining Union dominance in the Midwest and beyond.

This chapter honors the Cardwell soldiers of Illinois, ensuring their service and sacrifices are remembered as part of Cardwell Family history.

* * *

Aaron S. Cardwell (1841–1862) - *Private – Company C, 15th Illinois Volunteer Cavalry, USA* - **Died of Disease**

Aaron S. Cardwell was born in 1841 in McNairy County, Tennessee, the son of James L. Cardwell and Leah (Saunders) Cardwell. He appears in the 1850 U.S. Census in McNairy County, living in his parents' household.[1]

Around 1854, the family relocated to Franklin County, Illinois, where Aaron spent the remainder of his youth.

On 27 January 1859, Aaron married Sarah Catherine Clark in Franklin County.[2] The couple had one daughter, Narcissus S. Cardwell (1863–1924), who was born shortly after Aaron's death and never knew her father. He is recorded in the 1860 census for Franklin County, Illinois, where he worked as a laborer.[3]

Aaron enlisted in the Union Army on 06 September 1862 and was mustered in as a Private in Company C of the 15th Illinois Volunteer Cavalry. The regiment, organized that same year, was tasked with escort duty, reconnaissance missions, and cavalry support operations throughout the Western Theater. The 15th Illinois Cavalry operated primarily in Tennessee and Mississippi, playing a critical role in protecting Union supply lines, disrupting Confederate troop movements, and gathering intelligence during the lead-up to campaigns against Vicksburg and along vital river routes.

Aaron's military service was tragically brief. While stationed at Corinth, Mississippi—a strategic Union logistics base following its capture in 1862—he succumbed to disease on 25 December 1862. Fever and other camp-related illnesses were among the deadliest threats faced by Civil War soldiers, especially in densely occupied garrison towns like Corinth where sanitation was poor and outbreaks frequent.Aaron's death occurred just months after his enlistment, a loss felt deeply by his young wife and daughter. His widow, Sarah, received a federal pension in recognition of his service. Though the exact location of Aaron's grave remains unknown, it is likely he was interred near Corinth alongside other soldiers who died of disease during that period.

Aaron S. Cardwell's brief but honorable service exemplifies the sacrifice of thousands of men who gave their lives not in battle, but in the grueling and often overlooked hardships of military camp life. Cardwell Line I - Predicted.

* * *

Arthur Wellington Cardwell (1818-1887) - *Corporal - Company B, 17th Illinois Volunteer Cavalry, USA*

Arthur Wellington Cardwell was born in 1818 in Lancaster County, Pennsylvania. By 1850, he was residing in Philadelphia, living in the household of his likely older brother, Henry Cardwell, as recorded in the U.S. Census.[4]

Arthur enlisted in the U.S. Army on 06 March 1847, and served during the Mexican-American War, although details of that service remain uncertain. He later reenlisted in the Union Army during the Civil War, enlisting in Company B, 17th Regiment, Illinois Volunteer Cavalry on 22 January 1864 in Chicago, Cook County, Illinois, at the age of 45. He served as a Wagoner, a vital logistical role responsible for transporting supplies, ammunition, and rations, and later held the rank of Corporal until his discharge in December 1866.

The 17th Illinois Cavalry was organized during the winter of 1863–1864 and saw duty in Missouri, Kansas, and the western frontier, primarily focused on protecting Union supply lines, countering Confederate guerrilla activity, and managing unrest in border areas. Although the regiment was not heavily engaged in major battles, it played a critical part in securing Union-held territories during the final years of the war and in the early Reconstruction period. Cardwell's extended service beyond the war's end into late 1866 suggests involvement in postwar garrison duties, possibly tied to occupation or stabilization efforts in the West.

Arthur married Catherine Moore on 07 July 1852, in Reading, Berks County, Pennsylvania.[5] Together they had four children; Olivia Cardwell (1856-1947), Mary Helen Cardwell (1860-1934), Catherine E. "Kate" Cardwell (1861-1921), and Thomas Collier Cardwell (1865-1940). Arthur is listed in the 1860 Berks County, Pennsylvania census.[6]

Following his service, Arthur returned to Chicago, where he is listed in the 1870 Cook County census.[7] He worked as a Railroad Engineer according to the census record. He lived there until his death on 05 January 1887 and was buried in Graceland Cemetery in Chicago, Illinois.[8] <u>Ancestry Undetermined</u>.

* * *

Photo 2.1: *Hezekiah Cardwell - circa 1900 - Viro County, Indiana*

Hezekiah Cardwell (1829–1910) - *Private – Company H, 6th Illinois Infantry & 6th Missouri Infantry, USA*

Hezekiah Cardwell was born on 17 August 1829 in Claiborne County, Tennessee, the son of Thomas Cardwell and Mary Ann (Branson) Cardwell. Shortly after his birth, the family moved to Putnam County, Indiana, where they are listed in the 1830 U.S. Census.[9] He is listed in the 1850 Lee County, Iowa census, living in the home of N.D. Prouty, working as a farmer. By the mid-19th century, Hezekiah had settled in Illinois, where he would marry and raise a family.

Hezekiah married Kissiah A. Simmons on 24 June 1849 in Macoupin County, Illinois.[10] Their daughter Lorinda Jane Cardwell was born there on 18 April 1850. Though the details are unclear, it appears the marriage ended in divorce. On 12 December 1855, Hezekiah remarried Dorothia A. "Dolly" Sparks in Madison County, Illinois, and they had two children: Hester Cardwell (1855-) and Rachel Cardwell (1859-). He is listed with his young family in the 1860 Montgomery County, Illinois census.[11] Hezekiah later married twice more—Nettie Kepoo Legout in 1879 and Carissa Jane Yates in 1885.[12,13]

Hezekiah enlisted as a Private in Company H, 6th Illinois Infantry, United States Army. Unfortunately, only a single service record has been located, limiting our understanding of his time in that unit. He is also associated with service in the 6th Missouri Infantry, which may indicate a transfer, re-enlistment, or dual enlistment—common among volunteers who shifted between state regiments in neighboring regions. Both the 6th Illinois and 6th Missouri Infantry Regiments were active in the Western Theater, involved in guarding supply lines, engaging in regional skirmishes, and participating in operations supporting major campaigns such as the advance on Corinth and Vicksburg.

After the war, Hezekiah returned to Illinois and is listed in the 1880 Montgomery County census.[14] He moved to Vigo County, Indiana and is listed in the 1900 and 1910 census records. He died on 09 July 1910 in Center Creek, Vigo County, Indiana, and is buried at Markle Cemetery in Terre Haute.[15] His brother, James E. Cardwell, also served in the Union Army and is featured elsewhere in this volume. <u>Cardwell Line I - Predicted</u>. Photo Credit[16]

* * *

Photo 2.2: *James L. Cardwell (1845-1916) Headstone. Hollenback Cemetery, Wilkes-Barre, Luzerne County, Pennsylvania*

James L. Cardwell (1845—1916) - *Private - Company B, 146th Illinois Infantry, USA*

James L. Cardwell was born on 04 May 1845 in England, the son of William Cardwell and an unknown mother. He immigrated to the United States in 1863, arriving during the midst of the American Civil War. Just a year later, on 29 August 1864, he enlisted in Company B of the 146th Illinois Infantry, serving as a Private until his honorable discharge on 08 July 1865. He enlisted in Rockford, Winnabago County, Illinois.

The 146th Illinois Infantry was a 100-day service regiment raised late in the war to perform guard and garrison duties, freeing veteran troops for frontline service. The regiment was primarily stationed within Illinois and the Western Theater, where it was responsible for protecting key infrastructure such as railroads, supply depots, and military prisons. Though the 146th saw no major battles, its service was essential to maintaining the Union's logistical strength during the war's final year.

Following his military service, James married Charolette E. Clark around 1878. The couple had seven children: Rexford R. Cardwell (1879–1943), Ellen Cardwell (1885–1921), Jessie Cardwell (1888–1957), Irma Cardwell (b. 1891), John Hilbert Cardwell (1894–1929), Stanley Cardwell (1898–1959), and James Edgar Cardwell (1899–1954). They are listed in the 1910 Lackawanna County, Pennsylvania census record.[17]

By 09 September 1907, James was recorded as an invalid in federal pension records, indicating he suffered from illness or disability later in life. He passed away on 25 June 1916 in Scranton, Lackawanna County, Pennsylvania, and was laid to rest in Hollenback Cemetery, Wilkes-Barre, Luzerne County, Pennsylvania.[18] Ancestry undetermined. Photo Credit[19]

Indiana
Cardwell Union Soldiers

INDIANA WAS A KEY CONTRIBUTOR TO THE UNION WAR EFFORT, providing over 200,000 soldiers to the Union Army—one of the largest troop contributions of any Northern state. Indiana regiments played a crucial role in the Western Theater, participating in battles across Tennessee, Kentucky, and Georgia. The state also provided critical supplies, weaponry, and logistical support for the Union Army.

Though their service came during the final phase of the war, James E. Cardwell and Peter Cardwell contributed to Union victories and the preservation of the nation. Their regiments ensured the final destruction of Confederate resistance and the post-war stabilization of the South.

This chapter honors the Cardwell soldiers of Indiana, preserving their contributions to Union victory during the Civil War.

* * *

Photo 3.1: *James E. Cardwell (1836-1876) Headstone, Dayton National Cemetery, Dayton, Montgomery County, Ohio.*

James E. Cardwell (1836—1876) - *Private - Company B, 123rd Indiana Infantry, USA* - **Wounded in Action**

James E. Cardwell was born around 1833 in Indiana, the son of Thomas Cardwell and Mary Ann (Branson) Cardwell. On 03 March 1852, he married Nancy Ann C. Johnson in Parke County, Indiana.[1] Following Nancy's death, James married Martha E. Eddington on 06 March 1863, also in Parke County. He is documented in marriage records from that region, but has not been located in any census records of that period.[2]

James enlisted in the Union Army on 12 October 1863 at Roseville, Parke County, Indiana, and was mustered in as a Private in Company B of the 123rd Indiana Infantry. The regiment was organized during the fall of 1863 and became part of the Army of the Ohio. The 123rd Indiana played a key role in the Union campaigns across Tennessee and Georgia, notably participating in the Atlanta Campaign, one of the most decisive military operations in the Western Theater.

During the Atlanta Campaign, the regiment was engaged in intense combat, including actions at Resaca, Dallas, Kennesaw Mountain, and Peachtree Creek. On 06 August 1864, while fighting near Atlanta, James sustained a devastating gunshot wound to his left leg, necessitating amputation. His injury occurred during the grueling siege and daily skirmishes that characterized the push toward the fall of Atlanta.

James was honorably discharged on 23 May 1865 due to the severity of his wound. He applied for an Invalid Pension on 2 June 1865, which was granted in recognition of his permanent disability.

Following the war, James married for a third time—Sarah Reese—on 08 June 1870 in Clay County, Indiana, suggesting that his second wife had passed by that time. By 1871, he had entered the Home for Disabled Soldiers in Milwaukee, Wisconsin. In 1873, he was transferred to the National Home for Disabled Volunteer Soldiers in Hampton, Virginia, a facility better equipped for long-term care.

James E. Cardwell died on 30 October 1876 in Peoria County, Illinois. He was buried two days later in Dayton National Cemetery in Montgomery County, Ohio.[3] Pension records note that he fathered a child with Mary Adams, though no additional documentation survives regarding this relationship. One record states that Charles E. Cardwell was his minor child, dated on 08 February 1890, but additional research is needed.

His brother, Hezekiah Cardwell, also served in the Union Army and is profiled separately in this volume. Some military documents list James with the middle initial "C," likely a clerical error, as the records consistently identify his regiment and service history accurately. Cardwell Line I - Predicted. Photo Credit[4]

* * *

Photo 3.2: *Peter Cardwell (1825-1904) Headstone. Fairmont Cemetery, Denver, Arapahoe County, Colorado.*

Peter Cardwell (1825-1904) - *Captain - Company G, 147th Indiana Infantry, USA*

Peter Cardwell was born on 20 December 1825 in Rockingham County, North Carolina, to Noah Cardwell and Anna (Barnes) Cardwell. By 1830, the family had relocated to Jefferson County, Indiana, where Peter spent his early years. On 18 March 1852, he married Irene H. Davis in Washington, Hamilton County, Indiana.[5] They had five children together: Elvira Josephine Cardwell (1853–1900), Marshall W. Cardwell (1856–1939), Melvin L. Cardwell (1858–1943), Edgar Ellsworth Cardwell (1863–1864), and Arthur S. Cardwell (1867–1925). Peter is listed in the 1860, 1870, and 1880 Hamilton County, Indiana census records.[6,7,8]

During the final months of the Civil War, he enlisted as a Private in Company G of the 147th Indiana Infantry. The regiment was organized in early 1865 and assigned to garrison and provost duty in Georgia, playing a crucial role in maintaining order and supporting Reconstruction efforts in the South following the Confederate surrender. The 147th Indiana helped secure Union supply lines, protect freedmen, and enforce federal authority in a volatile postwar environment.

Although the regiment did not participate in large-scale combat, its mission was vital to the stability of occupied territories during the fragile transition to peace. On 04 August 1865, Peter was promoted to the rank of Captain. This promotion, documented in federal pension records, suggests he demonstrated exceptional leadership during his brief but important period of service.

After the war, Peter and his family eventually relocated to Colorado. By 1900, he was living in Denver, Arapahoe County, where he spent his later years.[9] Peter Cardwell died on 12 December 1904 and was buried in Fairmount Cemetery in Denver, Colorado.[10] <u>Cardwell Line I - Predicted</u>. Photo Credit[11]

Iowa
Cardwell Union Soldier

THOUGH GEOGRAPHICALLY REMOVED FROM THE FRONT LINES, IOWA played a vital role in the Union war effort, sending over 75,000 soldiers to fight in major campaigns across the country. Iowa's regiments were heavily involved in the Western Theater, fighting in battles from Missouri and Mississippi to Georgia and Virginia. Iowa soldiers gained a reputation for their tenacity and effectiveness in combat, particularly in Grant's and Sherman's campaigns.

Only one Cardwell man, Pleasant P. Cardwell, served in an Iowa regiment during the Civil War. His unit, the 22nd Iowa Infantry, was engaged in some of the war's most pivotal battles. Organized in 1862, the 22nd Iowa Infantry was heavily involved in the Vicksburg Campaign, where it participated in the siege and assault on the city in 1863.

This chapter honors the Cardwell soldier of Iowa, ensuring his service and sacrifices are remembered as part of Civil War history.

* * *

Photo 4.1: *Pleasant Perrin Cardwell (1820-1900). Circa 1880's - Republic County, Kansas. Photo enhanced.*

Photo 4.2: *Pleasant Perrin Cardwell (1820-1900) Headstone - Prairie Rose Cemetery, Republic, Republic County, Kansas.*

Pleasant Perrin Cardwell (1820—1900) - *Private - Company H, 22nd Iowa Infantry, USA* - **Wounded In Action**

Pleasant Perrin Cardwell was born on 05 September 1820 in Rockingham County, North Carolina, the son of Noah Cardwell and Anna (Barnes) Cardwell. By 1830, the family had relocated to Jefferson County, Indiana, where Pleasant came of age.

He married Sarah "Sally" Catt on 03 October 1844 in Hancock County, Indiana. Together, they raised a large family. Their children included: Joseph Henry Cardwell (1845–1885), Leah Ann "Legrand" Cardwell (1846–1942), Elmira Jane "Eco" Cardwell (1848-), Marshall Perrin "Marsh" Cardwell (1851–1940), Mary Ellen "Kell" Cardwell (1852–1936), James Pleasant

Cardwell (1852–1936), John Madison Cardwell (1856–1941), Sarah Emma Cardwell (1858–1935), Nelson Douglas Cardwell (1860–1948), Rebecca "Becky" Cardwell (1864-), Unison May Cardwell (1865–1942), and Ulysses Johnson "Jont" Cardwell (1866–1962). Pleasant appears in the 1850, 1860, 1870, and 1880 census records for Johnson County, Iowa, where he worked as a farmer. Pleasant is listed in the 1850, 1860, 1870, and 1880 o census records.[1,2,3,4]

At the age of 41, Pleasant enlisted on 6 August 1862 in Shueyville, Johnson County, Iowa, as a Private in Company I of the 22nd Iowa Infantry. He was described as 6 feet 1½ inches tall, with a dark complexion, gray eyes, and black hair. His occupation was listed as farmer.

The 22nd Iowa Infantry saw significant action in the Western Theater. The regiment participated in the campaign to capture Vicksburg, Mississippi, including engagements at Port Gibson, Champion Hill, and Big Black River Bridge. On 22 May 1863, during the final Union assault on the fortified heights at Vicksburg, Pleasant was shot in both feet, fracturing the right foot. He was initially treated at Union hospitals in Memphis, Tennessee, before being transferred to Benton Barracks in St. Louis and then to a hospital in Davenport, Iowa.

Pleasant was honorably discharged on 26 December 1864 due to disability from his wounds. In his pension declaration filed the following day, he confirmed that the injury occurred "while with his company and regiment, engaged in a charge on the enemy's works." His war injuries left him with permanent disabilities.

After the war, Pleasant moved west to Kansas, settling in the town of Union in Republic County. He remained there for the rest of his life. Pleasant Perrin Cardwell died on 23 February 1900 and was buried in Prairie Rose Cemetery in Republic County, Kansas. <u>Cardwell Line I - Confirmed</u>. Photo Credits[5,6]

Kansas
Cardwell Union Soldiers

KANSAS, HAVING ENTERED THE UNION AS A FREE STATE IN 1861, WAS A hotbed of conflict even before the Civil War began. The state was central to the "Bleeding Kansas" period, which saw violent skirmishes between pro-slavery and anti-slavery factions. During the war, Kansas troops played a key role in Union campaigns along the Missouri-Kansas border and in the Trans-Mississippi Theater, engaging in guerrilla warfare, raids, and full-scale battles against Confederate and pro-Southern guerrilla forces.

Two Cardwell brothers, George E. Cardwell and John T. Cardwell, served in Kansas regiments. Their service was marked by the brutal nature of warfare in the western territories, where Confederate forces and irregular combatants clashed frequently. Both men lost their lives in battle, making the ultimate sacrifice for the Union cause.

The Cardwell brothers from Kansas fought in the harsh and often lawless environment of the Trans-Mississippi West, where conventional warfare blended with irregular combat. The deaths of George E. Cardwell at Wilson's Creek and John T. Cardwell at Baxter Springs highlight the high price paid by Kansas soldiers who defended their state and the Union cause.

This chapter honors the Cardwell soldiers of Kansas, preserving their service and sacrifice as part of Cardwell Family history.

* * *

George E. Cardwell (1841-1861) - *Private - Company F, 1st Kansas Infantry, USA* - **Killed In Action**

George E. Cardwell was born in 1841 in Brown County, Indiana, the son of William Alexander Cardwell and Sarah Ann (Sparks) Cardwell. He appears in the 1850 U.S. Census residing in his parents' household in Brown County. Sometime between 1853 and 1856, the family relocated west to Douglas County, Kansas, where they are recorded in the 1860 census of the Kansas Territory.

When the Civil War began, George enlisted as a Private in Company F of the 1st Kansas Infantry, one of the earliest Union regiments raised west of the Mississippi River. Organized in 1861, the 1st Kansas Infantry was composed largely of antislavery settlers and Free-Staters. The regiment quickly moved into Missouri, where Union and Confederate forces were battling for control of the border state.

The 1st Kansas Infantry distinguished itself in the Battle of Wilson's Creek on 10 August 1861 in Greene County, Missouri—one of the first major engagements in the Western Theater. Although the Union forces ultimately retreated, the regiment was praised for its gallant stand during the battle, where it suffered heavy casualties. George E. Cardwell was among those killed in the fighting.

Due to the chaos of the battlefield and the high number of casualties at Wilson's Creek, George's remains were never identified, and his final resting place is unknown. His sacrifice came at a critical early moment in the war, when the future of Union control in Missouri and the broader Trans-Mississippi West was uncertain.

George's younger brother, John T. Cardwell, also served in the Union Army. He was killed in action at the Battle of Baxter Springs in Cherokee County, Kansas, in 1863—another tragic blow to the Cardwell family, who lost two sons in defense of the Union cause.[1] Cardwell Line I - Predicted.

* * *

Photo 5.1: *John T. Cardwell (1845-1863) Memorial. Baxter Springs City Cemetery Soldiers' Memorial, Baxter Springs, Cherokee County, Kansas.*

John T. Cardwell (1845-1863) - *Private - Company A, 14th Kansas Cavalry, USA -* **Killed In Action**

John T. Cardwell was born in 1845 in Brown County, Indiana, the son of William Alexander Cardwell and Sarah Ann (Sparks) Cardwell. He appears in the 1850 U.S. Census as a young child in his parents' household.[2] Between 1853 and 1856, the Cardwell family moved west to Douglas County, Kansas, where they were recorded in the 1860 census of the Kansas Territory.[3]

At age 18, John enlisted in the Union Army on 1 May 1863 and was mustered into service as a Private in Company A of the 14th Kansas Cavalry. This regiment was formed in response to ongoing Confederate threats and guerrilla activity in Kansas and Missouri. The 14th Kansas Cavalry was known for its mobility and effectiveness in irregular warfare. It was frequently assigned to patrols, reconnaissance missions, and anti-guerrilla operations in a region notorious for bushwhacker violence and shifting front lines.

On 06 October 1863, John was killed in action during the Battle of Baxter Springs in Cherokee County, Kansas.[4] The encounter began when Confederate guerrillas led by William Quantrill ambushed a Union column that included General James G. Blunt and his escort. The attack devolved into what became known as the Baxter Springs Massacre, as Quantrill's men killed scores of Union soldiers and support personnel, many of them after they had surrendered. John T. Cardwell was among those who died in the surprise assault.

He was buried in the Baxter Springs City Cemetery, in the Soldiers' Lot, alongside other Union casualties from the engagement.[5] His death represents one of many personal tragedies of the border war that ravaged Kansas and Missouri during the Civil War.

John's older brother, George E. Cardwell, was also killed in action while serving with the 1st Kansas Infantry at the Battle of Wilson's Creek in 1861. The Cardwell family thus endured the loss of two sons in the war, both falling in defense of the Union. <u>Cardwell Line I - Predicted</u>. Photo Credit[6]

Kentucky
Cardwell Union Soldiers

KENTUCKY WAS A BORDER STATE WITH DEEP TIES TO BOTH THE UNION and the Confederacy. Although it remained in the Union, the state was home to strong Confederate sympathies, leading to internal strife and violent skirmishes. Kentucky provided troops to both sides, making it one of the most divided states in the war. Unionist Kentuckians played an essential role in securing the state for the Union and participating in campaigns across the Western and Eastern Theaters.

The Cardwell men from Kentucky fought in both defensive and offensive operations, contributing to Union victories in key battles. Their service in infantry, cavalry, and artillery reflects the strategic importance of Kentucky in securing the Western Theater for the Union.

This chapter honors the Cardwell soldiers of Kentucky, ensuring their service is remembered as part of the broader Civil War history.

* * *

Dennis A. Cardwell, Jr. (1842—1882) **-** *Private - Company B, 6th Kentucky Infantry, USA -* **Prisoner of War**

Dennis A. Cardwell was born around 1842 in Oldham County, Kentucky, to Dennis A. Cardwell and Mary W. (Tucker) Cardwell. He is listed in the household of his parents in the 1850 and 1860 census for Oldham County, Kentucky.[1,2] On 26 October 1861, at the age of 19, Dennis enlisted in Company B of the 6th Kentucky Infantry (Union) at Louisville, Kentucky, for a term of three years. Dennis enlisted in the same unit as his brother, Henry C. Cardwell, but roughly a month later.

His early service record is marked by administrative gaps—he is listed as "not stated" for presence or absence on muster rolls between January and October 1862, a reflection of poor recordkeeping rather than actual inactivity. He is definitively marked present with his unit from November 1862 through September 1863. During this time, the 6th Kentucky Infantry was attached to the 1st Brigade, 1st Division, XXI Corps of the Army of the Cumberland and was actively engaged in the Battle of Stones River (December-January 1863), Tullahoma Campaign (June–July 1863) and the Chickamauga Campaign (September 1863).

On 19 September 1863, at the Battle of Chickamauga, Dennis was captured by Confederate forces. He was reported missing in action on 19 September and shortly thereafter confined in Confederate custody. He was initially sent to a Confederate prison hospital in Richmond, Virginia, arriving there on 26 November 1863. He was treated for diarrhea and then transferred to Andersonville Prison on 12 December 1863. Several records pertaining to Dennis appear in the service file of his brother, Henry C. Cardwell—an understandable error given that both men served in the same unit. These documents help clarify how Dennis was transported following his capture.

By December 1864, Dennis was among a group of paroled prisoners released at Charleston, South Carolina, and was sent to Camp Parole, Maryland, arriving there on 16 December. He received a 30-day furlough. At the end of January 1865, he was declared as having "deserted" for failing to report back at the end of his leave. However, Dennis voluntarily reported to Camp Chase, Ohio, on 03 February and was sent to the Provost Marshal in Columbus on 06 February. Due to his prompt reporting and absence of medical certification, the desertion charge was officially removed from his record. He was formally discharged from military service on 16 February 1865 in Louisville, Kentucky.

Raised four children He married Harriet A. Stutzer on 03 March 1869.[3] The couple had four children: Mary E. Cardwell (1871–1948), Elmo Dennis Cardwell (1874–1943), Margaret Cardwell (1875–1961), and Norvin H. Cardwell (1882–1966). The family is listed in the 1870 and 1880 census records for Jefferson County, Kentucky.[4,5]

Dennis A. Cardwell died on 02 April 1885 in Jefferson County at approximately 43 years of age. His widow applied for and received a pension based on his Union service. The exact location of his grave has not been found. Dennis was the brother of Henry C. Cardwell and Talbert V. Cardwell—both of whom also served in the Union army and are recorded in this chapter. Cardwell Line I - Predicted.

* * *

Henry C. Cardwell (1841—1862) - *Corporal - Company B, 6th Kentucky Infantry, USA* - **Killed in Action**

Henry C. Cardwell was born about 1841 in Oldham County, Kentucky, to Dennis A. Cardwell and Mary W. (Tucker) Cardwell. He appears in the household of his parents in the 1850 census of Oldham County, Kentucky, and is listed as a blacksmith, indicating that he had developed a trade skill by his teenage years.[6]

Henry enlisted on 23 September 1861 at Louisville, Kentucky, as a Private in Company B, 6th Regiment Kentucky Infantry, U.S. Army, for a three-year term of service. He was nineteen years old at the time of his enlistment. His younger brother, Dennis A. Cardwell Jr., enlisted in the same company about a month later.

The 6th Kentucky Infantry was formed in late 1861 and mustered into Federal service as part of the Union's "Orphan Brigade," though it soon served independently in numerous campaigns. Henry was appointed Corporal on 04 June 1862, and he remained with his company through a series of engagements throughout that year.

While Henry's service spanned several campaigns, the records show him present during the Kentucky Campaign in the fall of 1862 and during the lead-up to the Battle of Stones River. His regiment participated in the Battle of Perryville on 08 October 1862 but arrived too late to see major action. However, by December, the 6th Kentucky Infantry was actively engaged in the Union movement toward Murfreesboro, Tennessee, under the command of Major General William S. Rosecrans.

On 31 December 1862, during the opening day of the Battle of Stones River (also known as the Battle of Murfreesboro), Henry C. Cardwell was killed in action. The fighting was among the most brutal of the Western Theater, with severe casualties on both sides. The 6th Kentucky Infantry was heavily engaged, facing a powerful Confederate assault. It is likely that Henry died in the early stages of the battle when the Confederate army attempted to crush the Union right flank.

Due to the nature of battlefield burials during the war, and the intense fighting around Murfreesboro, it is probable that Henry was interred near where he fell and later reburied as an unknown soldier at Stones River National Cemetery in Rutherford County, Tennessee. His name does not appear on any surviving marked headstone, suggesting he lies in one of the many unmarked graves of Union soldiers buried there.

Of historical note, several documents pertaining to his brother, Dennis A. Cardwell Jr., were mistakenly filed in Henry's service record. This error is understandable, as both brothers served in the same company, and their military paths overlapped significantly.

Henry C. Cardwell was the brother of Talbert V. Cardwell and Dennis A. Cardwell, Jr., both of whom are also recorded in this chapter. His sacrifice at Stones River marked the ultimate cost paid by many families during the Civil War and stands as a testament to the Cardwell family's service to the Union cause. <u>Cardwell Line I - Predicted</u>.

* * *

Photo 6.1: *Major Isaac Newton Cardwell - circa 1880 - Estill County, Kentucky.*

Photo 6.2: *Isaac Newton Cardwell (1827-1899) Headstone. Frankfort Cemetery, Frankfort, Franklin County, Kentucky.*

Issac Newton Cardwell (1827-1899) - Major - *Company F, 7th Kentucky Infantry, USA*

Isaac Newton Cardwell was born on 27 September 1827 in Knox County, Tennessee, the third son of John Cardwell and Arminta Ariana "Ara" (Watkins) Cardwell. He is listed in the home of his parents in the 1850 Breathitt County, Kentucky census.[7] His family had deep roots in the South: his father was born in Fauquier County, Virginia in 1790 and served in the

War of 1812. His paternal grandfather, Reverend Perrin Cardwell, a wealthy planter and Methodist minister, also served in the Revolutionary War before relocating to Tennessee, where he died in 1850 at nearly 98 years of age. Isaac's mother, Ara Watkins, was the daughter of Colonel Thomas Watkins, and lived to the advanced age of eighty-seven.

In 1840, John Cardwell moved the family to Jackson, Breathitt County, Kentucky, where he entered into mercantile trade and served as postmaster from 1844 to 1877. Isaac, meanwhile, received a classical education and graduated from the University of Tennessee in 1850. He read law with Judge Reese in Knoxville and was admitted to the bar that same year.

By 1853, Isaac Cardwell had relocated to Booneville, Owsley County, Kentucky, where he opened a law practice and quickly established a reputation for legal acumen. On 25 December 1855, he married Joanna Gale.[8] The couple had three children: Florence Cardwell (1859–1873), Lena Cardwell (1862–1951), and Fox Cardwell (1880–1880). He is listed in the 1860 Owsley Couty, Kentucky census.[9]

Joanna died in July 1881, and Isaac later remarried to Jennie Logan Todd in Frankfort, Kentucky, in November 1882.[10] Jennie was the granddaughter of Kentucky Governor John J. Crittenden and a member of the Presbyterian Church.

Before the outbreak of the Civil War, Isaac had already seen military service. In the final year of the Mexican-American War, he served as Orderly Sergeant in Captain John J. Reese's company of the 5th Tennessee Infantry.

Isaac was among the American volunteers who joined William Walker's ill-fated filibustering expedition to Central America in the 1850s. Walker, a Tennessee-born adventurer, sought to establish English-speaking colonies under his control in Latin America, beginning with Nicaragua. Although the details of Cardwell's involvement remain sparse, records confirm his participation in the expedition, likely during Walker's 1855–1857 campaign. This experience, combining both military action and political intrigue, reflected the boldness and ambition that marked much of Cardwell's early career. His service under Walker, which followed his earlier enlistment during the Mexican-American War, added to a lifetime of varied and often hazardous military undertakings.

In 1860, with the secession crisis deepening, Cardwell accepted a commission from President Abraham Lincoln as Major of the 7th Kentucky Infantry (Union) on 20 August 1861. The regiment served in Kentucky and

East Tennessee, and was active in the Cumberland Gap Campaign. While stationed at the Gap, Union supply lines collapsed, and General George W. Morgan selected a mounted detachment of 400 men to seek provisions. Colonel Theophilus T. Garrard initially led the group, but command soon fell to Major Cardwell. The detachment rode toward Richmond, Kentucky, and encountered Confederate forces at the Battle of Richmond in August 1862. Scott's Louisiana Cavalry struck the detachment from the rear, scattering many of the men. Some rejoined Union lines at Cumberland Gap, others made their way to Louisville, and several were captured and paroled.

Cardwell continued to serve until 15 February 1863, when he resigned his commission due to a serious case of rheumatism. Returning to Lexington, he remained there until relocating in the fall of 1864 to Irvine, Estill County, Kentucky, where he resumed his legal practice. Isaac is listed in the 1870 and 1880 Estill County, Kentucky census records.[11,12]

He remained active in civic life and was twice elected as a state representative in the Kentucky Legislature, serving Estill County during the terms of 1872–73 and 1881–82. In 1884, he moved to Winchester, Clark County, Kentucky, where he continued practicing law until his death.

Known in legal circles as "Judge Cardwell," he was respected for both his intellect and public service. A lifelong Republican after the Civil War, he was not affiliated with any religious denomination but belonged to the Masonic Order.

Major Isaac Newton Cardwell died in June 1899 at the age of 71 in Frankfort, Franklin County, Kentucky. He was buried at the Frankfort Cemetery.[13] His life spanned service in three wars—the Mexican War, the Civil War, and the Walker Filibuster in Central America—and his record reflects both civic dedication and a long family tradition of military service. His brother, William Daniel Cardwell, also served in the Union during the conflict and is recorded in this chapter. Cardwell Line I - Predicted. Photo Credits[14,15]

* * *

Talbot V. Cardwell (1833->1880) - *Private - 54th Kentucky Infantry, USA*
Talbot V. Cardwell was born about 1833 in Oldham County, Kentucky, the eldest son of Dennis A. Cardwell and Mary W. (Tucker) Cardwell. He is listed in the household of his parents in the 1850 census for Oldham Coun-

ty.[16] Like his father, Talbot was a blacksmith by trade—a profession that was also passed down to two of his younger brothers. From a young age, Talbot exhibited an independent streak, and evidence from newspaper accounts shows that he had already developed a reputation for toughness and frontier resilience by the time he was in his early twenties.

In November 1854, Talbot was involved in a violent altercation on the Ohio River near Six-Mile Island, opposite Louisville, Kentucky. According to an article published in the *Louisville Daily Courier*, a fight broke out between two groups—hunters and rafters—after a confrontation turned physical. Talbot, identified as "Tolbert V. Cardwell" of Westport, Kentucky, was among the rafters returning from a hunting expedition. Armed with short sixes (revolvers), he and his companions found themselves in a running gunfight across skiffs, resulting in multiple wounds. Talbot himself was shot in the arm, neck, and breast, reportedly receiving fifty-eight shot in total. Though seriously injured, he survived the incident. The event became local lore, illustrating both the lawlessness of the river frontier and Talbot's gritty resilience.[17]

He married Quintilla Curtis Allnut on 19 January 1858 in Carroll County, Kentucky.[18] The couple had the following children: Vineyard Vergillius "Vinnie" Cardwell (1858–1895), Henry Thomas Cardwell (1861–1939), Alfred Alpheus Cardwell (1865–), Julius Iria Cardwell (1868–1870), Quintilla Curtis Cardwell (1870–1923), John Willis Cardwell (1873–1953), Argenta B. Cardwell (1875–1952), and one infant child who died in 1880. Talbot and his family are listed in the 1860 Oldham County census prior to his enlistment.[19]

Talbot enlisted as a Private in Company F of the 54th Kentucky Infantry on 27 September 1864 at the age of 30. His enlistment papers record that he was born in Oldham County, Kentucky, stood 5 feet 9 inches tall, had blue eyes, light hair, a fair complexion, and was a blacksmith by occupation. The 54th Kentucky Infantry was a short-term regiment organized in late 1864 for one year of service. Talbot's regiment was primarily tasked with guard and garrison duty in Kentucky during the final months of the war. The unit operated within the District of Kentucky and saw scattered skirmishes, including duties along the Louisville & Nashville Railroad and other key Union supply routes. Given his enlistment date and the movements of his company, Talbot would likely have participated in local patrol and garrison duties rather than any large-scale engagements. He is marked present throughout his service, although no specific discharge date has been located in available records.

After the war, Talbot returned to Kentucky and settled in Jefferson County, where he is listed in the 1870 census.[20] By 1880, he had moved his family to Amite County, Mississippi, where he continued working as a blacksmith and raising his children.[21]

The circumstances surrounding his death, passed down through oral family history, tell a somber story. According to descendants, a man brought a thoroughbred stallion to Talbot for shoeing, insisting the horse not be tied, hobbled, or restrained in any way. Talbot accepted the challenge and successfully completed the work. However, for reasons unknown, he moved behind the animal afterward and was fatally kicked. His death left the family in difficult circumstances.

Shortly after his passing, a legal partner—described in the family's account as an attorney who had worked with Talbot on a millworks and agricultural harrow design—took sole ownership of their joint enterprise. The business and patent had reportedly been filed only in the partner's name. Widow Quintilla Cardwell and her children were forced out of the business and denied any share in its proceeds. As a result, she sold the family home and relocated to live with her daughter, Quintilla Cardwell Pemble, in East Feliciana Parish, Louisiana.

Talbot's burial site has not been located, and he does not appear in the 1900 census, suggesting that he died sometime between 1880 and 1900. His legacy, however, is etched into both public record and family memory—a Union soldier, frontier blacksmith, survivor of gun violence, and a man whose tragic end left a mark on his descendants.

His younger brothers, Dennis A. Cardwell Jr. and Henry C. Cardwell, both served in the Union Army and are also recorded in this chapter. <u>Cardwell Line I - Confirmed</u>.

* * *

Thomas Wilcher Cardwell (1832-1913) - Private - *Company E, 21st Kentucky Infantry & Company H, 4th Kentucky Mounted Infantry, USA*

Thomas Wilcher Cardwell was born about 1832 in Anderson County, Kentucky. According to his Kentucky death certificate, his parents were John Cardwell and Frances Cardwell.[22] By 1850, he was residing in the household of Harvey Craig in Mercer County, Kentucky. Notably, his future wife, Frances H. Carter, was also living in that same home at the time.[23] The two were married on 11 December 1851 in Mercer County.[24]

Thomas and Frances had several children together: Lou Ella Cardwell (1853-1932), Josephine Cardwell (1854-1874), John C. Cardwell (1855-1937), Paralee Cardwell (1855-), Eugennie Cardwell (1859-), Jennie C. Cardwell (1861–1955), Robert Cardwell (1867-), and Silvester "Charley" Cardwell (1870-1956). He is listed in the 1860, 1870, 1880, 1900, and 1910 Jessamine County, Kentucky census.[25,26,27,28,29]

During the Civil War, Thomas first enlisted on 08 November 1861 as a Private in the 21st Kentucky Infantry (Union). However, military records show that he deserted on 15 October 1862. Despite this, he later received a pension—an unusual occurrence for someone with a desertion on record. Further research into his pension file reveals that he also served in Company H, 4th Kentucky Mounted Infantry. He enlisted with that unit on 31 March 1864 in Jessamine County, Kentucky. At the time of enlistment, he stated that he was 30 years old, born in Anderson County, and worked as a farmer. His physical description listed him as having brown hair, grey eyes, a dark complexion, and standing six feet tall. He was granted an Invalid Pension on 16 February 1889.

Following the war, Thomas remarried after the death of his wife in 1876. On 03 August 1887, he wed Martha J. Humphrey in Jessamine County.[30] They had one known child, Mary L. Cardwell (1889-1929).

Thomas Wilcher Cardwell died on 12 March 1913 in Jessamine County, Kentucky. His death certificate listed his parents as John and Frances Cardwell. Despite extensive research into the Cardwell families of Mercer County and surrounding areas, no definitive match for his parentage beyond these names has been identified. He is buried at Maple Grove Cemetery in Nicholasville, Jessamine County, Kentucky.[31] Ancestry Unlinked - Assumed Line I.

* * *

Photo 6.3: *Thomas Cardwell (1838-1862) Headstone. Nashville National Cemetery, Nashville, Davidson County, Tennessee.*

Thomas Cardwell (1838-1862) Private - *Company B, 7th Kentucky Cavalry, USA -* **Died of Disease**

Thomas Cardwell was born around 1838 in Hopkins County, Kentucky, the son of John Cardwell and Mary Ann (Carnahan) Cardwell. He appears in the 1850 U.S. Federal Census residing in the household of his parents in Hopkins County.[32]

During the Civil War, Thomas enlisted on 04 August 1862 in Paris, Bourbon County, Kentucky, for a three-year term of service. He was mustered in as a Private in Company G of the 7th Kentucky Cavalry, a Union regiment organized primarily to combat Confederate cavalry raids in Kentucky and Tennessee. The 7th Kentucky Cavalry operated under various commands, including those of General Burnside and General Stoneman, and played an active role in campaigns across Kentucky, Tennessee, and Georgia.

Shortly after his enlistment, Thomas was admitted to General Hospital No. 2 in Bowling Green, Kentucky, on 12 November 1862. His medical records state that he was suffering from congestion of the brain—a general term historically used for serious neurological symptoms, often indicating inflammation or high fever. His condition worsened, and he ultimately died of typhoid fever on 06 December 1862 while still in the hospital.

Thomas Cardwell was buried with honor at the Nashville National Cemetery in Nashville, Tennessee, a final resting place for many Union soldiers who died in the Western Theater.[33]

His younger brother, Charles T. Cardwell, served in the Confederate

Army and is detailed separately in the Confederate volume of this work. <u>Cardwell Line I - Predicted</u>. Photo Credit[34]

* * *

Photo 6.4: *William Benjamin Cardwell (1841-1926) circa 1861*

Photo 6.5: *William Benjamin Cardwell (1841-1926) circa 1915. He appears to be holding two service medals from his service with the 11th Kentucky Infantry, Union Army.*

Photo 6.6: *William Benjamin Cardwell (1841-1926) Headstone - Morgan-Smith Cemetery, Butler County, Kentucky.*

William Benjamin Cardwell (1841-1926) - *Sergeant - Company C, 11th Kentucky Infantry, USA*

William Benjamin Cardwell was born on 20 July 1841 in Butler County, Kentucky, the son of Robert Cardwell and Nancy J. (Moore) Cardwell. He appears in the 1850 census living with his parents in Butler County.[35]

He married Angeline Flener on 2 April 1860 in Ohio County, Kentucky.[36] Together they had the following children: Bedford W. Cardwell (1861–1876), William Harrison Cardwell (1863–1940), Martha Cardwell (1864–1877), James Cardwell (born 1866), Paradise A. Cardwell (1868–1955), Luvenna Angeline Cardwell (1870–1958), Sarah A. Cardwell (1872–1938), Azro Alison Cardwell (1874–1947), Howard Cardwell (born 1874), Alvarado "Alva" Rollo Cardwell (1876–1953), Syotha Jane Cardwell (1878–1937), Mary A. Cardwell (1880–1954), Sally M. Cardwell (born 1880), Leroy Latney Cardwell (1882–1968), and Robert Lincoln Cardwell (1884–1950). He is listed in the 1870, 1880, 1900, and 1910 Butler County and 1920 Owen County, Kentucky census records.[37,38,39,40]

William enlisted on 23 September 1861 in Butler County as a Private in Company C of the 11th Kentucky Infantry (Union) for a three-year term. The regiment saw extensive action throughout the Western Theater, including the Battles of Shiloh, Stones River, Lookout Mountain, Kenesaw Mountain, the Siege of Knoxville, and the Atlanta Campaign. The 11th Kentucky Infantry was known for its endurance and steadfastness across some of the most grueling campaigns in the region.

William was promoted to Sergeant on 15 August 1862. Despite suffering from illness that required hospitalization twice—once in May 1862 and again in September 1863, both times in Nashville—he remained with his regiment throughout the war. He was honorably discharged on 16 December 1864 at Bowling Green, Kentucky. His service record reflects continuous active duty with only brief interruptions for medical treatment.

Following the war, William filed for a federal invalid pension on 01 April 1876. His first wife, Angeline Flener, the mother of his fifteen children, passed away in 1910 in Butler County. In later years, William remarried to Nancy Fitch, the widow of Joseph Wilson. After William's death in 1926, Nancy was granted a federal widow's pension in recognition of his wartime service.

In civilian life, William first farmed on shares before acquiring 102 acres east of Aberdeen. He later expanded his holdings to 217 acres and engaged in general merchandising in Aberdeen beginning in 1884. Though he had limited formal education, he developed a strong business acumen over the years.

A devoted church member, William was active in the Methodist Episcopal Church, was a vocal advocate of temperance and a staunch Republican in political life.

William Benjamin Cardwell died on 01 May 1926 in Ohio County, Kentucky, at the age of 84. He is buried in Morgan-Smith Cemetery in Butler County, Kentucky.[41] Cardwell Line II - Confirmed. Photo Credits[42,43,44]

* * *

William Daniel Cardwell (1826-1887) - *Captain - Company G, Three Forks Battalion, Kentucky State Troops, USA*

William Daniel Cardwell was born on 05 January 1826 in Jefferson County, Tennessee, the second son of John Cardwell and Arminta Ariana "Ara" (Watkins) Cardwell. His family relocated to Breathitt County, Kentucky in 1840, part of a broader westward movement of the Cardwell family from Tennessee. In the 1850 census of Breathitt County, William is recorded as working as a coal miner, a common occupation in the rugged, resource-rich hills of eastern Kentucky.[45] By 1860, he was residing in the home of his aging parents in Jackson, Breathitt County, where he found work as a clerk in the general store owned by Thomas Sewell, located near what is now the site of the South Jackson Bridge.[46]

During the Civil War, William aligned with Unionist interests in eastern Kentucky and was appointed Captain of Company G, Three Forks Battalion, Kentucky State Troops. This battalion was a local home guard unit raised in July 1865, primarily for the purpose of maintaining post-war civil order in the mountainous regions of eastern Kentucky, where bushwhacking, feuds, and unrest continued after the formal close of hostilities. As a captain, William would have been responsible for leading and disciplining men from the local area, many of whom had previously served in both Union and Confederate armies, in an effort to stabilize the region during Reconstruction. The battalion's duties focused on protecting infrastructure, enforcing law, and securing isolated communities still vulnerable to violence and lawlessness.

In the years after the war, William remained active in his community. He was appointed Postmaster for Jackson, Breathitt County, serving from 20 February 1887 to 30 April 1887. Though his tenure was brief—lasting just over two months—it signaled his continued commitment to public service. He lived the remainder of his life along Cane Creek, where he managed his affairs and provided support to his extended family. William never married and was known to have lived as a bachelor. By the 1870 and 1880 census records, he is listed still residing in Breathitt County, and in 1880 he was living in the household of his widowed mother, Ara Cardwell.[47,48]

William was the older brother of Isaac Newton Cardwell, who served as Major of the 7th Kentucky Infantry (U.S.) during the Civil War and went on to become a state legislator and judge. William's service as a captain, though less known, reflected the same commitment to Unionist values and civic responsibility. He was also the brother-in-law of Lieutenant Alfred E. Little, who served in Company E of the Three Forks Battalion, further tying William to the network of community-based military leadership that held the region together in the unstable aftermath of the Civil War.

William Daniel Cardwell died on 30 April 1887 at Cane Creek, Breathitt County, Kentucky. The exact location of his burial is unknown, though it was likely near the family home or a local plot on the property. His life and service represent the quieter but no less meaningful legacy of local leadership during one of the most turbulent periods in Kentucky's history. Cardwell Line I - Predicted.

* * *

William Martin Cardwell (1823-1865) - *Private - Company F, 7th Kentucky Cavalry, USA -* **Prisoner of War - Died in Service**

William Martin Cardwell was born around 1823 in Grainger County, Tennessee, the son of Daniel Cardwell and Elizabeth (Abbott) Cardwell. His mother died either during childbirth or shortly thereafter, and his father later remarried to Martha Easley. William's father passed away around 1826, leaving the children to be raised by extended family members. As a result, William and his siblings are difficult to locate in early census records.

By 1860, William had moved to Kenton County, Kentucky, where he was listed in the federal census as a Tobacconist.[49] He had married Mary A. Cole, though the date of their marriage remains undocumented in surviving records.

On 19 October 1863, William enlisted in the Union Army at Covington, Kenton County, Kentucky. He was mustered in as a Private in Company F of the 7th Regiment Kentucky Cavalry. At enlistment, he gave his birthplace as Knoxville, Knox County, Tennessee, and described himself as 5 feet 7 inches tall, with grey eyes, black hair, and a dark complexion.

The 7th Kentucky Cavalry was organized in August 1862 and saw continuous action throughout the Western Theater. The regiment engaged in patrols, raids, and skirmishes across Kentucky, Tennessee, Georgia, and northern Alabama. By early 1864, they were operating in Union-controlled areas along key supply lines and railroads in Georgia, playing a vital role in disrupting Confederate movements.

William was marked present with his unit from enlistment until June 1864. On 24 June 1864, he was captured during a skirmish near Lafayette in Walker County, Georgia. The details of his captivity remain unclear. His name does not appear in the surviving records of Andersonville or other major Confederate prisons, and it is presumed he was held in one of the temporary or less-documented prison facilities in the South.

At the conclusion of the war in April 1865, William was among thousands of Union prisoners released in the South. He was sent to Vicksburg, Mississippi, where he boarded the *Sultana*, a steamboat contracted to transport recently paroled Union soldiers north. Tragically, on 27 April 1865, just nine miles above Memphis, Tennessee, the *Sultana's* boilers exploded, killing over 1,100 men in what remains the deadliest maritime disaster in United States history.

William Martin Cardwell was among those who perished in the explosion. His body was never recovered, and his final resting place is unknown. <u>Cardwell Line I - Predicted</u>.

* * *

Photo 6.7: *William W. Cardwell (1822-1885) and wife Headstone. Grapevine Cemetery, Madisonville, Hopkins County, Kentucky.*

William W. Cardwell (1822-1885), *Private - 2nd Kentucky Heavy Artillery, USA*

William W. Cardwell was born on 31 May 1822 in Hopkins County, Kentucky, the son of Thomas Cardwell and Catherine McGary. In the 1850 census, he is listed in the household of Stephen D. Rash in Hopkins County, likely working as a farm laborer or living with extended family. His parents resided nearby.

On 25 November 1851, he married Nancy J. Woodruff in Caldwell County, Kentucky. They had four children: Emma P. Cardwell (1852–1893), Thomas L. Cardwell (1852–1878), David E. Cardwell (1854–1880), and Cordelia E. "Corey" Cardwell (1857–1884).

William appears in the 1860, 1870, and 1880 U.S. Federal Census records, residing in Madisonville, Hopkins County, Kentucky, where he worked as a farmer.[50,51,52]

As the Civil War progressed and federal manpower demands increased, William was listed in the 01 July 1863 Draft Registration for Hopkins County. He was likely drafted and entered service shortly thereafter, enlisting on 19 October 1863 at Covington, Kenton County, Kentucky. He was mustered in as a Private in the 2nd Kentucky Heavy Artillery, a Union regiment tasked primarily with garrison duty, guarding supply lines, railroads, and strategic posts throughout Kentucky and Tennessee.

William's service record was marked by disciplinary issues. On 21 October 1864, he was reported as having deserted from a Union encampment near Tullahoma, Tennessee. He was later apprehended by Union authorities and arrested by the Provost Marshal in Louisville on 03 January 1865, for which a $30 reward had been posted. He was transported to Nashville on 06 January 1865 and returned to duty without formal trial.

Despite this reinstatement, William again deserted on 26 February 1865 near Huntsville, Alabama. After the war, he applied to have the charges of desertion removed and sought an honorable discharge. His request was denied, and the charges remained on his record.

Following his military service, William returned home to Madisonville in Hopkins County, where he resumed civilian life. He died on 26 May 1885 at the age of 62 and was buried at Grapevine Cemetery in Madisonville, Hopkins County, Kentucky.[53] <u>Cardwell Line I - Predicted</u>. Photo Credit[54]

Missouri
Cardwell Union Soldiers

MISSOURI WAS ONE OF THE MOST DIVIDED STATES DURING THE CIVIL War, with strong allegiances to both the Union and the Confederacy. While officially remaining in the Union, Missouri was also home to a Confederate government-in-exile. The state saw intense guerrilla warfare, skirmishes, and larger battles, such as Wilson's Creek, Lexington, and Westport. Unionist Missourians, including members of the Cardwell family, joined the fight to preserve the Union while also defending their home state from Confederate and guerrilla forces.

The Cardwell men from Missouri fought in a deeply divided state, serving in infantry, cavalry, and militia units that helped secure Missouri for the Union. Their contributions in anti-guerrilla operations, major battles, and local defense played a crucial role in maintaining federal control over the state.

This chapter honors the Cardwell soldiers of Missouri, preserving their service and dedication to the Union cause.

* * *

Photo 7.1: *Alexander Gaines Cardwell (1838-1914) Headstone - Cardwell Family Cemetery, Webster County, Missouri.*

Alexander Gaines Cardwell (1838-1914) - *Private - Capt. Bragg's Company (B), Webster County Regiment, Missouri Home Guard, USA*

Alexander Gaines Cardwell was born on 14 December 1838 in Greene County, Missouri, the son of Thomas Perrin Cardwell and Catherine (Steward) Cardwell. He is listed in the family home in the 1850 Greene County census, where he spent his early years in the rugged Ozark highlands of southwestern Missouri—a region marked by divided loyalties during the tumultuous years leading up to the Civil War.[1]

On 18 October 1858, Alexander married Sarah V. Mobley in Webster County, Missouri, where the couple would remain for much of their lives.[2] They appear together in the 1860 Webster County census, living as a young farming family just as Missouri's political and social climate began to fracture.[3] Over the course of their marriage, Alexander and Sarah had nine children: Mary C. Cardwell (1860–1878), William Thomas Cardwell (1864–1933), Perry W. Cardwell (1868–1917), John A. Cardwell (1871–1872), Melinda F. Cardwell (1874–), Samuel Tildon Cardwell (1876–1953), and three infant sons who died shortly after birth between 1879 and 1884. Sarah died in 1884, and Alexander later remarried to Elizabeth Denny on 06 June 1888 in Seymour, Webster County.[4]

With the outbreak of the Civil War in 1861, Missouri was immediately plunged into chaos. Although a slave state, it remained officially in the Union, and the state quickly became a battlefield of divided sympathies and internal conflict. On 10 June 1861, Alexander enlisted at Marshfield, Webster County, as a Private in Captain Bragg's Company, which was part of the

Webster County Regiment of the Missouri Home Guards. This militia-style force was one of several hastily organized local units raised under federal authority to protect Unionist communities and resist Confederate-leaning forces, bushwhackers, and pro-secession guerrillas within Missouri.

The Missouri Home Guards were not part of the regular Union Army but were sanctioned and supplied by the Union command in St. Louis during the earliest months of the war. They were assigned primarily to defensive and patrol duties within their own counties and surrounding regions, often operating without uniforms and using privately owned weapons. These local companies were crucial in countering early Confederate recruitment efforts and establishing Union control in contested areas like southwestern Missouri, which was home to significant Confederate sympathy.

Alexander served from 10 June to 11 August 1861, a period of only two months, but during a critical phase of the war in Missouri. His unit was likely involved in regional defense and local skirmishes rather than major engagements. One of the key events occurring during this time was the Battle of Wilson's Creek, fought on 10 August 1861 near Springfield—less than 50 miles from Marshfield. Although no direct record places Alexander at that battle, his service during this volatile period would have coincided with the preparation and mobilization of Unionist forces throughout the region.

While no additional service records for Alexander have been located beyond his brief enlistment, he was paid for his service in 1865, a common occurrence for early-war militia members whose official muster rolls and payrolls were later compiled for pension and reimbursement purposes. His short term of duty reflects the often-overlooked contributions of early-war Unionist Missourians who joined hastily formed home defense units before the Union Army was fully organized in the region.

After the war, Alexander returned to his life as a farmer in Webster County, where he raised his children and remained an active resident of the community. By the 1890 Veterans Schedule, many Missourians who had served briefly in local home guards began to apply for pensions or be recognized for their wartime roles, but there is no indication Alexander sought or received one.

Alexander Gaines Cardwell died on 15 April 1914 in Finley, Webster County, Missouri, at the age of 75. He was buried in the Cardwell Family Cemetery, a quiet resting place that bears testimony to the family's long-standing presence in the region.[5] His military service, though short in duration, reflects the urgency and uncertainty of Missouri's early Civil War months and the vital role played by men like him in holding the line for the Union in a deeply divided state. <u>Cardwell Line I - Predicted</u>. Photo Credit[6]

* * *

Photo 7.2: *Anderson H. Cardwell (1837-1905) Headstone - Mincy Cemetery, Taney County, Missouri.*

Anderson Huffman Cardwell (1837—1905) - *Wagoner/5th Sergeant - 5th Missouri State Militia Cavalry (2nd Organization), USA*

Anderson Huffman Cardwell was born in 1837 at Lone Mountain, Claiborne County, Tennessee, the son of Royal Cardwell and Anna (Claypole) Cardwell. His father died sometime between 1837 and 1840, leaving Anna a widow with several young children. By 1850, Anderson was listed in the household of his widowed mother in the Claiborne County census, alongside his siblings.[7] Over the next several years, Anderson and several of his adult siblings—John Wesley Cardwell, James Nelson Cardwell, Reuben Claypool Cardwell, and Royal Dowe Cardwell—relocated to Missouri, a frontier region at the time, likely drawn by new farmland and opportunity.

At the outbreak of the Civil War, Missouri quickly became a battleground of divided loyalties and guerrilla warfare. On 27 February 1862, Anderson enlisted as a Private in Company G, 5th Missouri State Militia Cavalry (Union) at Franklin County, Missouri. His enlistment came during a volatile phase of the war in the Trans-Mississippi theater, particularly across central and southern Missouri. The 5th Missouri S.M. Cavalry—also known in some sources as the 13th Missouri State Militia Cavalry—was organized to defend the Union cause within Missouri's borders and to suppress Confederate bushwhackers and irregular bands that terrorized the countryside.

On 2 September 1862, Anderson was promoted to the rank of 5th Sergeant, a non-commissioned officer position responsible for overseeing company logistics, guard duty assignments, and small detachments in field operations. This promotion reflected both his leadership ability and his steady presence in the field.

The 5th Missouri State Militia Cavalry primarily operated in south-central Missouri, particularly in the counties of Franklin, Phelps, Dent, Texas, Shannon, and Pulaski, where Confederate raids and guerrilla activity were common. During Anderson's time of service, the regiment was involved in scouting missions, escort details, and anti-guerrilla operations throughout the Ozarks region. While not engaged in large, set-piece battles, their work was no less dangerous. The constant exposure to skirmishes, ambushes, and harsh terrain made the regiment's service particularly grueling.

Among the regiment's more notable operations during Anderson's tenure was the defense of Unionist strongholds, including garrisons in Rolla and Houston, Missouri, and participation in regional expeditions designed to intercept Confederate recruiting parties and disrupt supply lines. Though records do not place Company G in any major battlefront outside Missouri, their service was essential in maintaining federal control in a region threatened by internal insurrection and Confederate sympathy.

Anderson served faithfully for the remainder of the war and was mustered out of service in April 1865, having completed three years, one month, and sixteen days of continuous duty. Like his brothers John Wesley and James Nelson, he survived the war and later received a Union pension, recognizing his service and its lasting effects on his health.

After the war, Anderson returned to civilian life and resumed farming. He married Eliza Jane Burlingame on 02 April 1865 in Phelps County, Missouri.[8] They raised a large family of eleven children: Ida Florence Cardwell (1866–1880), Ulysses Stanton Cardwell (1866–1870), Clara Augusta Cardwell (1870–1874), Lilian Aurora Cardwell (1873–1894), Olive Rosetta

Cardwell (1875–1921), Francis Allen Cardwell (1878–1954), Alma Myrtle Cardwell (1881–1967), Annie Laurel Cardwell (1883–1975), Edith Sophie Cardwell (1886–1934), Ivy Melinda Cardwell (1890–1976), and an unnamed infant son (1893–1893). His beloved wife Eliza died in 1893 following complications from childbirth.

The family appears in the 1860 census of Jefferson County, Missouri, and later in the 1880 and 1900 censuses of Texas County, Missouri.[9,10,11] By the end of his life, Anderson was living in Mincy, Taney County, Missouri, a quiet farming community near the Arkansas border. He died on 18 November 1905 and was buried at Mincy Cemetery, where his grave remains as a testament to his long service, both as a soldier and as a father.[12]

Anderson Huffman Cardwell was one of several sons of Royal Cardwell who served the Union during the Civil War. He, along with John Wesley and James Nelson Cardwell, served together in Company G of the 5th Missouri State Militia Cavalry. All three survived the conflict and are recorded in this volume. Another brother, Reuben Claypool Cardwell, died while serving in Company E of the 26th Missouri Infantry, and is buried in Elmwood Cemetery, Franklin County. Yet another, Royal (Rial) Dowe Cardwell, appears to have died while in service, though the details of his enlistment remain unconfirmed and his biography is not included here pending further research.[13,14,15,16,17]

Through their collective sacrifice, the Cardwell brothers of Missouri helped preserve the Union cause during a time when the state was fractured by violence and uncertainty. Their legacy endures in the communities they defended and the descendants they left behind. <u>Cardwell Line I - Predicted</u>. Photo Credit[18]

* * *

Photo 7.3: *Aurelius L. Cardwell (1833-1890) Headstone - Combs Cemetery, Clark County, Missouri.*

Aurelius L. Cardwell (1833-1890) - *Private - 2nd Missouri State Militia Cavalry; Capt. Silver's Company (K), 1st N. E. Cavalry Regiment Missouri Home Guard; & Company D, 2nd Missouri State Militia Cavalry, USA*

Aurelius L. Cardwell was born on 04 May 1833, most likely in Anderson County, Kentucky. While his exact parentage remains undetermined, records suggest he may have been connected to local Cardwell families living in the region. By 1850, he appears in the Hancock County, Illinois census in the household of Austin Hughes, a man who had previously lived in Anderson County, Kentucky. It is possible Aurelius was residing with relatives or family acquaintances, but no definitive documentation of his parents has been found.[19]

Aurelius relocated to Clark County, Missouri, where he would remain for the rest of his life. On 27 December 1863, he married Sarah H. Cottingham in Clark County.[20] They had four children: Henry James Cardwell (1865–1889), A. Edgar Cardwell (1868–), Maggie Cardwell (1869–1928), and Nellie M. Cardwell (1876–1900). The family lived in and around Luray, Missouri, a small agricultural community in the northeastern corner of the state.

At the outbreak of the Civil War, Missouri quickly devolved into a state of internal conflict and divided loyalties. In this context, Aurelius Cardwell enlisted as a Private on 17 June 1861 in Luray, Clark County, joining Captain Silver's Company of the 1st Northeast Missouri Cavalry Regiment, Missouri Home Guard. This unit was a short-term, emergency militia formed under the authority of the Union military command in St. Louis to protect local communities in northeast Missouri from Confederate sympathizers and guerrilla bands. These Home Guard companies were locally organized, lightly armed, and often saw action in county-level skirmishes rather than formal battles.

The 1st N.E. Missouri Cavalry Home Guard operated under the broader leadership of Colonel David Moore and participated in a number of anti-guerrilla operations throughout Clark, Lewis, and Scotland counties. They were active during the tense months of summer 1861, when Confederate-leaning raiders and recruiters sought to disrupt Union control in northeastern Missouri. Though there is no record placing Aurelius in a named engagement, the unit saw several skirmishes during this period, including at Athens, Missouri, in early August 1861. However, Aurelius is listed as having deserted his company on 01 August 1861, shortly before this action. No record explains the desertion, and such designations in early-war militia units were not uncommon, often resulting from miscommunication, disbandment of short-term forces, or dissatisfaction with irregular organization and uncertain leadership.

Despite the desertion listing, Aurelius reenlisted several months later, on 01 March 1862, in Alexandria, Clark County, as a Private in Company D of the 2nd Missouri State Militia Cavalry—a more formally organized unit operating under federal authority. The Missouri State Militia Cavalry regiments, including the 2nd, were created to provide long-term security in the state. These mounted troops were tasked with guarding Union interests, escorting supply trains, disrupting guerrilla operations, and ensuring control of communication routes across contested areas of Missouri.

The 2nd M.S.M. Cavalry was primarily engaged in scouting missions and local garrison work across northeast and north-central Missouri during the spring and summer of 1862. While Company D's full operational record during Cardwell's short tenure is limited, the unit was involved in small-scale engagements against bushwhackers and Confederate irregulars in Shelby, Knox, and Marion Counties, among others. Aurelius's name appears in records until June 1862, suggesting he served approximately three months before leaving the regiment. There are no records indicating he reenlisted or served beyond that time.

After the war, Aurelius resumed farming life near Luray, where he remained active in the community for the next three decades. Tragedy struck on 04 July 1890, when Aurelius was struck and killed by a locomotive on the M.I. & N. Railway, just west of Luray, during local Independence Day festivities. His sudden and tragic death at the age of 57 was recorded in local newspapers and mentioned in his daughter's later obituary. He was buried at Combs Cemetery in Clark County, a resting place close to his family and longtime home.[21]

Throughout official documents, Aurelius's middle initial varies between "L" and "H," but the balance of historical and military evidence strongly supports that he was the same man who served in both early-war Missouri units. His military career—brief and localized—reflects the experience of many rural Missourians who joined hastily assembled militia forces during the Civil War's chaotic early phase and later served in state-authorized cavalry units tasked with pacifying their own volatile homeland.

Aurelius L. Cardwell's story, though modest in scope, is a meaningful part of the broader narrative of Civil War Missouri—a state torn by internal division, irregular warfare, and civilian hardship. His life and service are preserved here alongside the stories of other Cardwells who answered the call in both Union and Confederate ranks. Ancestry Undetermined. Photo Credit[22]

* * *

Photo 7.4: *James Nelson Cardwell (1835-1907) and wife Headstone. Prospect Church Cemetery, Lonedell, Franklin County, Missouri.*

James Nelson Cardwell (1835—1907) **-** *Sergeant - Company G, 5th Missouri State Militia Cavalry, USA*

James Nelson Cardwell was born on 07 December 1835 in Lone Mountain, Claiborne County, Tennessee, the tenth of eleven children born to Royal Cardwell and Anna (Claypole) Cardwell. Following the death of his father between 1837 and 1840, James was raised in a single-parent household and appears with his mother and siblings in the 1850 census of Claiborne County.[23] From the age of fifteen, James worked to support her, demonstrating a strong sense of duty and responsibility from an early age.

In 1855, at age twenty, James left Tennessee and moved first to Indiana, then to Pacific, Missouri, where he spent a winter before settling briefly in Jefferson County. By 1860, he was living in Washington County, Missouri, along with several siblings who had also migrated west. He is recorded in that year's census as a farmer.[24]

James first entered military service in the fall of 1861, enlisting in the Missouri State Militia for a six-month term. He was mustered out on 08 January 1862. Just two months later, on 08 March 1862, he reenlisted in Company G of the 5th Missouri State Militia Cavalry at St. Joseph, Missouri. He was described at enlistment as 27 years of age, 5 feet 11 inches in height, with a light complexion, blue eyes, and light hair. His occupation was listed as farmer, and his birthplace as Claiborne County, Tennessee.

James advanced through the ranks during his service, being promoted to Corporal on 19 September 1862 and again to Sergeant on 01 July 1863. He eventually held the role of Quartermaster Sergeant for his company. The 5th Missouri State Militia Cavalry was largely engaged in counter-guerrilla operations and internal security duties across Missouri and parts of Arkansas during his term of service. While his unit was active throughout the war, James was not assigned to major field battles but was stationed in operations such as patrols, guard duty, and skirmishes aimed at suppressing Confederate guerrilla activity, particularly in the regions around Rolla, Jefferson City, and the Ozarks. He was mustered out of service on 13 April 1865 at Rolla, Missouri, after over three years of continuous military duty.

After the war, James returned to Franklin County, Missouri, and farmed for a season before opening a general store at Virginia Mines. He operated this business for four years before relocating to Texas County, Missouri, where he again ran a general store. In 1874, James moved back to Franklin County and settled on a 200-acre farm, where he spent the rest of his life.

He married Susan L. Worsham on 06 April 1873 in Texas County, Missouri. They had the following children; Ole Stanton Cardwell (1873-1941), Affie B. Cardwell (1877-1956), Nicholas Cardwell (1880-1956), and Roscoe C. Cardwell (1884-1902). The family is listed in the 1880 Franklin County, Missouri and the 1900 Franklin County, Missouri census records.[25,26]

In addition to his agricultural and business endeavors, James became involved in local government. He served as justice of the peace for about a year and a half. A committed Republican following the war, James had previously aligned with the Democratic Party.

James Nelson Cardwell died on 25 February 1907 in Franklin County, Missouri. He received a veteran's pension for his Civil War service. He is buried at Prospect Cemetery in Lonedell, Franklin County, Missouri.[27]

James was one of several Cardwell brothers who served the Union cause during the Civil War. His brothers—Anderson Huffman Cardwell and John Wesley Cardwell—served in the same company of the 5th Missouri State Militia Cavalry, and all survived the conflict. Another brother, Reuben Claypool Cardwell, died while in service with the 26th Missouri Infantry. James's grandfather, John Cardwell, served as a soldier in the American Revolution. His mother, Annie (Claypool) Cardwell, died in 1856 at the age of sixty. James's life reflects a legacy of military service, resilience, and dedication to both family and country. <u>Cardwell Line I - Predicted</u>. Photo Credit[28]

✳ ✳ ✳

Photo 7.5: *John Anthony Cardwell (1834-1898) Headstone - Minden Cemetery, Minden, Kearney County, Nebraska.*

John Anthony Cardwell (1834—1898) - *Corporal - Company K, 2nd*

Missouri State Militia Cavalry & Company L, 11th Missouri State Militia Cavalry, USA

John Anthony Cardwell was born on 26 October 1834 in Marion County, Missouri, to Anthony Cardwell and Martha "Patsy" (Stanford) Cardwell. He is recorded in their household in the 1850 census of Marion County and again in 1860, living in neighboring Shelby County.[29,30]

Raised in the rolling farmlands of northeastern Missouri, John likely assisted in the agricultural livelihood of his family until the outbreak of the Civil War.

John enlisted on 12 March 1862 in Newark, Knox County, Missouri, as a Private in Company K of the 2nd Missouri Cavalry, Union Army. At the time of his enlistment, he was 27 years of age and noted in the records as "having no horse," a common situation for newly joined cavalry recruits. He enlisted for the duration of the war and was promoted to the rank of Corporal on 18 April 1862. While he is briefly shown on the roster of Company L, 11th Missouri State Militia Cavalry, for July and August 1862, his primary service remained with the 2nd Missouri Cavalry.

During his term of service, John was consistently marked present on muster rolls, with only one known exception—his assignment to a detached military mail route to Jonesboro, Illinois, in September 1864. As a member of the 2nd Missouri Cavalry, he participated in the unit's operations in Missouri, Arkansas, and Tennessee. Notably, during the period of John's confirmed presence, the regiment was engaged in a series of operations against Confederate guerrillas and cavalry units in southern Missouri and northern Arkansas. This included participation in the Union's efforts to disrupt Confederate General Sterling Price's movements during his 1864 raid through Missouri. While John may not have been directly engaged in large-scale battles, his unit's continuous scouting, escort, and supply protection duties were vital to the Union's control of the region.

John was honorably discharged on 17 April 1865 at St. Louis, Missouri, just days after General Lee's surrender at Appomattox. He returned to civilian life and married Mary E. Mitchell on 09 February 1868 in Shelby County, Missouri. They had two sons: William Elbert Cardwell (1870–1961) and James Hartwell Cardwell (1875–1961). By 1880, John had moved with his family to Harlan County, Nebraska, where he resumed farming.[31] He received a pension for his wartime service, reflecting his honorable conduct and physical toll from three years of cavalry duty. Known in his later years as "a quiet, honest, hard-working man," his obituary praised him as "a good citizen, a kind husband, and an affectionate father."

John died of pneumonia on 18 November 1898 in Minden, Kearney County, Nebraska, at the age of 64. He is buried at Minden Cemetery.[32]His brother, William M. Cardwell, served in the Union Army and is recorded in this book. Cardwell Line I - Predicted. Photo Credit[33]

* * *

Photo 7.6: *John Hugh Curtis Cardwell (1829-1922) Headstone, Cardwell Chapel Cemetery, Webster County, Missouri.*

John Hugh Curtis Cardwell (1829—1922) - *Private - Capt. Bryan's Co. (E), Webster County Regiment, Missouri Home Guard, USA*

John Hugh Curtis Cardwell was born on 10 December 1829 in Roane County, Tennessee, to Thomas Perrin Cardwell and Catherine (Steward) Cardwell. The Cardwell family migrated westward and by 1834 had settled in what would become Webster County, Missouri. By the time of the 1850 census, John was listed in the household of his parents in Greene County, Missouri, during a period when the county boundaries were still shifting in the Ozarks region.[34]

Around 1854, John married Keisha E. Ellison, and together they raised a large family in the Missouri Ozarks. Their children included: Anna Francis Cardwell (1854–1936), Missouri Angeline Cardwell (1856–1901), Susan E. Cardwell (1858–1921), John Thomas Cardwell (1861–1920), John Lafayette Cardwell (1863–1911), Hettie C. Cardwell (1867–), Mary J. Cardwell (1873–1954), and Leva Mandy Cardwell (1888–1919). The family appears in the 1860, 1870, 1880, 1900, and 1910 census records for Taney County, Missouri, and in the 1920 census of Webster County.[35,36,37,38,39,40]

When the Civil War reached Missouri, John enlisted for Union service on 10 June 1861 at White Oak, Dunklin County, Missouri. He mustered into Company E of the Webster County Regiment of the Missouri Home Guard, a short-term defensive unit organized for emergency service in the early months of the war. This regiment was part of the broader effort to stabilize loyal Unionist control in central and southwestern Missouri during a period of great unrest, secessionist violence, and bushwhacker activity. Home Guard companies such as John's were tasked primarily with defending local infrastructure, suppressing Confederate sympathizers, and supporting Union recruitment efforts.

John's service in the Home Guard lasted through 11 August 1861, when the regiment was mustered out. His recorded duty period of just over two months occurred during a time of escalating tensions in Missouri, notably leading up to the Battle of Wilson's Creek (10 August 1861), although no records place him or his company directly in that engagement. His brief term likely involved local defense duties rather than formal battlefield action.[41]

Following the war, John returned to farming and family life. He continued to live in southern Missouri and remained active in his community. At some point, he may have applied for or received an Invalid Pension, which commenced on 23 July 1908; however, the unit designation listed in the pension record does not align with Company E of the Missouri Home Guard. Despite this discrepancy, no alternative matching service record has been found for another John Cardwell in that region, and it remains likely that the pension was granted for his brief but legitimate Home Guard service.

John lived a long life and remained in Missouri through his final years. He passed away on 24 January 1922 in Taney County at the age of 92. He was buried at Cardwell Chapel Cemetery in Webster County, Missouri—a resting place that connects his legacy with the community he helped shape before, during, and after the Civil War.[42]

His brother, Alexander Gaines Cardwell, also served briefly in the Union-aligned Missouri Home Guard, and is recorded elsewhere in this volume. Together, they were among the many Cardwell men who joined Union forces from southern Missouri during a time when loyalties were deeply divided and the region was wracked by guerrilla warfare and military uncertainty. <u>Cardwell Line I - Predicted</u>. Photo Credit[43]

Photo 7.7: *John T. Cardwell (1838-1903) Headstone, Fir Grove Cemetery, Cottage Grove, Lane County, Oregon*

John T. Cardwell (1838—1903) - *Private - Company B, 18th Missouri Cavalry, USA*

John T. Cardwell was born in January 1838 in Jackson County, Tennessee, to Wiltshire Cardwell and Mary (Campbell) Cardwell. During the westward migration of many frontier families, the Cardwells moved first to Keokuk County, Iowa, by the 1850 census, then on to Cass County, Nebraska Territory, by 1860.[44,45] By the mid-1860s, John and some members of the family had relocated again, this time to Andrew County, Missouri.

John was drafted into federal service late in the Civil War, entering the ranks as a Private in Company B, 18th Regiment Missouri Infantry, United States Army. His official induction date was 17 November 1864, at which time he was 26 years old and listed as born in Jackson County, Tennessee. The 18th Missouri Infantry had already seen significant action by the time of his conscription, having participated in major engagements including the battles of Shiloh, Corinth, and Atlanta. However, John did not join the regiment until its final phase of operations, which centered around garrison duties and post-war demobilization.

Shortly after his induction, John was reported to have suffered from an unspecified ailment or medical condition. He was sent to St. Louis, Missouri, where a military surgeon recommended his discharge due to disability. His official military service, therefore, was brief and did not include participation in any field operations or battles. He was likely discharged in early 1865, during a period when the Union Army was rapidly reducing its numbers as hostilities drew to a close.

After leaving the army, John eventually journeyed further west. In 1875, he married Josephine William in Elko, Nevada, a frontier community that had grown rapidly due to the expansion of the Central Pacific Railroad and mining interests.[46] The couple remained in Nevada for several years and were recorded in the 1880 federal census for Lander County, where John worked, likely as a laborer or in agriculture—though the exact occupation is unconfirmed.[47]

By the mid-1880s, the family had moved again—this time to the growing settlement of Cottage Grove in Lane County, Oregon, where many Civil War veterans sought new opportunities. It was there, in 1887, that their only known child, Della Irene Cardwell, was born.

John T. Cardwell spent his remaining years in Cottage Grove, where he lived near his brother George Washington Cardwell, who had also settled in Lane County after serving in the Union Army. Their other brothers, Daniel M. Cardwell and Hiram B. Cardwell, also served in Union regiments during the Civil War and are documented elsewhere in this volume.

John passed away on 06 January 1903 in Lane County, Oregon, and was laid to rest at Fir Grove Cemetery in Cottage Grove. Though his time in uniform was short and limited by health concerns, his journey—like that of many frontier soldiers—reflected the hardships and constant movement that defined the lives of those who came of age in the Civil War era and went on to shape the American West.[48] Cardwell Line I - Predicted. Photo Credit[49]

* * *

Photo 7.8: *John Wesley Cardwell (1822-1900) Headstone. Elmwood Cemetery, Prairie, Franklin County, Missouri.*

John Wesley Cardwell - (1822-1900) - *Veterinary Sergeant - Company G, 5th Missouri State Militia Cavalry (2nd Organization), USA*

John Wesley Cardwell was born around 1822 at Lone Mountain, Claiborne County, Tennessee, to Royal Cardwell and Anna (Claypole) Cardwell. His early life was marked by hardship, as his father died between 1837 and 1840, leaving Anna to raise the children alone. John appears with his widowed mother and siblings in the 1850 census of Claiborne County, Tennessee.[50]

He married Sarah Margaret Beeler on 19 May 1853 in Anderson County, Tennessee.[51] The couple had three children: Mary Ann Cardwell (1856–), Sarah C. Cardwell (1857–), and Lafayette Huffman Cardwell (1867–1918). During the 1850s, John joined a larger family migration westward and settled in Washington County, Missouri, where he and Sarah are recorded in the 1860 census. He worked as a farmer prior to the outbreak of the Civil War.[52]

On 21 February 1862, John enlisted in Company G, 5th Missouri State Militia Cavalry (2nd Organization), at Franklin County, Missouri, for service in the Union Army. At the time, he was 38 years of age, 5 feet 8 inches in height, with a dark complexion, grey eyes, and brown hair. His civilian occupation was listed as farmer. The 5th Missouri S.M. Cavalry was a Unionist unit formed to combat Confederate guerrilla activity and protect loyalist communities in Missouri.

Early in his service, John was designated a farrier—a specialist responsible for the care and shoeing of horses, a critical role in cavalry operations. On 24

May 1862, he was promoted to Veterinary Sergeant, a position authorized for each battalion within a cavalry regiment. In this role, he supervised other farriers and was responsible for the health and maintenance of horses, essential to mobility and effectiveness in the field. He received a monthly salary of $17, ranking on par with a sergeant of cavalry.

John's military service was largely spent performing duties critical to the support of cavalry operations rather than frontline combat. He is recorded absent as a witness in Rolla, Missouri in September 1863, likely appearing in a military or legal proceeding. In November 1863, he was assigned to escort duty, which may have involved safeguarding supply lines, couriers, or prisoners between federal posts in Missouri and adjacent regions. Though present with his unit during major operations in Missouri and Arkansas, there are no records indicating he was engaged in combat during large-scale battles. His service appears to have remained within Missouri during the conflict.

John was honorably discharged on 13 April 1865 at Rolla, Missouri, shortly before the official end of the war. Like many others in the Missouri State Militia, his role helped to stabilize the region during a time of extreme internal division and violence.

After the war, John remained in Franklin County, Missouri, where he continued his life as a farmer. He died in 1900 and was buried at Elmwood Cemetery, located in Prairie, Franklin County, Missouri.[53]

John Wesley Cardwell was one of several sons of Royal Cardwell who served in the Union Army during the Civil War. His brothers Anderson Huffman Cardwell and James Nelson Cardwell also served in Company G of the 5th Missouri State Militia Cavalry, while another brother, Reuben Claypool Cardwell, died in service with the 26th Missouri Infantry. Their collective participation reflects the commitment of the Cardwell family to the Union cause, despite their Southern roots in Tennessee. <u>Cardwell Line I - Predicted</u>. Photo Credit[54]

* * *

Photo 7.9: *Melville B. Cardwell (1846-1891) Headstone. Elmwood Church Cemetery, Lonedell, Franklin County, Missouri.*

Melville Beveridge Cardwell (1846-1891) - *Private - Company K, 40th Missouri Infantry, USA*

Melville Beveridge Cardwell was born on 31 December 1846 at Lone Mountain, Claiborne County, Tennessee, to Reuben Claypole Cardwell and Luritta (Sanders) Cardwell. His early years were spent in Tennessee, and he is listed in the 1850 Claiborne County census with his parents.[55] By 1860, the family had relocated to Jefferson County, Missouri, likely part of a larger migration of Unionist Tennessee families seeking safety and opportunity in the border states.[56]

Melville enlisted for Union service on 29 August 1864 at St. Louis, Missouri, joining Company K of the 40th Missouri Infantry Regiment. According to his enlistment records, he was 18 years old, though his birth year suggests he may have been slightly younger. He was described as standing 5 feet 5 inches, with blue eyes, light hair, and a fair complexion. His occupation at the time was listed as farmer, and his place of birth was incorrectly noted as Franklin County, Missouri, possibly due to family relocation or clerical error.

The 40th Missouri Infantry was a late-war regiment organized for one year of service, primarily tasked with defending Missouri and participating in Union operations in Tennessee and Mississippi. Melville is marked present for duty during the fall of 1864, which places him with the regiment during its most significant campaign: the Franklin-Nashville Campaign.

In November and December 1864, the 40th Missouri was involved in the Union counter-offensive against Confederate General John Bell Hood's Army of Tennessee. While much of the regiment was engaged in movements and skirmishes along supply lines, detachments supported actions near Columbia and Spring Hill, and were present during the Battle of Nashville on 15–16 December 1864. Though Melville's specific role is not detailed, records confirm he was marked present during this period, and it is likely he participated in rear-area defense or support roles that enabled the Union victory at Nashville.

Following the campaign, the regiment returned to Missouri in early 1865 and performed garrison duty until the end of their term. No official record of Melville's discharge has been found, but the regiment was mustered out in August 1865, suggesting he likely completed his service at that time.

After the war, Melville returned to civilian life in Missouri. He married Susan Tyler Hurt on 16 February 1870 in Franklin County, Missouri.[57] The couple is listed in the 1870 Washington County, Missouri census.[58] They eventually returned to Franklin County, appearing there in the 1880 census.[59] They had the following children: Oddie L. Cardwell (1876-), Louise Cardwell (1879-1940), Joseph Burnam Cardwell (1881-1942), and Frank Cornelius Cardwell (1883-1957).

Melville died on 24 March 1891 in Franklin County, Missouri, at the age of 44. He was laid to rest at Elmwood Church Cemetery in Lonedell, Franklin County, Missouri.[60] His service in the late-war defense of the Union, though brief, was part of a broader family contribution to the war effort—his father, Reuben Claypole Cardwell, also served and is recorded elsewhere in this volume. <u>Cardwell Line I - Predicted</u>. Photo Credit[61]

* * *

Photo 7.10: *Reuben Claypole Cardwell (1820-1862) Headstone - Elmwood Cemetery, Prairie, Franklin County, Missouri.*

Reuben Claypole Cardwell (1820—1862) - *Private - Company E, 26th Missouri Infantry, USA -* **Died of Disease**

Reuben Claypole Cardwell was born about 1820 at Lone Mountain, Claiborne County, Tennessee, to Royal Cardwell and Anna (Claypole) Cardwell. On 31 October 1844, he married Luritta Sanders in Claiborne County. By 1850, Reuben and Luritta had moved their growing family to Jefferson County, Missouri, where they appear in the 1860 census for Big River Township.[62,63] They had the children: Melville Beveridge Cardwell (1846-1891), Franklin "Frank" Cornelius Cardwell (1848-1937), Margaret Letitia Cardwell (1852-1940), Martha Emmaline Cardwell (1855-1940), Elizabeth Cornelia Cardwell (1857-1929), and Mary Alice Cardwell (1861-1948).

Reuben enlisted on 10 October 1861 at Moselle, Franklin County, Missouri, as a Private in Company K of the 26th Missouri Infantry, U.S. Army. At the time of his enlistment, the regiment had just been organized and was stationed primarily in southeast Missouri as part of efforts to secure that strategically vital region for the Union cause. The 26th Missouri Infantry was involved in stabilizing federal control during the chaotic months following the Battle of Wilson's Creek.

Reuben was marked present with his company from his enlistment through February 1862. However, beginning in March 1862, he began to suffer from chronic diarrhea—a common and often fatal condition in the army at that time due to poor sanitation and exposure. He was granted furlough to recover but never returned to duty. Pension records confirm that he remained ill for six months and died of disease on 16 August 1862 at his home in Franklin County while still officially on furlough.

His widow, Luritta, applied for a federal widow's pension on 12 August 1863. Her application was supported by fellow veterans and confirmed that Reuben died at home while suffering from ailments contracted during active service. She was ultimately awarded a pension for his service and sacrifice. A family descendant, Frank Cardwell Moffett, adds family tradition that Reuben had red hair and an aquiline nose.

Reuben is buried at Elmwood Cemetery in Prairie, Franklin County, Missouri, where several other members of the Cardwell family are interred.[64] His oldest son, Melville Beveridge Cardwell, would follow in his father's footsteps, enlisting in 1864 with the Union army and serving until the war's end.

Reuben Claypole Cardwell's brief but honorable service is a reminder of the many soldiers whose battles were fought not only in the field, but in the long struggle against disease—then one of the Civil War's deadliest enemies. Cardwell Line I - Predicted. Photo Credit[65]

* * *

Richard E. Cardwell (1828-) - *Private - Company H, 50th Missouri Infantry, USA*

Richard E. Cardwell was born about 1828 in Franklin County, Tennessee, to Perrin Cardwell and Catherine (Cook) Cardwell. His father died around 1830 in Greene County, Arkansas, where Richard spent his early years. He is listed in the 1840 Greene County census as a young member of the household.[66] Sometime in the early 1850s, Richard married Mary "Polly" Busby, likely in Arkansas, although no official record of their marriage has been located. Based on the birth of their first child in 1856, it is estimated they were married by 1855. They had two known daughters: Melissa Cardwell (1856-) and Mary Elizabeth "Betsy" Cardwell (1859–1944). The family was residing in Cache Township, Lawrence County, Arkansas, by the 1860 census, where Richard was listed as a farmer.[67]

Richard enlisted late in the war, joining the Union Army on 11 February 1865 at Cape Girardeau, Missouri. He was mustered into Company H of the 50th Missouri Infantry, a regiment organized in the final months of the conflict. At the time of his enlistment, he was 38 years old, stood 5 feet 10 inches tall, and had a red complexion, gray eyes, and dark hair. His occupation was listed as farmer, and he gave Franklin County, Tennessee as his place of birth. The 50th Missouri Infantry was primarily assigned to post duty in the Department of Missouri and Arkansas, guarding important supply routes, bridges, and railways from guerrilla activity. As Richard was marked present from enlistment through his discharge and the regiment saw no major engagements during this period, it is most likely he was involved in routine garrison duty and internal security.

Richard was honorably discharged on 05 August 1865 at Benton Barracks, near St. Louis, Missouri. The barracks served as a major Union training, hospital, and discharge center during the war's final years. His brief but honorable service came during a transitional time in the war, as hostilities drew to a close and soldiers were gradually mustered out.

Following his military service, Richard's trail grows cold. Despite exhaustive research, no further records of his life have been located. His wife, Mary "Polly" Busby Cardwell, appears to have died around 1865, perhaps shortly after the war's end. No grave has been located for either of them, and no records have been found in later census years. The fate of their daughter Melissa remains unknown, while their second daughter, Mary Elizabeth "Betsy," went on to marry and lived until 1944. It is likely the two girls are listed with Richard's brother, George Cardwell, in the 1870 census in Big Creek, Craighead County, Arkansas.[68]

Although Richard E. Cardwell's postwar life remains obscure, his wartime service—however brief—connects him to the greater history of the Cardwell family's contributions during the Civil War. His enlistment in the waning months of the conflict reflects the commitment of even those in remote areas to the Union cause. His story, like that of so many late-war enlistees, is one of quiet service and sacrifice at a pivotal moment in American history. Cardwell Line I - Predicted.

* * *

Photo 7.11: William McAfee Cardwell (1837-1920). Fresno, California
circa 1920

Photo 7.12: William McAfee Cardwell Cardwell (1837-1920) Headstone
- Mountain View Cemetery, Fresno, Fresno County, California.

William McAfee Cardwell (1837-1920) - *Lieutenant - Company L & G, 11th Missouri State Militia Cavalry, USA* - **Prisoner of War**

William McAfee Cardwell was born on 23 November 1837 in Shelby County, Missouri, to Anthony Cardwell and Martha "Patsy" (Stanford) Cardwell. He is listed in their household in the 1850 census of Marion County, Missouri, and again in the 1860 census of Shelby County.[69,70] His early years were spent in northeast Missouri, where the family moved frequently between counties bordering the Mississippi River.

William enlisted on 14 April 1862 in Shelbyville, Shelby County, Missouri, as a Private in Company L of the 11th Missouri State Militia Cavalry (Union). He stated his age as 25, his birthplace as Marion County, Missouri, and listed his occupation as artist. He was described in his enlistment records as 5 feet 11 ½ inches tall, with a dark complexion, blue eyes, and dark hair.

The 11th Missouri State Militia Cavalry was part of a specialized force assigned to internal security, patrolling Missouri's divided countryside, escorting supply trains, and engaging Confederate guerrillas. The unit saw frequent skirmishing across northeast and central Missouri. William was promoted to Bugler shortly after enlistment, on 16 April 1862. During the Battle of Kirksville in August 1862, he was captured by Confederate forces and held as a prisoner of war for approximately six months before being paroled.

Following his release, he returned to duty and was promoted to Sergeant on 12 June 1863. His service records note a loss of his horse during his initial capture. He was assigned to detached service in St. Louis during early 1864 and returned to his regular unit in April. He was again on special duty in the spring of 1865 and was promoted to First Lieutenant on 01 June 1865. His obituary later stated that he was mustered out at New Orleans, having served a total of three years and ten months. He was a member of the Grand Army of the Republic (G.A.R.).

After the war, William married Melissa Louisa Wharton on 08 October 1871 in Shelby County, Missouri.[71] They had two sons: Wilbert "Bert" Cardwell (1873–1936), and Frank Wharton Cardwell (1876–1953). By 1880, the family was living in Hastings, Adams County, Nebraska, where William worked in ranching. He left Nebraska in 1881 and arrived in Fresno, California, on his forty-fourth birthday—23 November 1881. He would remain in the Fresno area for the next thirty-nine years. He is listed in the 1900, 1910, and 1920 Fresno County, California census records.[72,73,74]

In Fresno, William pursued a career as a contractor and also owned and operated vineyards. One vineyard was located at West Park east of Fresno, and another later near Fowler. Eventually retiring from farming, he focused entirely on his contracting work. He ran for sheriff of Fresno County on the Populist ticket but was not elected, and though he remained politically active, he did not seek office again.

William died at his home at 357 Glenn Avenue, Fresno, on 26 November 1920, just three days after his eighty-third birthday. His obituary described him as a "pioneer contractor" and noted his Civil War service with distinction.[75] He is buried at Mountain View Cemetery in Fresno, Fresno County, California.[76] His brother, John Anthony Cardwell, also served in the Union Army and is included elsewhere in this volume. Cardwell Line I - Predicted. Photo Credits[77,78]

* * *

William Nimrod W. Cardwell (1838-1890) - *Private - Osage County Regiment, Missouri Home Guard & Company B, 8th Missouri State Militia Cavalry, USA*

William Nimrod W. Cardwell was born on 2 January 1838 in Calloway County, Kentucky, to William N. Cardwell and Sidney N. (Langford) Cardwell. He appears with his parents in the 1850 census for Calloway County. During the 1850s, the Cardwell family relocated to Benton County, Missouri, where they are listed in the 1860 census.[79,80] Like many young men swept up in the conflict, William answered the call to arms early in the war.

He first enlisted as a Private on 5 July 1861 in the Osage County Regiment, Missouri Home Guard, a short-term defensive unit raised during the early months of the Civil War to protect local communities from Confederate incursions and bushwhacker activity. The Home Guard units were active primarily in Missouri's central counties and were frequently engaged in skirmishes and patrol actions rather than formal battlefield engagements. William's term with the Home Guard ended on 20 December 1861.

Just nine days later, on 29 December 1861, William re-enlisted in Company B of the Missouri State Militia Cavalry at Jefferson City, Missouri. These state militia regiments were created under Federal authority to serve as full-time Unionist troops within the state of Missouri, tasked with counterinsurgency, scouting, and maintaining law and order in an area plagued by guerrilla warfare.

Although detailed records of his company's movements are limited, the Missouri State Militia Cavalry operated extensively throughout the central and southwestern parts of the state during the period of William's service. From late 1861 through early 1865, William would have participated in mounted patrols, escort duties, and small-scale engagements rather than large, set-piece battles. His unit likely engaged in operations against Confederate raiders and guerrilla bands such as those led by William Quantrill, "Bloody Bill" Anderson, and Joseph Shelby—whose attacks on Unionist civilians and infrastructure plagued Missouri's war-torn countryside.

He was marked as present for duty during his term and was discharged in February 1865, after over three years of continuous mounted service. His longevity in a cavalry role during Missouri's irregular warfare campaign attests to his endurance and reliability as a soldier during one of the Civil War's most dangerous and chaotic regional theaters.

After the war, William returned to Benton County, Missouri. On 14 April 1867, he married Margaret Rebecca Blake, and the couple began raising a family.[81] They had four known children: Nancy Josephine Cardwell (1869–1918), Mary Elizabeth Cardwell (1871–1890), Margaret Rebecca Cardwell (1873–), and Thomas L. Cardwell (1876–). William and Margaret appear in the 1870 federal census in Benton County.[82]

By 1880, the Cardwells had moved further southwest, settling in Fannin County, Texas, likely in search of better farmland and a new beginning in the postwar frontier economy. William is listed there in the 1880 census, continuing his work as a farmer.[83] In 1890, he appears again in Fannin County in the Veterans Schedule, which confirms his service with the Missouri State Militia Cavalry during the war.

William died in Fannin County, Texas, on 21 November 1890 at the age of 52.[84] The exact location of his burial remains unknown, and no marked grave has been located as of this writing. His life reflects that of many Southern Unionists from border states—men who were caught between conflicting loyalties, chose the Union cause, and served with distinction in the difficult and often-overlooked war fought within Missouri's borders. Cardwell Line III - Predicted.

Nebraska Territory
Cardwell Union Soldiers

As a sparsely populated territory far from the war's primary battlefields, Nebraska's contributions to the Civil War focused on protecting the frontier, securing trade routes, and preventing potential Confederate threats in the West. Although no major battles occurred within the territory, Nebraska soldiers were tasked with guarding settlements, escorting wagon trains, and engaging in skirmishes with hostile forces that threatened Union-aligned settlers and infrastructure.

Three Cardwell brothers, Daniel M. Cardwell, George W. Cardwell, and Hiram B. Cardwell, served together in the 1st Nebraska Cavalry, with Hiram also serving in the 2nd Nebraska Cavalry. Their service was vital in maintaining order in the vast frontier lands of the Nebraska Territory.

Though far from the war's largest battles, Daniel, George, and Hiram Cardwell played an essential role in securing the western frontier for the Union. Their service in the 1st and 2nd Nebraska Cavalry ensured that supply routes remained open, settlements were protected, and potential Confederate influences in the West were suppressed.

This chapter honors the Cardwell brothers of Nebraska, preserving their contributions to Union victory and frontier defense during the Civil War.

* * *

Daniel M. Cardwell (1840-1882) - *Private - Company K, 1st Nebraska Cavalry, USA*

Daniel Cardwell was born around 1840 in Jackson County, Tennessee, the son of Wiltshire Cardwell and Mary (Campbell) Cardwell. By 1850, the family had relocated to Keokuk County, Iowa, and by 1860 they were living in Cass County, Nebraska.[1,2] At the age of 24, Daniel enlisted in the Union Army on 05 September 1863 at St. Louis, Missouri, joining Company K of the 1st Nebraska Cavalry as a Private. His enlistment records describe him as 5 feet 6 inches tall, with a dark complexion, gray eyes, and black hair. He listed his birthplace as Jackson County, Tennessee, and his occupation as farmer.

The 1st Nebraska Cavalry was active throughout the Western frontier, tasked with protecting vital supply lines, escorting settlers, and engaging in skirmishes with Confederate raiders and Native American forces during the latter stages of the Civil War. The regiment saw extended duty in the Nebraska Territory, Dakota Territory, and surrounding regions, often operating in remote and rugged conditions. Although not engaged in large-scale battles like units in the Eastern Theater, their work was crucial in maintaining federal control across the Great Plains.

Daniel served faithfully until his discharge on 18 July 1866 at Omaha, Nebraska. Not long after his return to civilian life, he married Lavonia C. Webb around 1868. The couple had four children: Grant Cardwell (1869-), Adeline Cardwell (1870-), Nora Cardwell (1873–1919), and Cortez Cardwell (1875–1893). He is listed in the 1870 Andrew County, Missouri census.[3] Daniel is not listed with his family in 1880, as his wife Lavonia is listed without him in the Carbon County, Wyoming census.[4]

However, newly discovered evidence sheds light on the final chapter of Daniel's life. A newspaper article from Colorado reports that Daniel Cardwell died by suicide in Georgetown after a period of personal and financial hardship. Following years of unstable work in mining and labor jobs, Daniel had recently secured a steady position with the Colorado Central machine shops in Golden, Colorado. With newfound hope, he rented a home and returned to Georgetown in early 1875 to relocate his family. To his shock, he discovered that his wife had filed for divorce, citing cruelty and neglect.

Devastated by this revelation and the delay of court proceedings, Daniel purchased 30 grains of morphine—an amount sufficient to be fatal—and took his own life. Despite the efforts of a local physician, he was beyond saving.

Justice Post investigated the death and ruled no inquest was necessary. At the time of his death, Daniel was reported to be about 35 years old and originally from Kansas, matching the known details of his migration history. His body was likely buried locally in Georgetown, though no headstone or record has been found to confirm the exact site.

His service alongside his brothers—George Washington Cardwell and Hiram B. Cardwell, who also enlisted in the Union Army—is a testament to the family's strong contribution to the war effort, and all three are recognized within this volume. <u>Cardwell Line I - Predicted</u>.

* * *

Photo 8.1: *George Washington Cardwell (1836-1891) Headstone. Fir Grove Cemetery, Lane County, Oregon*

George Washington Cardwell (1836-1891) - *Corporal - Company K, 2nd Nebraska Cavalry, USA* - **Prisoner of War**

George Washington Cardwell was born in 1836 in Jackson County, Tennessee, the son of Wiltshire Cardwell and Mary (Campbell) Cardwell. Like many families seeking new opportunities in the expanding western frontier, the Cardwells moved steadily westward—first to Keokuk County, Iowa, where they appear in the 1850 census, and then to Cass County, Nebraska, by 1860.[5,6]

Around 1859, George married Charlotte T. Poole, and together they had two children: Martha M. Cardwell (1860–1936) and James Laurel Cardwell (1863–1927). By the start of the Civil War, George was a young farmer living in a newly admitted state on the edge of the western frontier.

On 19 September 1862, at the age of 25, George enlisted in the Union Army at Plattsmouth, Nebraska, joining as a Private in the 2nd Nebraska Cavalry (U.S.). His enlistment record describes him as 5 feet 11½ inches tall, with dark eyes, sandy hair, and a farmer by occupation. He listed his birthplace as Jackson County, Tennessee, but by the time of his enlistment, Nebraska had become his adopted home.

The 2nd Nebraska Cavalry was organized in late 1862 primarily to defend the Great Plains from escalating conflict with Native tribes following the Dakota War of 1862. The regiment's original term of service was set for nine months, and it was assigned to the Department of the Northwest under General Alfred Sully. Unlike many Civil War regiments deployed to the Southern battlefronts, the 2nd Nebraska was engaged in campaigns on the northern plains, largely focused on protecting settlers, escorting wagon trains, and responding to Native resistance spurred by broken treaties and federal encroachment.

The regiment participated in the Sully Expeditions across the Dakota Territory, culminating in the Battle of Whitestone Hill in September 1863. However, George Cardwell does not appear to have been with the regiment during this earlier campaign, as his enlistment took place in September 1862, and his documented service continued into 1864, when the unit operated in Arkansas. During this time, Union forces worked to secure supply lines and resist Confederate raids targeting outposts and foraging parties.

On 24 August 1864, George was captured by Confederate forces at or near Grand Prairie, Arkansas, during a period of heightened partisan and cavalry action in the region. His capture likely occurred during one of the many scattered encounters between Union patrols and Southern guerrilla bands or regular cavalry elements that continued operating despite the weakening of Confederate control in the Trans-Mississippi Theater. George was paroled just over a week later, on 01 September 1864, a fairly rapid release consistent with the declining ability of Confederate forces to maintain prisoners in the region during the war's final year.

Following the war, George and his family continued their westward migration. By 1870, they were living in Wyoming Territory, a region still sparsely populated and in transition from frontier to settlement. In the 1880 census, they appear in Montana Territory, before finally settling in Cottage Grove, Lane County, Oregon. George is listed there in the 1890 Veterans Schedule, which recorded Union veterans and their wartime service.[7,8,9]

George Washington Cardwell died on 26 April 1891 in Cottage Grove, Oregon, at the age of 55. He was buried at Fir Grove Cemetery in Lane County, where his grave marks the final resting place of a pioneer soldier who helped secure Union interests not in the bloody fields of Gettysburg or Antietam, but on the remote and volatile western frontier.[10]

George was part of a military family. His brothers, Daniel M. Cardwell and Hiram B. Cardwell, also served in the Union Army and are recorded in this volume. The Cardwells' combined service reflects the widespread sacrifice made by families across the country—North and South, urban and rural, Eastern and Western—in preserving the Union and shaping the future of a postwar nation. <u>Cardwell Line I - Predicted</u>. Photo Credit[11]

* * *

Hiram B. Cardwell (1846—1923) - *Private - Company H, 1st Nebraska Cavalry, USA*

Hiram B. Cardwell was born in July 1846 in Jefferson County, Iowa, the son of Wiltshire Cardwell and Mary (Campbell) Cardwell. His early years were marked by the family's westward movement across the frontier. By 1850, the Cardwells were recorded in Keokuk County, Iowa, and by 1860, they had moved farther west to the Nebraska Territory, settling in Cass County, where they appear in the census that year.[12,13]

At the age of 16, Hiram enlisted in the Union Army on 06 November 1862 at Plattsmouth, Nebraska, just weeks after his older brother, George Washington Cardwell, had joined the service. He mustered in as a Private in Company H of the 1st Nebraska Cavalry (U.S.). His enlistment papers list him as 18 years old (though he was likely younger), 5 feet 7 inches tall, with a light complexion, blue eyes, light hair, and a farmer by occupation. Though still a teenager, Hiram joined a regiment tasked with securing the western frontier during one of the most volatile periods in the Trans-Mississippi West.

The 1st Nebraska Cavalry had originally formed as an infantry regiment early in the war but was reorganized as a mounted unit in late 1863. By the time Hiram joined in late 1862, the regiment had begun transitioning to cavalry service and was tasked with a dual mission: to assist in securing Union supply lines in Arkansas and Missouri, and to patrol and protect settlements in the Nebraska and Kansas frontier against raids from Confederate bush-whackers and Native American resistance.

From 1863 through 1865, Hiram's regiment was primarily engaged in garrison duty, scouting missions, and escort service across wide portions of Nebraska, Kansas, western Missouri, and eastern Colorado Territory. During this period, the 1st Nebraska Cavalry helped secure the overland mail routes, protected Union supply trains, and patrolled regions vulnerable to guerrilla attacks. While not often engaged in formal large-scale battles, the regiment saw frequent skirmishes with Confederate irregulars, particularly in western Missouri, and took part in expeditions to suppress hostile activity along the Platte River corridor.

Unlike soldiers in the Eastern Theater, Hiram's experience was shaped by long patrols through sparsely settled terrain, difficult weather conditions, and the constant threat of ambush from both Confederate sympathizers and unset-tled Native tribes. The demanding nature of frontier cavalry service required endurance and self-reliance, especially for younger enlistees like Hiram.

He remained on active duty throughout the remainder of the war and into the early postwar occupation period, when Union forces continued to monitor and secure western territories during Reconstruction and ongoing tribal unrest. Hiram B. Cardwell was honorably discharged on 01 July 1866 at Omaha, Nebraska, having served for nearly four years—an unusually long enlistment for someone who entered service so young.

Following his discharge, Hiram B. Cardwell returned to civilian life and married Frances Elizabeth Coffman on 15 December 1867 in Andrew County, Missouri.[14] The couple went on to have five children: Cora M. Card-well (1869–), Leona D. Cardwell (1873–1932), Columbus L. Cardwell (1876–1934), William C. Cardwell (1879–), and Edith M. Cardwell (1881–). Over the following decades, the Cardwell family relocated several times, likely in search of farmland, employment, or improved living conditions as the frontier transitioned into more established communities. By 1870, Hiram and his young family were living in Atchison County, Kansas. A decade later, they had returned to Andrew County, Missouri, where they are listed in the 1880 census. By 1900, Hiram—then a veteran suffering from the long-term effects of his service—was a patient at a Home for Disabled Volunteer Soldiers in Leavenworth County, Kansas. In the 1910 census, he appears in Mill Creek, Polk County, Arkansas, boarding in the home of Mr. Cross. By 1920, he was recorded as a widowed boarder in the household of Dogan Cotton in Le Flore County, Oklahoma. These records reflect a life of frequent movement across the American heartland, likely shaped by changing health, economic necessity, and the availability of care and housing for aging veterans.[15,16,17,18,19]

Later in life, Hiram applied for and received a Civil War pension, indicating the long-term physical toll of his military service. According to pension records, Hiram B. Cardwell died on 17 May 1923 in Opal, Polk County, Arkansas, a small rural community in the western part of the state. His exact place of burial is unknown, though it was likely in or near Opal.

Hiram's long service on the frontier placed him among the thousands of young men whose Civil War experience was not defined by Gettysburg or Antietam, but by the equally vital and grueling task of preserving Union authority in the vast and often lawless West. His brothers, George Washington Cardwell and Daniel M. Cardwell, also served in the Union Army, and together they represent a family deeply embedded in the fabric of both the war effort and the nation's westward expansion. Cardwell Line I - Predicted.

New York
Cardwell Union Soldiers

As the most populous state in the Union, New York played a crucial role in the Civil War, supplying more men, money, and resources than any other state. New York soldiers fought in every major campaign of the war, from the Eastern Theater's battles in Virginia to operations along the Mississippi River. The state's industrial centers produced weapons, uniforms, and supplies, while its ports helped sustain the Union war effort. New York also saw significant wartime unrest, including the infamous Draft Riots of 1863.

The Cardwell men from New York fought in both the Eastern and Western Theaters, serving in cavalry and infantry units that played vital roles in securing Union victories. Whether in Louisiana, Virginia, or Texas, they contributed to key military operations that helped bring about the war's end.

This chapter honors the Cardwell soldiers of New York, preserving their service and dedication to the Union cause.

* * *

Photo 9.1: *Lucius Demster Cardwell (1830-1911) Headstone - Grove Cemetery, Bath, Steuben County, New York.*

Lucius Demster Cardwell (1830-1911) - *Private - Company E, 161st New York Infantry, USA*

Lucius Demster Cardwell was born on 26 March 1830 in Carenvia, Madison County, New York, the son of John Jacob Cardwell and Rachel (Paine) Cardwell, according to his death certificate. His early life remains partially undocumented; he does not appear in the 1850 federal census, though later records confirm his presence in Steuben County, New York. By 1880, Lucius is recorded in the census as the head of household with his widowed mother Rachel living with him, indicating a continued family connection in his adult years.

On 19 September 1864, at the age of 34, Lucius enlisted in the Union Army as a Private in Company E, 161st New York Infantry, at Jasper, Steuben County, New York. His enlistment record describes him as 5 feet 10 inches tall, with blue eyes, dark hair, and a light complexion. He listed his occupation as Mechanic, suggesting skilled labor, possibly in metal or wood-working trades—occupations in high demand both during and after the war.

The 161st New York Infantry was originally organized in the fall of 1862 and had already seen extensive service in the Department of the Gulf before Lucius joined its ranks. By the time of his enlistment in September 1864, the regiment was stationed in Louisiana, assigned to XIX Corps, part of the Union Army's presence in the Gulf region. During this late phase of the war, the 161st was primarily engaged in occupation duties, garrison service, and security operations in and around New Orleans, as well as in Baton Rouge and the Red River area.

Lucius arrived too late to take part in earlier major battles such as Port Hudson, Sabine Cross Roads, or the Red River Campaign, in which the 161st had played significant roles. However, during his period of service, the regiment remained active in stabilizing Union control over southern Louisiana and safeguarding key transportation and supply points along the Mississippi River. These were important strategic tasks during the final months of the war, as Union forces sought to prevent any resurgence of Confederate resistance and to protect newly freed populations and infrastructure.

On 11 January 1865, Lucius was listed as sick in New Orleans, where the regiment had established quarters and maintained a long-term military presence. Illness was rampant among Union troops stationed in the Gulf region due to the humid climate, poor sanitation, and exposure to diseases such as dysentery, malaria, and yellow fever. His condition was evidently serious enough to warrant relocation, and on 30 April 1865, he was transferred back to New York. He was ultimately discharged on 29 May 1865 at Elmira, New York, likely from a convalescent facility or military hospital following the end of hostilities.

After the war, Lucius returned to Steuben County, where he resumed civilian life. He had married Isabell LNU (last name unknown) around 1856, based on the birth year of their eldest child. Together, they had at least five children: John F. Cardwell (1857–), Charles H. Cardwell (1859–1916), Edward Cardwell (1861–), Minnie Cardwell (1864–), and Lucius D. Cardwell, Jr. (–1909). The family is found in the 1860, 1870, 1880, 1900, and 1910 census records, all in Steuben County.[1,2,3,4,5]

Late in life, Lucius was admitted to the National Home for Disabled Volunteer Soldiers in Bath, Steuben County, on 14 November 1910, a reflection of the long-term health effects of his wartime service. These homes served as federal residences and hospitals for aging veterans who required care or had limited means of support.

Lucius Demster Cardwell died on 11 September 1911 at the age of 81. He was buried at Grove Cemetery in Bath, Steuben County, New York, among fellow Union veterans and local community members.[6] His life spanned from the early days of westward migration and industrial expansion to the postwar era of Reconstruction and reconciliation.

Lucius's story is especially significant within his family. His father, John Jacob Cardwell, served in a Pennsylvania militia unit during the Gettysburg Campaign, and his brother, John William Cardwell, served in the 27th Pennsylvania Militia Infantry and was later honorably discharged in 1864. Together, this branch of the Cardwell family represents a deep and varied participation in the Union cause—each man answering the call to service in his own way, in separate theaters of the war. Ancestry Undetermined. Photo Credit[7]

* * *

Photo 9.2: *Walker C. "Dock" Cardwell (1833-1905) Headstone - Cardwell Family Cemetery, Ayersville, Rockingham County, North Carolina.*

Walker C. "Dock" Cardwell (1835–1905) - *Private – Company L, 21st North Carolina Infantry, CSA & Private - Company M, 2nd New York Cavalry, USA*

Walker C. Cardwell, known by the nickname "Dock," was born in March 1835 in Rockingham County, North Carolina. He was the son of Gabriel Cardwell and Cynthia (Humphrey) Cardwell. He appears in the household of his parents in both the 1840 Rockingham County and 1850 Stokes County, North Carolina census records.[8,9] By 1860, Walker was likely residing in Polk County, Tennessee.[10]

During the Civil War, Walker became one of only three Cardwell men known to have served on both sides of the conflict. He initially enlisted as a Private in Company L, 21st North Carolina Infantry, Confederate States Army, on 3 June 1861 in Wentworth, Rockingham County. The 21st North Carolina Infantry was organized in June 1861 and was part of the Army of Northern Virginia. It saw action in many of the major battles of the Eastern Theater, including First Manassas, Antietam, Fredericksburg, and Chancellorsville. The regiment participated in Stonewall Jackson's Valley Campaign and suffered heavily at Gettysburg. Walker's brothers—Wyatt Cardwell, Parker Cardwell (KIA at the Battle of Chancellorsville), Hiram Henry Cardwell, and Thomas Cardwell (died of disease in 1863)—all served in the Confederate Army, some in the same or associated regiments.

Walker's Confederate service ended when he "deserted to the enemy" on 01 June 1863, according to his Confederate records. The exact circumstances or motivations for his desertion are unknown, though desertions among soldiers were not uncommon due to the hardships of war, disillusionment, or shifting political sentiments.

More than a year later, Walker enlisted in the Union Army on 30 August 1864 as a Private in Company M, 2nd New York Cavalry. This unit was also known as the "Harris Light Cavalry." The 2nd New York Cavalry participated in numerous cavalry raids and skirmishes during the later stages of the war, especially in the Shenandoah Valley under General Philip Sheridan. Walker served with this regiment until he was discharged on 5 June 1865 at Alexandria, Virginia, shortly after the conclusion of the war. The reason for Walker making this decision is not known.

After returning home to Rockingham County, Walker resumed civilian life. On 13 September 1866, he married Nancy "Nannie" Fair in Rockingham County.[11] Together, they raised a large family that included: William Jackson "Will" Cardwell (1868–1942), George Thomas Cardwell (1868–1945), Mary Magdeline Cardwell (1871–1931), Lou Settie Cardwell (1872–1965), Ella Fountaine Cardwell (1877–1931), Virginia "Jennie" Cardwell (1880–1962), James Andrew Cardwell (1882–1957), and Jesse W. Cardwell (1885–1918). He appears in the 1870, 1880, and 1900 Rockingham County, North Carolina census records.[12,13,14]

Walker died on 14 February 1905 in Rockingham County. He is buried at the Cardwell Family Cemetery in Ayersville, Rockingham County, North Carolina.[15] His complex military history—serving both the Confederacy and the Union—makes him a particularly notable figure among the many Cardwells who fought in the war. He is also featured in *Brothers in Gray*, the first volume in this series. <u>Cardwell Line I - Predicted</u>. Photo Credit[16]

* * *

Photo 9.3: *William Newton Cardwell (1841-1880) Headstone - Mount Moriah Cemetery, Philadelphia, Philadelphia County, Pennsylvania.*

William Newton Cardwell (1841-1880) - *Private - Company C, 14th New York Cavalry & 18th New York Cavalry, USA*

William Newton Cardwell was born around 1841 in Manchester, Lancashire, England, the son of John Cardwell and Margaret (Nuttall) Cardwell. The Cardwell family immigrated to the United States around 1849, settling in Philadelphia, Pennsylvania, where William's younger brother was later born. He appears in the household of his parents in the 1850 and 1860 federal census records for Philadelphia, where his father worked as a laborer and the family established itself in one of the city's working-class neighborhoods.

On 01 April 1863, William married Mary Ellen Logan in Philadelphia, and together they had six children: John Logan Cardwell (1864–1946), Margaret Cardwell (1866–1871), Mary Ella Cardwell (1869–1871), Asher William Cardwell (1873–1957), Joseph Charles Cardwell (1875–1949), and Martha Cardwell (1880–1880). Like many young families during the war years, William and Mary faced frequent economic and emotional strain as the nation remained divided in conflict.

Despite having already married and begun a family, William enlisted in the Union Army on 26 February 1864, joining as a Private in Company C of the 14th New York Cavalry. His enlistment took place in New York, likely through a recruitment program offering enlistment bonuses or bounties for Philadelphia-area residents willing to serve under New York regimental designations. His enlistment record lists him as a Printer by trade, with blue eyes, light hair, light complexion, and a height of 5 feet 3 inches.[17]

The 14th New York Cavalry, organized in 1863, was primarily assigned to the Department of the Gulf, a wide-ranging command covering Louisiana and parts of the Gulf Coast. Upon William's enlistment in early 1864, the regiment was engaged in active operations throughout southern Louisiana, particularly during the closing phases of the Red River Campaign and in anti-guerrilla actions near New Iberia, Opelousas, and Bayou Teche. The regiment's responsibilities included scouting enemy positions, disrupting Confederate supply lines, and engaging irregular Confederate cavalry units operating in the backcountry of Louisiana.

Although his time in uniform was brief, William was present with the regiment during a demanding period of mounted operations in a region plagued by disease, extreme heat, and poor supply conditions. On 29 September 1864, he was discharged for disability at the General Hospital in Baton Rouge, Louisiana. The nature of his illness is not specified in surviving records, but it was likely related to tropical disease or physical exhaustion common among cavalrymen in the Gulf theater. His early discharge—just seven months after enlistment—indicates the severity of his condition and marked the end of his brief but earnest military service.

After returning to Philadelphia, William resumed civilian life and appears in both the 1870 and 1880 federal census records. He continued to provide for his family as best he could while managing the lingering effects of his wartime health issues. Unfortunately, his postwar years were cut short. On 06 July 1880, William Newton Cardwell died in Philadelphia at the age of 39. He was buried at Mount Moriah Cemetery, one of the city's largest burial grounds and final resting place to many Union veterans.[18]

Though his service was short, William's decision to enlist during a time of personal and national challenge reflects the commitment of many first-generation immigrants to the Union cause. His participation in the 14th New York Cavalry, a unit operating in the rugged, disease-prone region of the Deep South, placed him in one of the war's most difficult environments. His sacrifice is memorialized both by his military record and by the generations of descendants that followed. Ancestry Undetermined. Photo Credit[19]

Oregon Territory
Cardwell Union Soldiers

ALTHOUGH FAR FROM THE MAJOR BATTLEFIELDS OF THE CIVIL WAR, Oregon played a strategic role in protecting Union interests in the West. The Oregon Territory was sparsely populated, and much of its military activity focused on defending settlers, securing trade routes, and preventing potential Confederate influence in the region. The 1st Oregon Cavalry was raised to patrol the vast frontier, engaging in skirmishes with hostile forces and ensuring the continued safety of Union-aligned settlers.

While Julius and Zachariah Cardwell did not see the large-scale battles that defined the Civil War, their service in the 1st Oregon Cavalry was essential in maintaining stability in the western territories. Their efforts contributed to the Union's broader war strategy by ensuring security in the frontier regions.

This chapter honors the Cardwell soldiers of Oregon, recognizing their unique contributions to the Civil War effort in the Pacific Northwest.

* * *

Photo 10.1: *Julius C. Cardwell (1838-1915) Headstone. Oakland Masonic and Old Town Oakland Cemeteries, Oakland, Douglas County, Oregon.*

Julius C. "Doc" Cardwell (1838-1915) - *Private - Company C, 1st Oregon Cavalry, USA*

Julius C. "Doc" Cardwell was born on 31 March 1838 in White County, Tennessee, the son of George Washington Cardwell and Mary "Polly" (Hitchcock) Cardwell. Like many families of the antebellum South, the Cardwells joined the great westward migration, first settling in Wapello County, Iowa by 1850, and then continuing on to the frontier town of Canyonville, Douglas County, Oregon, where they appear in the 1860 census. By the eve of the Civil War, Julius was living and working as a young farmer in Oregon's rugged and rapidly developing interior.[1,2]

On 21 November 1861, at the age of 23, Julius enlisted as a Private in Company C of the 1st Oregon Cavalry (U.S.) at Canyonville. His enlistment record lists him as 5 feet 10¾ inches tall, with a fair complexion, blue eyes, and light hair. He identified his birthplace as Tennessee and his occupation as farmer.

The 1st Oregon Cavalry was created during the early months of the Civil War to provide local defense and security throughout the vast, thinly settled Oregon Territory and surrounding frontier areas. With regular U.S. Army troops withdrawn for service in the East, the regiment took on the essential duties of guarding travel routes, escorting supply trains, protecting settlers, and conducting scouting missions across eastern Oregon, southern Idaho, eastern Washington, and northern California. Their service, while far from the large-scale battles of the Eastern Theater, was crucial to maintaining federal authority and regional stability in a time of national division.

Company C, Julius's unit, operated primarily out of Fort Walla Walla, Fort Dalles, and Camp Baker, often spending months on patrol in remote and hostile environments. These soldiers endured isolation, harsh weather, and the dangers of both hostile encounters and rugged terrain, often far removed from conventional support. Julius remained consistently present with his company throughout his term of enlistment and was honorably discharged on 27 January 1865, having served over three years in defense of the Pacific frontier.

After the war, Julius traveled south into California, where he appears on voter rolls for Siskiyou County in 1867 and 1868, a region just south of the Oregon border that attracted many former soldiers and miners. In 1869, he was listed again, this time on the voter rolls for Santa Clara County, suggesting a period of movement, perhaps in search of employment or a more settled postwar life. These records are among the few known references to him in the immediate aftermath of the war.[3]

By 1870, Julius had returned to Canyonville, Oregon, where he is recorded in the federal census living in the household of his father, George W. Cardwell.[4] In that entry, he is listed as a Saloon Keeper, a profession not uncommon among former soldiers in frontier towns, where commercial opportunities often included taverns, supply shops, and lodging houses. This role, combined with his local reputation, may have contributed to the nickname "Doc," though the precise origin of the moniker remains undocumented.

No record has been found indicating that Julius ever married, and he appears to have lived a quiet, bachelor's life following his return to Douglas County. Scant documentation survives for his later years, but it is clear that he remained in Canyonville, surrounded by the familiar ridges and river valleys he had known since youth.

Julius C. Cardwell died on 18 November 1915 in Canyonville, at the age of 77. He was buried at the Oakland Masonic and Old Town Oakland Cemeteries, resting among the early settlers and Civil War veterans of southern Oregon. His grave marks the final chapter of a man who helped secure the western frontier during the Civil War and whose quiet postwar life was lived in the same land he once helped defend.[5] <u>Cardwell Line I - Predicted</u>. Photo Credit[6]

* * *

Zachariah Cardwell (1832-1909). Douglas County, Oregon - circa 1900

Zachariah Cardwell (1832-1909) Headstone. Stephens Cemetery, Myrtle Creek, Douglas County, Oregon.

Zachariah Cardwell (1832-1909) - *Private - Company C, 1st Oregon Cavalry, USA*

Zachariah Cardwell was born on 5 April 1832 in White County, Tennessee, the son of George Washington Cardwell and Mary "Polly"

(Hitchcock) Cardwell. Like many frontier families of their generation, the Cardwells joined the great westward movement that characterized the mid-19th century. By 1850, they had relocated to Wapello County, Iowa, and by the end of the decade, they had continued further west, settling in Douglas County, Oregon, as the Oregon Territory opened to broader settlement.[7]

In the 1860 census, Zachariah appears in the household of Thomas Parker, likely working as a laborer or hired hand, as was common for unmarried men of his age and background.[8] On 11 January 1862, amid growing national conflict, Zachariah enlisted as a Private in Company C, 1st Oregon Cavalry (U.S.) at Canyonville, Douglas County, Oregon, the same community where his family had made their home. His enlistment record describes him as 30 years of age, 5 feet 7 inches tall, with a dark complexion, gray eyes, dark hair, and a stated occupation of farmer.

The 1st Oregon Cavalry was organized in late 1861 and early 1862 to fill the void left in the Pacific Northwest after regular U.S. Army troops had been reassigned to the major battlefronts of the Civil War. While not engaged in traditional Eastern battles, the regiment was essential to protecting the Oregon frontier from lawlessness, Confederate sympathizers, and conflict with Indigenous peoples.

Zachariah's unit, Company C, spent the bulk of its service patrolling remote settlements, guarding emigrant trails, and protecting supply trains across eastern Oregon, southern Idaho, eastern Washington, and northern California. Though the regiment did not participate in any major battles, it was involved in frequent field operations and skirmishes, often in remote terrain with minimal support. Zachariah would have experienced the harsh realities of wilderness patrols, prolonged detachment from fixed posts, and the constant demands of keeping the frontier stable during a time of national upheaval.

His service spanned the regiment's most active years, during which it garrisoned posts such as Fort Walla Walla, Camp Baker, and Fort Dalles, while also sending scouting parties as far east as Fort Boise and the Snake River Valley. Unlike soldiers in Eastern campaigns, Zachariah's duties involved months of isolation and hardship in rugged terrain, often far removed from supply lines or medical support.

Zachariah was honorably discharged on 11 January 1865 at Fort Vancouver, in the Washington Territory, having completed exactly three years of active duty. His consistent service record, with no known absences or disciplinary issues, indicates a dependable and resilient soldier who fulfilled his responsibilities in one of the most challenging and underrecognized theaters of the war.

After the war, Zachariah returned to civilian life in Oregon. On 22 October 1865, he married Susan Jane Stephens in Jacksonville, Douglas County. The couple went on to raise a large family, with the following known children: Mary E. Cardwell (1866–), Ina Dammarrus Cardwell (1868–1951), Edwin Cardwell (1870–1950), Judith Cardwell (1875–1893), Benjamin W. Cardwell (1875–1879), John E. Cardwell (1878–1900), Henry Lester Cardwell (1881–1962), and Alfred Cardwell (1883–1926).

Zachariah appears in the 1880 and 1900 federal censuses, residing in Douglas County, where he worked as a farmer.[9,10] In his later years, he applied for and received an Invalid Pension beginning on 09 February 1891, recognition of the toll that his military service and frontier hardships had taken on his health. His steady presence in the Myrtle Creek area marks him as one of the early settlers who remained to help build and sustain the postwar community.

Zachariah Cardwell died on 25 December 1909, Christmas Day, in Myrtle Creek, Douglas County, Oregon, at the age of 77. He was laid to rest at Stephens Cemetery in Myrtle Creek, surrounded by family and the same valleys he had once helped to protect as a cavalryman.[11] His brother, Julius C. "Doc" Cardwell, also served in Company C of the 1st Oregon Cavalry, and their dual service stands as a testament to the Cardwell family's role in preserving order and Union authority on the far western frontier during the American Civil War. Cardwell Line I - Predicted. Photo Credit[12,13]

Pennsylvania
Cardwell Union Soldiers

PENNSYLVANIA WAS A VITAL STATE FOR THE UNION DURING THE CIVIL War, serving as an industrial and logistical hub while also providing a significant number of troops. The state was home to some of the war's largest training camps, iron foundries, and munitions factories. Pennsylvania also became the site of Gettysburg, one of the most decisive battles of the war. Its soldiers fought in every major theater of the conflict, contributing to Union victories in both the Eastern and Western campaigns.

A significant portion of the Cardwell men who served from Pennsylvania during the Civil War were either immigrants from Ireland and England or the sons of immigrants who had arrived in the decades leading up to the conflict. Philadelphia, in particular, experienced a surge of immigration during the mid-nineteenth century, driven largely by political unrest, economic hardship, and famine abroad—especially the Great Famine in Ireland (1845–1852) and industrial decline in England. These conditions led many families to seek new opportunities in the United States, and cities like Philadelphia, with its growing industrial economy and active port, became key destinations.

Immigrants who settled in Pennsylvania quickly became part of the labor force and community fabric, and many were eager to prove their loyalty to their new homeland when war broke out. For the Cardwells, their service was not only a contribution to the Union cause but also a reflection of their integration into American civic life. The presence of multiple Cardwell men with

Irish or English birthplaces or heritage within the Pennsylvania regiments underscores this broader historical trend.

While the vast majority of Cardwell veterans across the nation come from long-established American families—those categorized under Lines I, II, III, and IV with roots extending back before the Revolutionary War—many of the men from Pennsylvania represent a distinct demographic. Their service not only reflects the demographic shifts of the era but also highlights the commitment of new Americans to the defense and unity of their adopted country. Though some volunteered, others were conscripted into federal military service.

The Cardwell men from Pennsylvania fought in defensive militia, frontline infantry, and heavy artillery units, contributing to major Union victories. Their service helped protect Pennsylvania from invasion while also reinforcing Union forces in key campaigns across the Eastern Theater.

This chapter honors the Cardwell soldiers of Pennsylvania, preserving their dedication and sacrifices as part of Cardwell Family history.

* * *

Photo 11.1: *Calvert Owen Cardwell (1820-1895) Headstone - Upland Baptist Church Cemetery, Delaware County, Pennsylvania*

Calvert Owen Cardwell (1820-1895) - *Commissioner Sergeant - Company A, 58th Pennsylvania Infantry, USA*

Calvert Owen Cardwell was born on 26 November 1820 in Ireland, the assumed son of Samuel Cardwell and Sarah (Calvert) Cardwell. He is listed in the 1850 and 1860 Middletown, Delaware County, Pennsylvania census records.[1,2] Located near him are Samuel Cardwell, born about 1777 in Ireland. Also, an assumed brother, John Jacob Cardwell, born about 1808 in Ireland. Given this grouping in the same geographic area, it is assumed that they are all kin, but more research is needed. The Cardwell family immigrated to the United States in 1839, arriving in Philadelphia, Pennsylvania, where they settled amid a growing Irish immigrant community in the Delaware Valley.

Calvert married Ann Elliot on 02 July 1841 in Rockdale, Delaware County, Pennsylvania. Together, they raised a large family of nine children: Robert E. Cardwell (1842–1900), Julia L. Cardwell (1845–), Edward E. Cardwell (1847–1938), Ann Cardwell (1849–), John E. Cardwell (1850–1879), James Elliot Cardwell (1853–1906), Sarah J. Cardwell (1855–1916), William C. Cardwell (1858–1933), and Benjamin J. Cardwell (1864–1945). The family remained rooted in Upland, a borough in Delaware County, where Calvert worked to support his growing household. He is recorded there in the 1870 and 1880 U.S. censuses.[3,4]

At the age of 40, Calvert enlisted in the Union Army on 12 September 1861 at Philadelphia, joining the 58th Pennsylvania Volunteer Infantry as a Private. This regiment was composed largely of men from Philadelphia and surrounding counties, with many enlistees—like Calvert—being older tradesmen or working-class laborers. The regiment mustered into service under Colonel John Richter Jones and was assigned to the Army of the Potomac before later transferring to the Department of North Carolina and Department of Virginia.

In its early months, the 58th Pennsylvania was stationed in eastern Virginia and coastal North Carolina, where it performed picket duty, garrison assignments, and support operations for Union forces securing the Outer Banks and nearby inland positions. These early deployments were grueling but often lacked large-scale combat, as the Union prioritized fortification and control of Confederate coastal supply lines.

By February 1863, Calvert had been promoted to Commissary Sergeant, a non-commissioned officer position responsible for overseeing the distribution of rations and supplies within the regiment. His advancement into this logistical role suggests a degree of literacy, trustworthiness, and reliability that was highly valued in managing essential support functions for an infantry unit on campaign.

During this time, the 58th Pennsylvania took part in several significant operations. In May 1863, the regiment was involved in the expedition to Gum Swamp, near Kinston, North Carolina, which involved skirmishes against Confederate outposts. Throughout 1863 and 1864, the unit supported operations along the Albemarle and Pamlico Sounds, helping secure Union control of key waterways and rail hubs. While Calvert would not have participated in direct combat as a commissary sergeant, he would have been attached to regimental headquarters, coordinating logistical support during active campaigns and troop movements.

In the spring of 1864, the 58th was transferred to participate in General Benjamin Butler's operations south of the James River. The regiment was engaged in the Bermuda Hundred Campaign in May 1864, where Union forces attempted to sever Confederate supply lines into Richmond and Petersburg. The 58th Pennsylvania manned defensive positions and supported engagements at Port Walthall Junction, Swift Creek, and Drewry's Bluff, although losses were relatively light.

From June 1864 through early 1865, the 58th Pennsylvania Infantry was positioned at City Point, Virginia, General Ulysses S. Grant's primary logistical base during the Siege of Petersburg. As Commissary Sergeant, Calvert's responsibilities would have been vital—ensuring food stores, forage, and supplies were adequately distributed to maintain the effectiveness of the regiment under prolonged siege conditions.

Calvert was honorably discharged on 24 January 1866 at City Point, Prince George County, Virginia, after over four years of continuous service. His longevity in the army, especially in a non-combat but critical administrative role, was unusual for a man who had enlisted at age 40. His commitment to duty until the close of hostilities reflects his dedication to the Union cause and to his regiment.

In the years following the war, Calvert returned to Upland, where he resumed civilian life and remained active in his community. He was recorded in the 1890 Veterans Census as a resident of Delaware County and received a Federal pension for his service, which acknowledged the long-term impact of his years in uniform.[5]

Calvert Owen Cardwell died on 11 February 1895 in Upland, at the age of 74, and was buried at Upland Baptist Church Cemetery.[6] His grave remains a testament to the service of an Irish immigrant who, having made a new life in America, stood in defense of his adopted country during its most perilous hour. His nephews, John Henry Cardwell and Lucius Demster Cardwell, and his likely brother, John Jacob Cardwell, also served and are listed in this volume. <u>Ancestry Undetermined</u>. Photo Credit[7]

*　*　*

Photo 11.2: *John Cardwell (1829-1897) Headstone - Shamokin Cemetery, Shamokin, Northumberland County, Pennsylvania*

John Cardwell (1829-1897) - *Private - Company I, 27th Pennsylvania Militia Infantry, USA*

John Cardwell was born on 29 October 1829 in Manchester, England, a region known for its industrial heritage and textile production. While the precise date of his immigration to the United States remains unknown, it is likely that John arrived in Pennsylvania by the early 1850s, part of a wave of British working-class immigrants who came to the anthracite coal regions in search of economic opportunity.

By circa 1856, John had married Hannah Butterwick, also born in Manchester, England. It is possible that they were married in England, prior to immigrating to the United States. Together they raised a large family in Northumberland County, Pennsylvania, a region that would remain their home for the rest of their lives. Their known children were: Sarah J. Cardwell (1857–1889), Arthur Cardwell (1862–1946) and his twin John W. Cardwell (1862–1928), Mary E. Cardwell (1868–1932), and Annie Cardwell (1876–1960). John appears in the 1870 census living in Coal Township, Northumberland County, and in the 1880 census residing in Bear Valley, also within Northumberland County, reflecting his long-standing ties to Pennsylvania's anthracite coal region.[8,9]

Amid the turbulence of the Civil War, John enlisted as a Private in the Union Army on 16 June 1863 at Schuylkill County, Pennsylvania, when he was 32 years old. His enlistment coincided with the Emergency Militia mobilization called by Governor Andrew Curtin in response to General Robert E.

Lee's invasion of Pennsylvania, which culminated in the Battle of Gettysburg from 01 to 03 July 1863.

John was assigned to a unit of the Pennsylvania Emergency Militia, raised to defend the state against Confederate incursion. These regiments were formed quickly in June 1863 and included men from the mining regions, towns, and rural communities of central and eastern Pennsylvania. Their primary role was to guard roads, bridges, and potential invasion routes while the Army of the Potomac pursued Lee's advancing army. Many of these short-term units saw no direct combat but performed vital defensive tasks that freed up regular Union forces for front-line duties.

John served during the most intense weeks of the Gettysburg Campaign but was discharged on 31 July 1863, shortly after the Confederate army had retreated into Virginia. His 45-day term of service was typical of the emergency regiments, which were mustered in for short periods during state crises. No detailed regimental record survives naming his specific unit assignment or engagement location, which is not unusual for militia units activated during a rapid mobilization. However, his participation during this high-alert period contributed to the overall success of Pennsylvania's defensive efforts.

Decades after the war, John applied for and received a Federal Invalid Pension, granted on 23 July 1890. While the nature of his disability is not specified in the available records, it likely related to lingering health issues from his life as both a soldier and coal miner. His pension suggests that despite the brevity of his military service, his contribution was formally recognized by the federal government.

John Cardwell died on 31 July 1891 in Northumberland County, exactly 28 years to the day after his military discharge. He was buried at Shamokin Cemetery in Shamokin, a community that had grown from a coal camp into a bustling industrial town during his lifetime.[10] His wife, Hannah, and several of their children remained in the area, contributing to the fabric of Northumberland County life for decades afterward.

It should be noted that Civil War records for Pennsylvania men named John Cardwell are scarce and often difficult to distinguish. Extensive research, including comparisons of census data, pension files, and cemetery records, was conducted to ensure that the service details attributed here are correct and that this John Cardwell—miner, immigrant, father, and Union veteran—is properly represented in this work. Ancestry undetermined. Photo Credit[11]

* * *

John Jacob Cardwell (1808-1878) - *Private - Company B, 45th Pennsylvania Militia Infantry, USA*

John Jacob Cardwell was born around 1808 in Ireland, the son of Samuel Cardwell and Sarah (Calvert) Cardwell. The Cardwell family immigrated to the United States in 1839, arriving at Philadelphia, Pennsylvania, as part of a broader wave of Irish migration seeking economic opportunity and religious freedom. Like many skilled and working-class immigrants of the era, John and his family settled in Delaware County, a region that would remain their home for several decades.

Prior to their immigration, John had married Rachel Paine in 1836 in Trevethin, Monmouthshire (Gwent), Wales, suggesting a period of residence in the United Kingdom before settling in America.[12] Together, John and Rachel raised a large family, including: Lucius Demster Cardwell (1830–1911), Sarah Jane Cardwell (1841–1909), John William Cardwell (1842–1919), Thomas A. Cardwell (1845–), Hannah A. Cardwell (1845–1918), George Washington Cardwell (1847–1915), Martha Cardwell (1850–), Rachel M. Cardwell (1854–1891), and Alexander Paine Cardwell (1857–1922).

The 1840, 1850, and 1860 federal census records list John residing in Middletown, Delaware County, where he worked to support his growing household.[13,14,15] At the time of the Civil War, he was in his mid-50s—older than the typical soldier—but like many Pennsylvania men of all ages, he answered the call during the Gettysburg Campaign of 1863.

On 29 June 1863, just days before the Battle of Gettysburg, John enlisted in a unit of the Pennsylvania Emergency Militia at Upland, Delaware County. This mobilization was part of Governor Andrew Curtin's statewide call for temporary forces to defend Pennsylvania from the advancing Confederate Army under General Robert E. Lee. The state's eastern counties, including Delaware County, responded swiftly, organizing short-term infantry regiments composed of farmers, merchants, and laborers—many of them older men or teenage boys—who stepped forward during the crisis.

These emergency regiments, including the one in which John served, were assigned to guard strategic railroads, patrol transportation corridors, and defend key supply depots in the region. While not engaged directly at Gettysburg, their presence helped free up regular Union troops for battlefield engagements and provided vital local security during one of the most critical moments of the war.

John was discharged on 29 August 1863, after completing two months of emergency service. No location is listed for his discharge, which was common for short-term state militia units that were mustered out near their home communities. His willingness to serve despite his age reflected the deep loyalty felt by many Pennsylvania citizens during the Confederate invasion of their state.

After the war, John relocated to Wabasha County, Minnesota, where he is listed in the 1870 federal census, residing near Lake City in neighboring Goodhue County.[16] The move westward may have been influenced by postwar opportunities or by connections to family members who had already begun relocating. He lived there during the final years of his life and died in 1878 in Lake City. The location of his grave remains unknown.

John's military service is part of a broader family legacy of patriotism and sacrifice. His brother, Calvert Owen Cardwell, served as Commissary Sergeant in the 58th Pennsylvania Infantry, and his sons, Lucius Demster Cardwell and John William Cardwell, both served in the Union Army—the former in New York and the latter in Pennsylvania. These connections highlight the deep involvement of the Cardwell family in the preservation of the Union during the nation's most pivotal conflict.

Due to the commonality of the name and the often-fragmentary nature of militia records, extensive genealogical and military research was required to positively identify this John Jacob Cardwell and distinguish him from other Pennsylvania men with similar names. This research also confirmed his middle name and established the connections to his children and extended family noted throughout this volume. <u>Ancestry undetermined.</u>

* * *

Photo 11.3: *John William Cardwell (1842-1919) Headstone - Westminster Cemetery, Montgomery County, Pennsylvania.*

John William Cardwell (1842-1919) - *Private - Company F, 1st Pennsylvania Reserve Infantry & Company I, 27th Pennsylvania Militia Infantry, USA*

John William Cardwell was born on 28 October 1842 in Pennsylvania, the son of John Jacob Cardwell and Rachel (Paine) Cardwell. He is listed in the household of his parents in the 1850 census for Middletown, Delaware County, where he appears under his middle name, William. In the 1860 census, he is again found in the family home in Middletown, this time listed as John, the name used in all subsequent records related to his life and military service.[17,18]

At age 19, John enlisted as a Private in the Union Army on 30 May 1861, during the earliest phase of Pennsylvania's mobilization for the Civil War. His enlistment record describes him as 5 feet 5½ inches tall, with a light complexion, brown hair, and gray eyes. He was residing in Delaware County, and his occupation at the time was listed as operative, likely indicating work in one of the region's textile or manufacturing mills.

While his original enlistment records did not specify a unit, further research confirms that John served in Company I of the 27th Pennsylvania Militia Infantry, a unit organized in response to Governor Andrew Curtin's call for emergency troops during the Gettysburg Campaign of 1863. The 27th Pennsylvania Militia was formed in June 1863, as Confederate forces under General Robert E. Lee advanced into Pennsylvania. The regiment was mustered for short-term service to defend against the invasion and was tasked with guard duty, emergency mobilization, and protecting key transportation routes and supply depots. Though the regiment did not engage in any major battles, its presence was part of the broader effort that allowed Union forces to concentrate at Gettysburg.

Following this period of emergency militia service, John reenlisted or continued his service in a three-year regiment, remaining on active duty until his honorable discharge on 13 June 1864. Though his service records do not specify the second unit in which he served during this longer term, the timeline places him squarely within the Army of the Potomac's operational campaigns of 1862 through 1864, including the Peninsula Campaign, the Maryland Campaign, and the eventual push toward Richmond and Petersburg. However, without confirmed unit designation for the latter portion of his enlistment, no specific battles can be directly attributed to him beyond his militia service in 1863.

After returning home from the war, John married Emma L. Shronk around 1866. The couple settled in Philadelphia, where they raised four children: Emily Cardwell (1869–), Emma Cardwell (1869–), George Cardwell (1870–1931), and Christine Cardwell (1877–). John remained a resident of Philadelphia for the rest of his life, and he is listed in the 1870, 1880, 1900, and 1910 federal census records for Philadelphia County.[19,20,21,22] Like many Civil War veterans, he transitioned from military to civilian life during a period of rapid urban growth and industrialization in the city.

On 26 July 1890, John was awarded a Federal Invalid Pension, recognizing the toll his military service had taken on his long-term health. The pension ensured that he received compensation for his disabilities, and his inclusion in the pension rolls confirmed the federal government's acknowledgment of his wartime contributions. He lived long enough to see his family grow into adulthood and maintained ties to his fellow veterans in a city where numerous Grand Army of the Republic (G.A.R.) posts supported Union veterans. His obituary noted that he was a member of Union Veteran Legion No. 63.[23]

John William Cardwell died on 14 October 1919 in Philadelphia, just two weeks shy of his 77th birthday. He was buried at Westminster Cemetery in Bala Cynwyd, Montgomery County, where many veterans of the Civil War were laid to rest.[24] His headstone marks his life and legacy as one of Pennsylvania's early volunteers who stood in defense of the Union.

John came from a family with deep wartime ties. His father, John Jacob Cardwell, and uncle, Calvert Owen Cardwell, also served in the Union Army, making theirs one of the few documented Cardwell families in Pennsylvania with multiple members in uniform. Due to the number of men named John Cardwell in Pennsylvania during the Civil War era, extensive research was necessary to confirm and correctly attribute this individual's records. That research also helped clarify his middle name and link him to both emergency militia service and his longer-term enlistment during the war's early years. <u>Ancestry undetermined</u>. Photo Credit[25]

* * *

Robert E. Cardwell (1843-1899) - *Private - Company A, 59th Virginia Infantry, CSA & Company B, 45th Pennsylvania Militia Infantry, USA*

Robert E. Cardwell was born on 20 June 1842 in Pennsylvania, the son of Calvert Owen Cardwell and Ann (Elliot) Cardwell. He is listed in the home of his parents in both the 1850 and 1860 Delaware County, Pennsylvania census records.[26,27] His early life was spent in the North, making his appearance in Confederate service records both unusual and intriguing. While definitive proof remains elusive, there is strong circumstantial evidence suggesting that the Robert Cardwell who served briefly in the 59th Regiment, Virginia Infantry, CSA was the same individual from Delaware County, Pennsylvania.

According to Confederate service records, "Robert Cardwell," "R.E. Cardwell," and "R.P. Cardwell" enlisted or were conscripted into Company A, 59th Virginia Infantry in June 1861 at Chaffin's Farm, a key Confederate position just east of Richmond. The 59th Virginia Infantry, originally organized as a battalion of state troops in southeastern Virginia, was later mustered into Confederate service. The unit operated under the Department of Norfolk and took part in the defense of Virginia's coastline and interior rivers, including actions in North Carolina, most notably the Roanoke Island campaign in early 1862.

Robert's military record suggests that he ran afoul of military discipline. He was charged with being absent without leave and disobedience of orders, ultimately escaping from a guardhouse near Elizabeth City, North Carolina, in February 1862. The records list him as deserted, and a later note indicates his "whereabouts are unknown." No further Confederate documentation regarding his service has been located.

There is no known match for this Robert Cardwell among native

Virginians or Marylanders in Confederate records—an oddity, given the detail typically available in muster rolls. The best and perhaps only fitting candidate from the region is the Robert E. Cardwell of Delaware County, Pennsylvania. If he had found himself in Virginia at the war's outset—whether visiting, studying, or working—he may have been conscripted into Confederate service during the early, chaotic months of the war when manpower was critically needed and records sometimes incomplete or hastily prepared. Given the unusual birthplace listed in the Confederate rolls—Maryland—it is possible that Cardwell, if indeed a Northern-born man, claimed a border-state origin to avoid suspicion or worse treatment during his brief conscription.

The theory continues that after deserting from the Confederate army, Robert made his way back to Pennsylvania, where he resumed civilian life until new demands arose. With the Gettysburg Campaign in full motion during the summer of 1863, Pennsylvania called up militia units to defend against the Confederate advance into the Commonwealth. Robert was conscripted as a Private in Company B, 45th Regiment, Pennsylvania Militia, USA, on 29 June 1863, at Upland, Pennsylvania.

The 45th Pennsylvania Militia was a 90-day emergency unit, activated specifically in response to General Robert E. Lee's invasion of Pennsylvania. The regiment was tasked with guarding infrastructure, defending transportation lines, and supplementing the state's defensive readiness. Although it did not see direct action at Gettysburg, its presence contributed to the broader strategic mobilization that helped protect Philadelphia and other critical areas.

While Robert's time in both the Confederate and Union military was brief, his case is a rare and complex example of the war's deep social and regional entanglements. He appears to be one of the very few Cardwell men to have served in both armies, and perhaps the only one to have done so under such uncertain and conflicting circumstances. The absence of clear documentary continuity means that this account rests largely on well-reasoned assumptions rather than confirmed facts. However, the match of name, age, and region provides strong justification for his inclusion in the record of Cardwell men of Virginia during the Civil War.

Following the war, Robert returned to life in Delaware County, Pennsylvania, where he is believed to have lived quietly for the remainder of his years. He died on 16 September 1899, and is possibly buried at Chester Rural

Cemetery, Chester, Delaware County, Pennsylvania, though a grave marker has not been conclusively verified.[28]

Though his military service was short and troubled, Robert E. Cardwell's wartime story stands as a testament to the complexity of individual experience during the Civil War—a conflict where geography, circumstance, and identity often blurred the lines of allegiance. Cardwell Line - Undetermined.

* * *

William Cardwell (1818-) - *Private - Company L, 2nd Pennsylvania Heavy Artillery (112th Volunteers), USA*

William Cardwell was born about 1818 in Ireland. Though definitive records are lacking, it is assumed that he was the son of Samuel Cardwell and Sarah (Calvert) Cardwell, which would make him the brother of two other veterans recorded in this chapter, John Jacob Cardwell and Calvert Owen Cardwell, both of whom served during the Civil War. William married Sarah Hawthorne around 1847, based on the birth of their eldest known child. Together, they had six children: William John Cardwell (1848–1867), Robert Cardwell (1850–1911), Calvert Cardwell (1852–1911), Elisa Cardwell (born 1855), Charles Cardwell (born 1860), and George Cardwell (1860–1861). His son William John Cardwell served in Company G of the 183rd Pennsylvania Infantry and is also included in this volume.

By 1860, William and his family were living in Philadelphia's 19th Ward, where he worked as a laborer. In the 1870 census, he is found residing in the 24th Ward with two of his sons, still employed in manual labor, a common occupation among Irish immigrants in the city at the time.[29,30]

William enlisted as a Private in Company L of the 2nd Pennsylvania Heavy Artillery, also designated as the 112th Pennsylvania Volunteers, on 01 October 1861 in Philadelphia. He was 43 years of age at the time of his enlistment, a relatively advanced age for a volunteer soldier. The 2nd Pennsylvania Heavy Artillery was among the largest regiments in Union service, initially organized for the defense of Washington, D.C. Its companies were stationed at various forts around the capital. Company L, to which William was assigned, was primarily engaged in garrison duty, manning artillery positions at key defensive installations protecting the capital during the early stages of the war.

Though the regiment would later see significant action—especially during the Siege of Petersburg and the Appomattox Campaign—William was discharged early in the war. He received a Surgeon's Certificate of Disability and was mustered out on 01 April 1862, having served just six months. The specific nature of his disability is not documented in surviving service records, but the early discharge suggests he likely never left the Washington defenses nor participated in any major campaigns.

The 2nd Pennsylvania Heavy Artillery was raised largely in Philadelphia, where William lived, and the unit drew heavily from the city's working-class neighborhoods. The city's industrial strength and significant immigrant population—particularly Irish and German—made it a prime recruiting center for heavy artillery and support units. William's enlistment fits the pattern of many older laborers seeking steady pay, patriotic purpose, or community standing through brief military service.

Following his discharge, William returned to civilian life in Philadelphia. Given the prevalence of men with the name William Cardwell in Philadelphia during this period, pinpointing his exact date of death remains uncertain. One possibility is a William Cardwell who died in March 1890 and was interred at Cathedral Cemetery, but further documentation is needed to confirm this identification.[31]

William Cardwell's military service, though brief, reflects the early enthusiasm and high enlistment rates among immigrants during the first year of the war. His connection to multiple family members who also served underscores the commitment of the Cardwell family to the Union cause. Ancestry Undetermined.

* * *

William Henry Cardwell (1819-1887) - *Private - Company E, 68th Pennsylvania Infantry & Possibly Company I, 59th Massachusetts Infantry, USA*

William Henry Cardwell was born about 1819 in Ireland, though the names of his parents have not been determined. According to family researcher Georgia Gander, William first immigrated to Canada, where he appears in the 1851 Census of Addington, Canada West (modern-day Ontario).[32] Sometime before or during his time in Canada, he married Mary Jane Johnston. Whether the marriage occurred in Ireland or Canada is not known. They had the following: Mary Jane Cardwell (1849-1883), Alice

Cardwell (1850-1934), John Cardwell (1852-1884), William H. Cardwell, Jr, (1856-1902), Susan Cardwell (1860-1926), and Samuel Cardwell (1861-).

Sometime in the late 1850s or early 1860s, the Cardwell family relocated to the United States, settling in Pennsylvania. William appears in the 1870 census for Montgomery County and again in the 1880 census for Philadelphia County, where he is listed as a blacksmith—an occupation he maintained throughout his life and one that may have contributed to his physical endurance during military service.[33,34]

William Henry Cardwell enlisted in the Union Army on 18 August 1862 in Philadelphia, Pennsylvania, joining Company K of the 68th Pennsylvania Infantry. At the time of enlistment, his age was recorded as 43, though a later annotation on his Pennsylvania Veterans Index Card noted that the original roll listed his age as 52. His actual birth year, based on census records and family research, is believed to be 1819, which aligns with the older age.

The 68th Pennsylvania Infantry saw significant action during the war. At the time William enlisted, the regiment was engaged in the Maryland Campaign and later participated in the Battle of Fredericksburg (December 1862) and the Chancellorsville Campaign (May 1863). They were also heavily involved in the pivotal Battle of Gettysburg (July 01–03, 1863), where they fought in the Peach Orchard and Wheatfield sectors. The regiment continued service through the Overland Campaign and the Siege of Petersburg, including engagements at the Wilderness, Spotsylvania, and Cold Harbor. While it is not confirmed in which battles William participated, his service records indicate he remained with the unit until the end of the war, making it likely that he saw at least some of this combat.

On 09 June 1865, William was discharged at Hart's Island, New York Harbor, a common discharge and processing center for Union soldiers at war's end. Shortly thereafter, on 22 June 1865, he was awarded an invalid pension, indicating that he may have suffered wounds, chronic illness, or other impairments connected to his military service.

An interesting complication arises from records that also attribute service in the 59th Massachusetts Infantry to a William H. Cardwell.[35] That man enlisted on 21 March 1864, raising questions about whether this is the same individual or another man with the same name. Further confusing the matter is the existence of multiple William Cardwells living in Philadelphia during this period. While William's consistent occupation as a blacksmith in census and service records supports a link between the two records, no definitive evidence has yet clarified the dual enlistments. For this reason, information pertaining to the 59th Massachusetts Infantry service is addressed separately in the Miscellaneous chapter of this volume.

After the war, William returned to civilian life in Philadelphia. His name appears in connection with Ellis Post, Number 6 of the Grand Army of the Republic, confirming his identity as a Union veteran. He died on 09 July 1887 in Germantown, Philadelphia County, Pennsylvania, and was buried at Ivy Hill Cemetery in Philadelphia.[36] Though questions about his dual enlistment remain unresolved, William Henry Cardwell's service in the 68th Pennsylvania Infantry and his postwar recognition as a veteran firmly establish his role in the preservation of the Union. <u>Ancestry Undetermined</u>.

* * *

William John Cardwell (1845-1867) - *Private - Company G, 183rd Pennsylvania Infantry, USA*

William John Cardwell was born in 1845 in Philadelphia, Pennsylvania, the eldest son of William Cardwell and Sarah (Hawthorne) Cardwell. His parents were both natives of Ireland who immigrated to the United States prior to William's birth. By 1860, the family is documented in the Philadelphia census, residing together in the city.[37] His father was a laborer, and William would have come of age as sectional tensions erupted into full civil war.

Although the exact date of William's enlistment has not been located, he is confirmed to have served as a Private in Company G, 183rd Regiment, Pennsylvania Infantry. The 183rd Pennsylvania was organized during the latter years of the war, mustering in at Camp Curtin in Harrisburg between December 1863 and May 1864, suggesting that William likely enlisted as a teenager around late 1863 or early 1864.

The 183rd Pennsylvania Infantry was quickly thrown into the heart of combat. It was assigned to the Army of the Potomac, where it took part in some of the fiercest engagements of the Overland Campaign. William's company would have been engaged at the Battle of the Wilderness (May 05–07, 1864) and shortly thereafter at Spotsylvania Court House (May 08–21, 1864). The regiment suffered considerable losses and continued through the brutal fighting at Cold Harbor (June 01–12) and the long siege operations against Petersburg, Virginia. Though specific company-level records for

William are sparse, his presence with Company G during this period means he was likely a participant in these actions, enduring both the hardships of battle and the toll of camp disease.

Tragically, William John Cardwell died on 08 May 1867, just two years after the war's end, in Philadelphia at the young age of about twenty-two. The cause of death is not recorded, but given the timing and common patterns among Civil War veterans, it is reasonable to speculate that his death may have been related to lingering effects of illness or injury sustained during his service. Unfortunately, the limited and fragmentary state of his service records leaves this question unresolved. His Civil War records state his name as William J. Cardwell, but a newspaper account of his passing provided his middle name and parents.[38]

Interestingly, William was commemorated with a U.S. Government-issued veteran's headstone, which was ordered from supplier D. W. Whitney on 29 November 1879. The intended burial site was Franklin Cemetery in Philadelphia, yet no documentation has been found confirming that the headstone was ever installed.[39] Today, his final resting place remains uncertain, and the stone's whereabouts are unknown.

Though little is documented about his short life, William John Cardwell's inclusion in the ranks of the 183rd Pennsylvania places him among those who endured the brutal final year of the war and whose sacrifice may have extended beyond the battlefield. His legacy, like many young soldiers of that time, is preserved through records of duty and memory of loss. Ancestry undetermined.

Tennessee
Cardwell Union Soldiers

TENNESSEE WAS ONE OF THE MOST CONTESTED STATES IN THE CIVIL War, with strong allegiances to both the Union and the Confederacy. Though it officially joined the Confederacy in 1861, large portions of East Tennessee remained pro-Union, contributing thousands of soldiers to the Union cause. The state saw some of the war's most intense battles, including Shiloh, Stones River, Chattanooga, and Franklin. Unionist Tennesseans, including members of the Cardwell family, fought to restore federal control over their home state.

The Cardwell men from Tennessee who served in Union regiments were part of a larger movement of pro-Union Tennesseans who fought to restore their state to federal control. Their service in infantry, cavalry, and artillery units contributed to key victories in the Western Theater, helping turn the tide of the war in favor of the Union.

This chapter honors the Cardwell Union soldiers of Tennessee, ensuring their commitment and sacrifices are preserved in the Cardwell Family history.

* * *

Photo 12.1: *Alfred Cardwell (1843-1913) Headstone - Little Flat Creek Cemetery, Corryton, Knox County, Tennessee.*

Alfred Cardwell (1843-1913) - *Private - Company B, 1st Tennessee Infantry, USA*

Alfred Cardwell was born on 01 December 1843 in Grainger County, Tennessee, the eldest son of Daniel J. Cardwell and Frances (Norris) Cardwell. He spent his early years in the rugged hills of East Tennessee, a region known for its strong opposition to secession and deep loyalty to the federal Union. This pro-Union sentiment was so pronounced that in 1856, local residents petitioned to create a new county named Union County, carved from parts of Grainger, Claiborne, Knox, Anderson, and Campbell Counties—a symbolic expression of their allegiance to the United States, even before the war began.

Alfred is listed with his family in the 1850 census for Grainger County and again in Union County in the 1860 census, just a year before the first shots were fired at Fort Sumter.[1,2] As the Civil War unfolded, East Tennessee remained a hotbed of Unionist resistance in a Confederate state, and thousands of its young men crossed mountains or dodged Confederate patrols to enlist in Federal service.

At the age of 19, Alfred Cardwell joined their ranks. He enlisted as a Private in Company B, 1st Tennessee Infantry (U.S.) on 25 February 1863 at Murfreesboro, Rutherford County, Tennessee, for a term of three years. His enlistment records describe him as 5 feet 6 inches tall, with a dark complexion, light hair, and distinctive yellow eyes—a rare detail in surviving Union records.

The 1st Tennessee Infantry (Union) had been organized in late 1861 at Camp Dick Robinson, Kentucky, by Unionist Tennesseans who fled Confederate-held territory. The regiment was attached to the Army of the Ohio and later the Army of the Cumberland, performing essential duties such as garrison work, railroad protection, and provost assignments across Kentucky, Middle Tennessee, and Northern Georgia. While not often engaged in major combat, the regiment's role in holding and stabilizing critical supply lines in hostile territory was vital to the broader Union war effort.

Alfred appears consistently on unit rolls from his enlistment through 05 December 1864, at which point he was assigned to detached service under Special Order #186. He returned to regular duty on 02 January 1865, when he was transferred to Company A of the same regiment. He remained on active duty until his honorable discharge on 03 August 1865 at Nashville, Tennessee, having seen the conflict through to its conclusion.

After the war, Alfred returned to Union County, where he married Marinda J. Dyer on 31 July 1869.[3] The couple had two children: Paralee Cardwell (1874–1913) and Francis Cardwell (1879–1913). Alfred appears in the 1870 census for Grainger County and the 1880 census for Union County, working as a farmer during the difficult Reconstruction years.[4,5]

Marinda died on 01 April 1883, leaving Alfred a widower with young children. Later that year, on 31 August 1883, he married Sarah Jane Mitchell. Alfred fathered three more children: Pearl D. Cardwell (born 1894), Lillie G. Cardwell (1897–1911), and Beulah Katherine Cardwell (1899–1921).

Alfred applied for a Union pension on 25 February 1890 in Grainger County, reporting a service-related disability beginning 27 August 1886. His pension records cite rheumatism contracted during the harsh winter of 1863. He was awarded a pension of $17 per month, a modest but critical support for aging veterans.

By 1900, Alfred had settled in Corryton, Knox County, Tennessee, where he appears in both the 1900 and 1910 census records.[6,7] His second wife, Sarah Jane, died on 19 December 1903, and by 1910 he was a widower once again, living with two of his children.

Alfred Cardwell died of influenza on 22 July 1913 in Knox County, and was buried at Little Flat Creek Baptist Church Cemetery in Corryton. His death occurred the same year as that of his adult children Paralee and Francis. His daughter Lillie had died two years earlier, and Beulah would pass away in 1921.

Alfred's wartime service in the 1st Tennessee Infantry, U.S. Volunteers, and his postwar life reflect the journey of many East Tennessee Unionists. Raised in a community that valued loyalty to the United States above sectional allegiance, he answered the call to preserve the Union and lived long enough to see its preservation secure. His brother, James Calvin Cardwell, also served in the Union Army and is profiled in this volume.[8] Cardwell Line I - Predicted. Photo Credit[9]

Photo 12.2: *Anthony Warren Cardwell (1836-1904) - Roane County, Tennessee - circa 1872.*

Photo 12.3: *Anthony Warren Cardwell (1836-1904) - Oral, Roane County, Tennessee - circa 1900.*

Photo 12.4: *Anthony Warren Cardwell (1836-1904) Headstone. Oral Cemetery, Oral, Roane County, Tennessee.*

Anthony Warren Cardwell (1836-1904) - *5th Sergeant - Company D, 5th Tennessee Infantry, USA*

Anthony Warren Cardwell was born on 20 November 1836 in Grainger County, Tennessee, the son of John Wesley Cardwell and Sarah (Smith)

121

Cardwell. He appears in the 1850 census in his parents' household in Jefferson County, Tennessee. The entire family moved southwest of Knoxville, to Roane County, Tennessee in the 1850's. Anthony married Sarena Ellen Carter on 20 May 1857 in Roane County, Tennessee.[10] Together they had the following children: Martha Elizabeth Cardwell (1858-1930), Mary E. Cardwell (1860-1937), James H. Cardwell (1864-1864), Laura Lavada Cardwell (1866-1928), William R. Cardwell (1868-1870), Thomas Oscar Cardwell (1871-1933), and Joseph Schultz "Joe" Cardwell (1874-1943). Anthony and his family appear in both the 1860 and 1870 federal censuses for Roane County.[11,12]

In early 1862, as the war intensified across the upper South, Anthony joined the ranks of East Tennessee Unionists determined to preserve the United States. On 26 February 1862, he enlisted as a Private in Company D of the 5th Tennessee Infantry, U.S. Volunteers, at Barboursville, Knox County, Kentucky. He was promoted to the rank of 5th Sergeant the following month, in March 1862.

The 5th Tennessee Infantry (U.S.) was composed primarily of Union loyalists from East Tennessee, many of whom had fled Confederate-held areas to enlist. The regiment was organized under Colonel James T. Shelley and saw service under the Army of the Ohio, later becoming part of the Army of the Cumberland. Initially assigned to secure East Tennessee and southern Kentucky, the 5th Tennessee conducted reconnaissance and guard duty in critical mountain passes and river corridors during 1862.

Anthony was present for all activities until 15 September 1862, when he became ill and was admitted to a Union hospital in Bowling Green, Kentucky. The specifics of his illness were not recorded. As the 5th Tennessee moved with Union forces toward Cumberland Gap, Anthony was transferred to a hospital there on 17 December 1862, and during this period, his rank was reduced from Sergeant back to Private, likely due to extended absence from duty.

In January 1863, Anthony returned to his regiment and resumed active service. He is recorded as present from January 1863 through June 1864, and his rank of Sergeant was restored in March 1863. During this time, the 5th Tennessee Infantry became heavily involved in the war's major operations across Tennessee and Georgia. In the summer of 1863, the regiment partici-pated in the Tullahoma Campaign, helping to drive Confederate forces from

Middle Tennessee in a series of swift, coordinated maneuvers under General Rosecrans.

Later that year, Anthony would have taken part in the Battle of Chickamauga (19–20 September 1863), one of the bloodiest battles of the war. The 5th Tennessee served in Brigadier General James G. Spears's Brigade, defending Union lines along the southern edge of the field. Though ultimately a Confederate victory, the regiment fought with distinction during the retreat toward Chattanooga.

In the first half of 1864, the regiment became part of General Sherman's forces advancing into Georgia. Anthony would have participated in the early phases of the Atlanta Campaign, including the grueling marches and constant skirmishes through rugged terrain near Tunnel Hill, Rocky Face Ridge, and Resaca, as Union troops pressed into the heart of the Deep South.

On 05 June 1864, Anthony was hospitalized again—this time in Altoona, Georgia, shortly after the Battle of New Hope Church. He was later moved to a hospital in Chattanooga, Tennessee, where he remained until November 1864, recovering from an unspecified ailment. Following his return to duty, he remained with the regiment through the war's conclusion and was honorably discharged on 30 June 1865 at Nashville, Davidson County, Tennessee.

After his return home, Anthony moved with his family briefly to neighboring Loudon County, where they appear in the 1880 census. By 1890, they had returned to Oral, a small community in Roane County, where he is listed in the 1890 Veterans Census. In his later years, Anthony was widowed and lived with his daughter Mary E. (Cardwell) Waller, as shown in the 1900 Roane County census.[13,14,15] He was granted an Invalid Pension by the United States government, on 25 January 1869.

Anthony Warren Cardwell died on 23 March 1904 in Oral, Roane County, Tennessee, and was laid to rest at Oral Cemetery, not far from where he had spent much of his life.[16] His journey—from the mountains of East Tennessee, through the fields of Chickamauga and the ridges of North Georgia, and back home—mirrors that of many Unionist Tennesseans who fought to preserve the nation despite living in a seceded state. His loyalty, endurance, and long postwar life mark him as a quiet but steadfast representative of East Tennessee's wartime legacy. <u>Cardwell Line II - Predicted</u>. Photo Credits[17,18,19]

* * *

Photo 12.5: *Clisby Austin Cardwell (1843-1905) Headstone. Glades Lebanon Baptist Church Cemetery, Sevier County, Tennessee.*

Clisby Austin Cardwell (1843-1905) - *Private - Company C & L, 1st Tennessee Cavalry, USA*

Clisby Austin Cardwell was born in July 1843 in Grainger County, Tennessee, the son of James Thompson Cardwell and Mary Alice (Austin) Cardwell. He appears in both the 1850 and 1860 census records for Grainger County, residing in his parents' household.[20,21] Sometime after 1860, the family relocated to Gatlinburg in Sevier County, nestled deep within East Tennessee's mountainous terrain—a region noted for its strong Unionist sympathies despite Tennessee's Confederate alignment.

On 11 January 1863, at the age of 19, Clisby enlisted as a Private in Company C, 1st Tennessee Cavalry (U.S.), at Louisville, Jefferson County, Kentucky. His enlistment records describe him as 5 feet 9 inches tall, with a fair complexion, blue eyes, and light hair. He reported his birthplace as Grainger County and listed his occupation as farmer. His decision to join a Union cavalry unit in Kentucky reflects the reality faced by many East Tennessee Unionists, who had to leave their home counties—then under Confederate control—in order to enlist with Federal forces.

The 1st Tennessee Cavalry (U.S.) was organized between November 1862 and March 1863, drawing heavily from Unionist strongholds in East Tennessee. Once fully assembled, the regiment was attached to the Army of the Ohio and later to the Army of the Cumberland, performing a mix of scouting, raiding, and escort duties. In its early operations, the regiment helped secure supply lines across Middle Tennessee and southern Kentucky, contributing to the Union's strategic hold on the region.

Clisby was present with the regiment during its active campaigning in late 1863 and early 1864, when the unit participated in Federal efforts to control East Tennessee following the successful capture of Knoxville in December 1863. In April 1864, Clisby was recorded as being on detachment duty in Chattanooga, then a key Union logistics hub in southeastern Tennessee. From May to July 1864, he was assigned to guard duty at an unspecified railroad bridge in Georgia, most likely protecting Union supply lines in support of General Sherman's Atlanta Campaign. These duties, while less visible than front-line battles, were vital to the campaign's success, as they secured the railroads that moved men, weapons, and rations through hostile territory.

He returned to his company sometime in July 1864, rejoining the 1st Tennessee Cavalry as the unit moved into more aggressive operations against Confederate cavalry and supply trains in northern Georgia and southeastern Tennessee. The regiment took part in anti-guerrilla actions, railroad patrols, and small-scale raids aimed at weakening Confederate mobility during the height of Sherman's Atlanta operations.

In March 1865, Clisby was transferred from Company C to Company L, a common administrative adjustment within cavalry regiments as men were consolidated in the war's final months. He remained with Company L until he was honorably discharged on 19 June 1865 at Nashville, Tennessee, having fulfilled the terms of his enlistment.

Following the war, Clisby returned to Sevier County and married Arena Cochran on 18 September 1865.[22] The couple had three daughters: Mary Etta Cardwell (1869–1940), Eliza J. Cardwell (1872–1888), and Alice Cardwell (1873–1919). Clisby is listed in the 1870 census for Sevier County, but by 1880 had moved westward to Loudon County, where he appears again in census records. He eventually returned to Sevier County by 1900, where he spent his remaining years.[23,24,25]

Clisby applied for and received a Union pension beginning on 03 June 1882, part of the first generation of Civil War veterans to benefit from federal compensation. He appears in the 1890 Veterans Census, listed as a resident of Sevier County, Tennessee, and noted his Civil War service in the 1st Tennessee Cavalry.

He died on 25 June 1905 in Sevier County at the age of 61, and was buried at

Glades Lebanon Baptist Church Cemetery, a quiet burial ground nestled in the Smoky Mountains.[26] His service, though not marked by famous battles, was part of the essential and often dangerous infrastructure of the Union war effort in the South—guarding supply lines, holding railways, and patrolling contested terrain.

Clisby was the brother of William C. Cardwell, another Union veteran whose service is detailed in this chapter. Together, they reflect the resolve of East Tennessee's Unionists, men who risked arrest, exile, or worse to enlist under the flag of the United States, and whose service helped secure Federal control in one of the war's most strategically valuable—and politically divided —regions. <u>Cardwell Line II - Predicted</u>. Photo Credit[27]

* * *

Henry Cardwell (1837-) - *Private - Company D, 4th Tennessee Cavalry, USA*

Henry Cardwell enlisted in the Union Army on 21 December 1862 at London, Laurel County, Kentucky, joining as a Private in Company D of the 4th Tennessee Cavalry (U.S.). According to his enlistment records, Henry was 26 years old, stood 5 feet 8 inches tall, and had a brown complexion, dark hair, and dark eyes. He listed his birthplace as Davidson County, Tennessee, and his occupation as farmer.

The 4th Tennessee Cavalry (Union) was organized between October 1862 and April 1863, drawing largely from East and Middle Tennessee men loyal to the Union. As Confederate authorities retained control over large portions of the state, many enlistees—like Henry—fled to nearby Kentucky to muster into Federal service. The regiment was formed with the intention of conducting scouting operations, raiding, and reconnaissance behind enemy lines, often in cooperation with the Army of the Ohio and later the Army of the Cumberland.

Henry's enlistment in late December 1862 coincided with the early stages of the regiment's organization. At the time, the unit was still being recruited and outfitted for active field service and had not yet entered into sustained combat operations. However, within weeks, detachments of the 4th Tennessee Cavalry would begin escorting supply trains, skirmishing with Confederate raiders in southern Kentucky and East Tennessee, and establishing a presence in key towns such as Columbia and Gallatin in Middle Tennessee.

Henry Cardwell's time in uniform, however, appears to have been brief. His service record indicates that he deserted on 08 January 1863, less than three weeks after enlistment, while stationed at Louisville, Kentucky. No additional military documents have been located that clarify whether he returned to duty, reenlisted under a different name or unit, or faced disciplinary action. With no further muster rolls, pension applications, or service-related correspondence attached to his file, the nature and circumstances of his desertion remain unknown.

There is tentative evidence that a man by the name of Henry Cardwell appears in the 1880 federal census for Davidson County, Tennessee, listed as a farm laborer.[28] However, due to the commonality of the surname and the absence of matching family records or pension applications, it cannot be confirmed that this is the same individual. No known record of marriage, death, or burial has been located for him.

Henry's case reflects a lesser-known aspect of Union military service in Tennessee—namely, the high rate of early desertions among enlistees from Middle Tennessee, where Confederate sympathies were stronger and social pressures more severe. Many Union regiments suffered significant manpower losses from men who either grew disillusioned with army life, feared reprisal from Confederate neighbors, or were unwilling to serve under unfamiliar officers far from home.

Though his time in uniform was short and his later life remains uncertain, Henry Cardwell's enlistment stands as part of the larger and more complex story of Tennessee's divided loyalties. He joined the Union Army at a critical moment when the future of the state and the nation was being contested by neighbors, kin, and communities. Whether his decision to leave the army was driven by hardship, hesitation, or a change of heart, his name—briefly entered into the rolls of the 4th Tennessee Cavalry—remains preserved among the records of a deeply fractured and deeply human war. <u>Ancestry undetermined.</u>

* * *

Photo 12.6: *Henry H. Cardwell (1836-1923) Headstone. Kelley Cemetery, Ash Grove, Greene County, Missouri.*

Henry H. Cardwell (1836-1923) - *Private - Company F, 1st Tennessee Cavalry, USA*

Henry H. Cardwell was born on 02 November 1836 in Grainger County, Tennessee, the son of Perrin Cardwell and Louisa (Norris) Cardwell. His father died in 1854, leaving Louisa a widow with several children. By the time of the 1860 census, Henry was still residing in Grainger County, listed in the household of his widowed mother, along with his siblings.[29,30] Like many families in East Tennessee, the Cardwells lived in a region deeply divided by the coming war—where loyalties often split households and communities.

On 02 June 1861, as Tennessee moved to join the Confederacy, Henry married Elizabeth Minerva Corum in Grainger County.[31] The couple would have three children: Anna Cardwell (1862–1863), John Wesley Cardwell (1865–1866), and James William Cardwell (1868–1953). Only their youngest son lived beyond childhood.

Determined to support the Union cause despite Confederate control over his home region, Henry enlisted in the Union Army on 01 March 1862 at Cumberland Gap, Claiborne County, Tennessee, as a Private in Company F, 1st Tennessee Cavalry (U.S.). His enlistment papers describe him as 5 feet 8 inches tall, with a dark complexion, dark eyes, and dark hair. A farmer by trade, he gave his birthplace as Grainger County.

The 1st Tennessee Cavalry (U.S.) was formed in Kentucky and East Tennessee, composed almost entirely of Unionist refugees who had escaped Confederate control. The regiment was attached to the Army of the Ohio, and later the Army of the Cumberland, tasked with vital operations including reconnaissance, raiding, and railroad protection. Early in the war, the unit patrolled the mountainous corridors along the Tennessee-Kentucky border, securing strategic passes and escorting Union supply trains.

Henry is listed as present for duty from March 1862 through January 1864, with a single exception in January 1864, when he was reported as sick in Knoxville, Tennessee. He returned to duty shortly thereafter, rejoining his regiment in time to participate in the spring and summer operations of 1864.

In April 1864, Henry was detached to guard duty on a railroad bridge in Georgia, a critical role during General William T. Sherman's Atlanta Campaign. Though the precise location of the bridge is not specified in the records, guarding Union rail lines in Georgia was essential to ensuring the continuous movement of troops and supplies during the campaign. He remained on detached duty until late June 1864, after which he rejoined his unit.

Following his return, Henry served with the 1st Tennessee Cavalry as it conducted skirmishes, scouting missions, and rail disruption operations in north Georgia and southeast Tennessee. These efforts helped isolate Atlanta and harass Confederate movements in the waning months of the campaign. Henry remained on duty until the expiration of his term and was honorably discharged on 30 March 1865 at Nashville, Davidson County, Tennessee.

After the war, Henry returned to Grainger County, where he appears in both the 1870 and 1880 census records.[32,33] Sometime after 1880, he and his family moved west to Boone, Greene County, Missouri, a common destination for Tennessee families seeking land and opportunity in the postwar period. He appears in the 1890 Veterans Census in Missouri and applied for a Union pension on 23 July 1890, which was approved and granted during his residence there.[34]

Henry spent the remainder of his life in Ash Grove, Greene County, Missouri and is listed in the 1900 and 1910 census records.[35,36] Henry H. Cardwell, Union veteran of the Civil War, died on 03 December 1923 at the age of 87. He was buried at Kelley Cemetery in Ash Grove, Missouri.[37]

Henry H. Cardwell's life bridges the two worlds of Civil War-era Tennessee: that of a fiercely divided homeland and the steadfast conviction of those who chose to fight for Union preservation. His service in the 1st Tennessee Cavalry (U.S.), particularly during the critical phases of the Atlanta Campaign, placed him among those whose contributions helped tip the balance in the Western Theater. His endurance through war, loss, and westward migration stands as a testament to the resilience of East Tennessee's Unionist soldiers. <u>Cardwell Line I - Predicted</u>. Photo Credit[38]

* * *

James Calvin Cardwell (1845-1893) - *Private - Company B&A, 1st Tennessee Infantry, USA*

James Calvin Cardwell, known by family and neighbors as "Cal," was born in 1845 in Grainger County, Tennessee, the son of Daniel J. Cardwell and Frances (Norris) Cardwell. He is listed in his parents' household in the 1850 census for Grainger County and again in the 1860 census for Union County, Tennessee. Like many young men in East Tennessee—where loyalty to the Union ran deep—James came of age in a region marked by divided allegiances and the growing strain of civil conflict.

Though only a single surviving military record confirms his service, it identifies James Cardwell as a Private in Companies A and B of the 1st Regiment Tennessee Infantry, U.S. Volunteers. His enlistment date is not recorded, and there are no accompanying muster rolls or pension files. However, the unit assignment corresponds with the regiment in which his brother, Alfred Cardwell, served—a regiment composed almost entirely of East Tennessee Unionists.

The 1st Tennessee Infantry (U.S.) was organized between August and October 1861 in Barbourville and Camp Dick Robinson, Kentucky, with many recruits coming from Unionist families in East Tennessee who had crossed into Kentucky to escape Confederate control. The regiment served under the Army of the Ohio and later the Army of the Cumberland, engaging in guard, garrison, and supply line security duties throughout Kentucky, Middle Tennessee, and Northern Georgia.

Assuming James Calvin's service aligned with that of his brother Alfred—who enlisted in February 1863—he likely joined the regiment during its mid-war service phase. During this period, the 1st Tennessee Infantry was assigned to railroad protection duties, defended key Union supply routes, and engaged in small-scale skirmishes throughout the Upper Cumberland region. While the regiment did not participate in large-scale battles like Chickamauga or Atlanta until later, its role was essential to ensuring operational support for larger campaigns.

James was likely part of Company B, which served in Middle Tennessee, conducting patrols, guarding Union supply lines, and preventing Confederate cavalry raids. He was later transferred or attached to Company A, a typical administrative move within regiments that sustained casualties or required reorganization. Though we cannot pinpoint the specific battles he may have witnessed, his presence in the 1st Tennessee Infantry during its active years suggests he participated in the defense of Nashville, the Tullahoma campaign logistics, and garrison operations in occupied Tennessee towns.

After the war, James returned to Union County, where he married Elizabeth Jane Dyer on 19 January 1869. The couple raised eight children: John Wesley Cardwell (1870–1964), Samuel Cardwell (1872–1954), Martha Jane Cardwell (1873–1969), Maude Cardwell (1877–1924), James D. Cardwell (1878–1880), Mary Emily Cardwell (1882–1964), Marquis Lafayette Cardwell (1885–1956), and Frances D. Cardwell (1890–1973). Like many East Tennessee families of the Reconstruction era, they built a life rooted in hard work, community ties, and quiet resilience.

Though James Calvin Cardwell did not apply for a federal pension, and his grave location is unknown, family tradition has long preserved his memory as a Union veteran. He is believed to have died around 1893, most likely in Union County, Tennessee. His absence from pension rolls may stem from administrative oversights, incomplete discharge documentation, or personal choice—a common fate for many veterans who served briefly or whose service was poorly documented.

His brother, Alfred Cardwell, whose service in Company B of the same regiment is well-recorded, appears elsewhere in this chapter and reinforces the family's contribution to the Union cause. Together, their names are tied to one of the earliest and most dedicated Union regiments from a Confederate state—a distinction that reflects the courage and convictions of East Tennessee Unionists during the nation's most trying hour. <u>Cardwell Line I - Confirmed</u>.

* * *

Photo 12.7: *John Preston Cardwell (1846-1891) Headstone. Emerts Cove Cemetery, Sevier County, Tennessee.*

John Preston Cardwell (1846-1891) - *Private - Company D, 2nd Tennessee Cavalry, USA*

John Preston Cardwell was born on 16 February 1846 in Grainger County, Tennessee, the son of Robert Cardwell and Nancy (Mayes) Cardwell. He appears with his family in the 1850 census for Grainger County, but by the late 1850s the family had relocated to Sevier County, in the Smoky Mountain foothills of East Tennessee. In the 1860 census, John is recorded again in the home of his parents in Sevier County, where he worked as a young farm laborer amid the rising tensions of a nation at war.[39,40]

On 17 July 1863, at the age of 18, John enlisted in the Union Army as a Private in Company D, 2nd Tennessee Cavalry (U.S.), at Jasper, Marion County, Tennessee. He stood 5 feet 8 inches tall, with a fair complexion, blue eyes, and light hair, and listed his birthplace as Grainger County. Like many East Tennessee men, he joined the Union cause despite his state's official allegiance to the Confederacy. The mountainous regions of Tennessee remained fiercely loyal to the United States, and many young men like John traveled across difficult terrain to enlist in Federal service.

The 2nd Tennessee Cavalry (U.S.) was originally formed in Kentucky in late 1862, with its ranks filled by East Tennesseans who had escaped Confederate conscription. By the time John joined in mid-1863, the regiment was already engaged in raiding operations and cavalry screening missions across Middle Tennessee. The 2nd Tennessee Cavalry played a vital role in pursuing Confederate cavalry under General Joseph Wheeler and securing Union supply lines during the Chattanooga Campaign.

John was listed as present with his unit from his enlistment in July 1863 through June 1864, a period during which the regiment participated in several skirmishes and support operations. In August and September 1863, his company was likely involved in scouting and raiding missions in support of

General Rosecrans's movement toward Chattanooga, though the unit's role remained largely in a support and harassment capacity rather than direct engagement at Chickamauga.

On 14 June 1864, John was placed on detached duty in Chattanooga, where cavalry troops were often assigned to escort duties, picket lines, or railroad defense as the Union consolidated its control over southeastern Tennessee. He returned to his company by July 1864, just as the 2nd Tennessee Cavalry became active in General William T. Sherman's Atlanta Campaign, primarily through reconnaissance, rear guard duties, and small-unit raids designed to disrupt Confederate communication and supply.

On 10 October 1864, John was again sent on detached duty, this time to Decatur Junction, Georgia, a strategic location along the Western & Atlantic Railroad. There, his responsibilities would have included protecting key rail infrastructure vital to Sherman's army as it prepared for the final push into central Georgia.

In early 1865, during the winding down of active campaigning in the Western Theater, John became ill and was sent to a Union hospital in Columbia, Tennessee, where he was listed as sick on 15 January 1865. He recovered and returned to duty, continuing to serve through the final months of the war. He was honorably discharged on 06 July 1865 at Nashville, Davidson County, Tennessee, after completing his full term of enlistment.

Returning to civilian life in Sevier County, John wasted no time in rebuilding. On 28 December 1865, he married Margaret Whaley, and together they had two sons: Robert Harrison Cardwell (1867–1936) and John W. Cardwell (1868–1931). Margaret died in 1878, and the following year, on 21 June 1879, John married Sarah C. Bradley. Their union produced four more children: Phoebe E. (1881–1969), Isabell Cordelia (1882–1916), William Preston "Bill" (1885–1970), and Martha Ann Cardwell (1888–1960).[41]

John was a lifelong resident of Emerts Cove, a small mountain community in Sevier County, where he worked the land and raised his children. He appears in the 1870 and 1880 federal censuses, both times listed as a farmer.[42,43] His health, like that of many Civil War veterans, may have declined in the years following his service, and on 23 June 1883, he was awarded a federal pension for his military service in the Union Army.

John Preston Cardwell died on 30 October 1891 at the age of 45, and was buried at Emerts Cove Cemetery in Sevier County, Tennessee.[44] Following his death, his widow, Sarah C. Cardwell, applied for and was granted a Widow's Pension.

Notably, his Civil War service records list him only as "John Cardwell," with no middle name, but extensive research and family documentation confirm his full name as John Preston Cardwell. His dedication, even as a young enlistee, placed him in the ranks of the thousands of East Tennesseans who risked their lives in defense of the Union during a bitterly divided time. His legacy continues in the hills of Emerts Cove, where his descendants still recall his service with quiet pride. Cardwell Line II - Predicted. Photo Credit[45]

* * *

Richard Cardwell (1845-1916) - *Private - Company B, 1st East Tennessee Infantry & Company K & G, 8th East Tennessee Cavalry, USA*

Richard Cardwell was born on 17 December 1845 in Grainger County, Tennessee, the son of Peter A. Cardwell and Susan Anna (Dyer) Cardwell. He appears with his parents in the 1850 census for Grainger County.[46] Raised in a region of complex loyalties and frequent division during the Civil War, Richard's family history reflected both deep roots in military service and conflicting political sympathies.

His paternal grandfather had served in the War of 1812, and his eldest paternal uncle and namesake, Richard Cardwell, was killed in action during the Mexican-American War in 1847. However, during the Civil War, two other uncles—James R. Cardwell and William T. Cardwell—enlisted in the Confederate Army. In contrast, Richard chose to fight for the Union, a decision that likely introduced significant tension within his extended family. Such internal divisions were not uncommon in East Tennessee, where loyalty often split along generational or regional lines. That Richard eventually relocated to Obion County, on the opposite side of the state, may reflect the long-term consequences of this family divide.

On 03 August 1862, at the age of 16, Richard enlisted in Company B of the 1st East Tennessee Infantry (U.S.) at Cumberland Gap, Claiborne County, Tennessee. The 1st East Tennessee Infantry, one of the earliest Union regiments raised in the state, was composed largely of East Tennessee Unionists who had slipped into Kentucky to avoid Confederate conscription. At the time of Richard's enlistment, the regiment was tasked with guarding

Cumberland Gap, then a critical mountain pass under Union control. However, shortly after his enlistment, the situation at the Gap deteriorated.

In September 1862, Union forces were forced to evacuate Cumberland Gap after a Confederate advance cut off their supply lines. The 1st East Tennessee Infantry retreated through Kentucky, engaging in a long and difficult march to Union-held territory. Richard's records indicate he was still with the regiment when it passed through Louisville, Kentucky, but on 16 December 1862, he was listed as having deserted. The specific circumstances are unknown, but his age—only 17 at the time—and the severe hardships of the campaign may have contributed to his withdrawal.

Despite the desertion charge, Richard reenlisted the following year. On 24 July 1863, he joined Company G of the 8th East Tennessee Cavalry (U.S.) at Union County, Tennessee. His enlistment papers describe him as 5 feet 6 inches tall, with a dark complexion, gray eyes, and dark hair. He gave his occupation as farmer and enlisted for a three-year term. The 8th East Tennessee Cavalry was organized in the summer of 1863 and was attached to the Department of the Ohio, conducting raids, escort duty, and scouting operations across East Tennessee and southeastern Kentucky.

However, Richard did not serve long in the field. Later that year, he was hospitalized at Camp Nelson, Kentucky, a large Union recruiting and medical facility. His condition is not specified in surviving records, but he remained at Camp Nelson from December 1863 until the end of the war, indicating a serious or chronic illness. During his time in the hospital, he was transferred from Company G to Company K, likely an administrative measure due to his prolonged absence from active field service. Richard was ultimately discharged on 11 September 1865 at Knoxville, Tennessee.

Despite his illness, Richard made efforts years later to rectify his military record. On 22 December 1889, nearly a quarter-century after his initial enlistment, he submitted a petition to the War Department requesting the removal of the desertion charge and an honorable discharge for his service in the 1st East Tennessee Infantry. His request was denied, and the charge remained on his record.

Following the war, Richard returned to Union County, Tennessee, where he married Sarah Catherine Boles on 01 November 1866.[47] They had three children: Joseph "Joe" Henry Cardwell (1867–), Peter A. Cardwell (1872–1891), and James G. Cardwell (1875–1948). The couple appears to have later divorced, and on 02 January 1888, Richard married Cordelia "Cordie" P.

Donehew, also of Union County.[48] Together, they had five children: Myrtle "Bertie" A. Cardwell (1889–), Benjamin Floyd Cardwell (1891–), Winnie C. Cardwell (1894–1925), Lawrence Chester Cardwell (1897–1980), and Menton Sims Cardwell (1900–1921).

Richard is listed in the 1870, 1880, and 1900 federal census records for Union County, working primarily as a farmer.[49,50,51] By 1900, he had relocated to Obion County, in northwest Tennessee, where he lived as a boarder—a move that may have been influenced by lingering divisions in his home region or the presence of extended family who had also resettled there.[52]

He died on 15 May 1916 in Union City, Obion County, Tennessee, at the age of 70. His body was cremated, and the location of his remains is unknown.[53] Though his service was marred by illness and administrative complications, Richard Cardwell's military story is still emblematic of the conflicted loyalties and difficult choices faced by men from East Tennessee. He was one of several Cardwells who served during the Civil War—some for the Union, others for the Confederacy—reflecting the divided nature of families during America's most devastating conflict. The location of remains is unknown. <u>Cardwell Line I - Predicted</u>.

* * *

Photo 12.8: *Samuel Sullivan Cardwell (1841-1906), Smith County, Tennessee, circa 1900*

Photo 12.9: *Samuel Sullivan Cardwell (1841-1906) Memorial Marker. Cardwell Family Cemetery, Chestnut Mound, Smith County, Tennessee.*

Samuel Sullivan Cardwell (1841-1906) - Private - *Company H, 28th Tennessee Infantry (2nd Tennessee Mountain Volunteers), CSA & Company A, 8th Tennessee Mounted Infantry, USA*

Samuel Sullivan Cardwell was born on 08 December 1841 in Smith County, Tennessee, the son of Leonard H. Cardwell and Martha (Cornwell) Cardwell. He was raised in a farming family in the Upper Cumberland region and appears in his parents' household in both the 1850 and 1860 federal censuses for Smith County.[54,55] When war came, Samuel's choices would place him among a very small number of Cardwell men known to have served in both the Confederate and Union armies during the Civil War—a distinction that underscores the divided nature of Tennessee loyalties during the conflict.

On 18 December 1861, at the age of 20, Samuel enlisted as a Private in Company H of the 28th Tennessee Infantry, Confederate States Army, also known as the 2nd Tennessee Mountain Volunteers. His enlistment took place at Red Springs, Tennessee. The regiment was formed under the command of Colonel John P. Murray and drew recruits largely from Middle Tennessee, especially from Smith and surrounding counties. Initially tasked with protecting Tennessee's northern frontier, the 28th saw light action along the Kentucky-Tennessee border through early 1862.

By the spring of 1862, the 28th Tennessee was placed under General John C. Breckinridge's Brigade, part of the Army of Mississippi. The regiment moved into central Tennessee, preparing for major engagements as Confederate forces sought to reassert control in the region. However, Samuel Cardwell was discharged on 17 July 1862, according to his Confederate service records—more than five months before the regiment's significant participation in the Battle of Stones River near Murfreesboro (31 December 1862 to 02 January 1863). His discharge came during a period of transition for the Confederate army, but no explanation for his release is provided in the surviving records. Whether due to illness, injury, or hardship is unknown.

Following his brief Confederate service, Samuel returned to Smith County. On 04 April 1863, during the heart of the war, he married Marjorie Eugenia Robinson, also of Smith County.[56] The couple would go on to raise nine children, establishing a large and enduring family in the Chestnut Mound area: William Henry Cardwell (1869-1952), Mary Victoria Cardwell (1870-1960), Susan Ova Cardwell (1873-1945), Martha Charlotte Cardwell (18756-1915), Leonard Henton "Lennie" Cardwell (1879-1957), Joseph Allen "Joe" Cardwell (1881-1958), Anna Elizabeth Cardwell (1884-1959), Floy Eugenia Cardwell (1887-1985), and Fannie Bob Cardwell (1890-1982).

In a striking postscript to his earlier military service, Samuel enlisted again on 10 January 1865, this time as a Private in Company A, 8th Tennessee Mounted Infantry (U.S.), at Carthage, Tennessee. This unit, formed late in the war in a region known for its Unionist leanings, was created to help stabilize the region and suppress guerrilla activity that had flourished in Middle Tennessee after regular Confederate forces had retreated.

The 8th Tennessee Mounted Infantry (U.S.) was primarily engaged in garrison duties, scouting missions, and counter-guerrilla operations across Smith, Jackson, Putnam, and neighboring counties. By early 1865, Confederate resistance in Tennessee was largely limited to small bands of irregular fighters, and units like the 8th were instrumental in re-establishing Union authority in areas previously contested or left lawless.

Samuel is listed as present from the date of his enlistment through the end of his service, with no absences or illnesses reported. He was honorably discharged on 17 August 1865 in Nashville, Davidson County, Tennessee, having served in the final months of the war during the Union's occupation and stabilization phase.

Decades later, Samuel applied for a Federal Invalid Pension, which was approved on 03 September 1890. While the specific cause is not noted in available records, this pension suggests lasting physical hardship related to his wartime service. He appears in the 1880 and 1900 censuses for Smith County, residing in Chestnut Mound, where he worked as a farmer and raised his large family.[57,58]

Samuel died on 27 September 1906 in Smith County at the age of 64. He was buried in the Cardwell Family Cemetery, located in Chestnut Mound, where several generations of his family have been aid to rest.[59] His widow, Marjorie, survived him and later applied for a widow's pension, preserving his record as a two-service veteran of the war.

Though his service on both sides of the conflict may appear contradictory to modern readers, Samuel Sullivan Cardwell's story reflects the complex and often personal decisions made by men in a border state like Tennessee. His shift in allegiance—whatever its motive—was not uncommon among those who faced conflicting regional pressures, family dynamics, and the need to survive in a deeply fractured land. His life stands as a reminder of the blurred lines and lived realities of civil war in America. <u>Cardwell Line III - Predicted</u>. Photo Credits[60,61]

* * *

William Cardwell (1840-) - *Private - Company D, 4th Tennessee Cavalry, USA*

William Cardwell was born around 1840 in Davidson County, Tennessee, according to his Union enlistment record. Unfortunately, no documentation has yet been located to clarify his parentage or early life. He does not appear in the 1850 or 1860 census records for Davidson County, nor has research uncovered any local records—such as land deeds, court filings, or probate entries—that might link him to other Cardwell families in the region. Whether he was part of a transient household, living with non-family members, or simply missed in enumeration is unknown. His early life remains a mystery, and research into his origins is ongoing.

William enlisted in the Union Army on 21 December 1862 at London, Laurel County, Kentucky, joining as a Private in Company D of the 4th Tennessee Cavalry (U.S.). At the time of enlistment, he gave his age as 22, his birthplace as Davidson County, and his occupation as farmer. He was described as 5 feet 6 inches tall, with a fair complexion, yellow eyes, and fair hair. Like many Tennesseans loyal to the Union cause—particularly those from regions under Confederate control—William traveled to Union-held Kentucky to enlist.

The 4th Tennessee Cavalry (Union) had only recently begun organizing in late 1862, formed from East and Middle Tennessee Unionists who had escaped Confederate-held areas. It was attached to the Army of the Ohio and began its service performing scouting, screening, and guard duties, primarily along supply lines and in contested areas of southern Kentucky and northern Tennessee. At the time William enlisted, the regiment was still being mustered and equipped. Company D would have been engaged in training and light patrols in the area around London, Kentucky, with some elements moving toward Louisville as they prepared for broader deployment.

However, William's time in uniform was short-lived. He is recorded as having deserted on 08 January 1863, just 18 days after his enlistment, while stationed at Louisville, Kentucky. No other military or civilian records have been found to clarify what happened to him after this date. His name does not appear in subsequent muster rolls, hospital logs, pension applications, or postwar census records. His date of death, place of burial, and any subsequent life history remain unknown.

Desertion during this stage of the war was not uncommon. In newly raised regiments like the 4th Tennessee Cavalry, many men enlisted under difficult personal circumstances—fleeing Confederate conscription, seeking economic stability, or following local political leaders—only to find themselves disillusioned or overwhelmed by army life. Harsh winter conditions, illness, or confusion over assignments sometimes resulted in men being marked as deserters, even in cases where illness or miscommunication may have played a role.

William Cardwell's story, though brief, reflects the uncertainty and fluid nature of enlistment during the Civil War, particularly in border states like Tennessee where loyalties were often divided even within families. His name survives in the official records of the 4th Tennessee Cavalry, and although no more is currently known about his life, his enlistment adds another thread to the broader fabric of Unionist service from a state that officially joined the Confederacy.[62]

* * *

Photo 12.10: *William C. Cardwell (1840-1864) Headstone,*
Andersonville National Cemetery, Macon County, Georgia.

William C. Cardwell (1840-1864) - *Private - Company G, 6th Tennessee Infantry, USA -* **Prisoner of War - Died in Captivity**

William C. Cardwell was born around 1840 in Grainger County, Tennessee, the son of James Thompson Cardwell and Mary Alice (Austin) Cardwell. He appears in the household of his parents in both the 1850 and 1860 federal census records for Grainger County.[63,64] Raised in East Tennessee, a region known for its strong Unionist sentiment during the Civil War, William came of age as sectional tensions intensified, ultimately leading to national conflict.

On 10 May 1862, at the age of 22, William enlisted in the Union Army as a Private in Company G, 6th Tennessee Infantry (U.S.), at Knoxville, Knox County, Tennessee. His enlistment papers describe him as 6 feet 2½ inches tall, with blue eyes, light hair, and a fair complexion—a notably tall man for his time. He listed his occupation as farmer and his birthplace as Grainger County. He joined the Union ranks approximately seven months before his younger brother, Clisby Austin Cardwell, who would later enlist in the 1st Tennessee Cavalry (U.S.) and whose biography is included in this volume.

The 6th Tennessee Infantry (U.S.) was organized during the spring of 1862 and composed primarily of Union loyalists from East Tennessee and southern Kentucky. The regiment was mustered into service under the command of Colonel Joseph Alexander Cooper, a staunch Unionist, and was attached to various commands within the Army of the Ohio and later the Army of the Cumberland. Its duties initially involved picket duty, railroad protection, and small-unit engagements across East Tennessee, a region contested throughout the war by Confederate cavalry and partisan raiders.

From the date of his enlistment in May 1862 through early 1864, William was consistently listed as present for duty, with one exception. Between 27 June and 08 August 1862, he was detailed as a cook at a Union hospital, likely in Knoxville or Cumberland Gap, where Union forces were actively establishing field hospitals to treat sick and wounded soldiers during the summer campaigns.

Throughout late 1862 and into 1863, the 6th Tennessee Infantry took part in the East Tennessee Campaign, supporting efforts to secure the region and drive Confederate forces out of Knoxville. During this time, the regiment was involved in skirmishes and reconnaissance missions across the mountain passes and river valleys that defined the rugged terrain of the area. In the fall of 1863, the regiment participated in the defense of Knoxville, a critical stand that helped preserve Union control over East Tennessee following the Confederate siege led by General James Longstreet.

On 05 February 1864, William was sent out on a scouting mission by order of General James G. Spears, a prominent Union commander in East Tennessee. During this operation, he was captured by Confederate forces somewhere near Knoxville, a region still fraught with guerrilla activity and patrol skirmishes even after major Confederate armies had withdrawn.

Following his capture, William was transported south and eventually confined at Camp Sumter, more commonly known as Andersonville Prison, in Macon County, Georgia. One of the most infamous of the Confederate prisoner-of-war camps, Andersonville was overcrowded, under-supplied, and wracked by disease, malnutrition, and exposure. William was admitted to the prison hospital on 14 March 1864, suffering from an unspecified illness. Like so many others held at Andersonville, he did not survive.

William C. Cardwell died in captivity on 27 March 1864, just over a year before the war ended. He was buried at Andersonville National Cemetery, now part of the Andersonville National Historic Site in Georgia.[65] His grave is among the thousands of Union soldiers who perished in one of the war's most tragic and historically significant settings.

Years after the war, on 21 March 1882, William's mother, Mary Alice (Austin) Cardwell, applied for and received a pension for her son's Union service, recognizing the sacrifice he made for the preservation of the United

States. Her application affirmed the details of William's death in enemy hands and ensured that his memory would be honored in the public record.

William C. Cardwell's life and military service reflect the courage and conviction of East Tennessee Unionists—men who enlisted to defend their country even as their state joined the Confederacy. His ultimate sacrifice at Andersonville stands as a solemn reminder of the cost of war and the personal tragedies endured by families on both sides of the divide. Cardwell Line II - Predicted. Photo Credit[66]

* * *

Photo 12.11: *William J. Cardwell (1841-1863) Headstone. Nashville National Cemetery, Madison, Davidson County, Tennessee.*

William J. Cardwell (1841-1863) - *Private - Company F, 1st Tennessee Cavalry, USA -* **Died of Disease**

William J. Cardwell was born around 1841 in Grainger County, Tennessee, the son of Perrin Cardwell and Louisa (Norris) Cardwell. He appears in his father's household in the 1850 census for Grainger County, part of a large farming family in the ridgelines of East Tennessee.[67]William's father, Perrin, died in 1854, leaving Louisa a widow with several children. By the time of the 1860 census, she is recorded as head of household, with her children—William among them—still living in Grainger County. Like many East Tennessee families, the Cardwells lived in a region known for its strong Unionist leanings despite Tennessee's official secession.[68]

On 01 March 1862, at the age of 22, William J. Cardwell enlisted as a Private in Company F, 1st Tennessee Cavalry (U.S.), alongside his older brother Henry H. Cardwell, who joined the same day. According to his enlistment papers, William was 5 feet 11 inches tall, with a light complexion, blue eyes, light hair, and worked as a farmer. His birthplace was listed as Grainger County, Tennessee. Like many East Tennesseans, he likely traveled north to join a Union regiment due to the Confederate presence that dominated much of the state in the war's early years.

The 1st Tennessee Cavalry (U.S.) was one of the first loyalist units raised from Tennessee, mustered in Kentucky and composed primarily of Unionist refugees from East Tennessee counties. The regiment was attached to the Army of the Ohio, and later the Army of the Cumberland, where it served in cavalry screening, reconnaissance, and raiding operations throughout Tennessee, Kentucky, and northern Alabama. Its men endured difficult early service, operating in mountainous terrain against Confederate guerrillas, raiders, and mobile cavalry forces.

From his enlistment in March 1862 through mid-1863, William is recorded as present for duty. During this time, the 1st Tennessee Cavalry was assigned to guard and patrol duties in Middle Tennessee, helping to secure Union supply lines and suppress Confederate cavalry movements. The regiment also supported the advance on Nashville and was active during the Union's consolidation of control over Murfreesboro and Triune, both key transportation hubs along the Nashville & Chattanooga Railroad.

In the spring of 1863, the 1st Tennessee Cavalry took part in the Middle Tennessee operations that preceded the Tullahoma Campaign, a critical Union maneuver that forced Confederate General Braxton Bragg to retreat from Middle Tennessee without a major engagement. Though not involved in any major battles during this stretch, the regiment saw constant movement, fatigue duty, and exposure as it pushed deep into contested areas. The strain of such conditions, combined with limited medical care, led to widespread illness in Union camps.

On 22 June 1863, William J. Cardwell died of consumption (tuberculosis) at the Regimental Hospital near Triune, in Williamson County, Tennessee. Disease was the most common cause of death among Civil War soldiers, and regimental hospitals—often ill-equipped and exposed to the elements—were frequent sites of fatal outbreaks. William's passing came during a critical time for Union forces in Tennessee, just days before the Tullahoma Campaign would begin in earnest.

He was buried at Nashville National Cemetery, located in Madison,

Davidson County, Tennessee, where his grave remains marked among thousands of others who perished during the war.[69] Though he died without seeing the end of the conflict, William's service helped secure East and Middle Tennessee for the Union and supported the broader efforts of the Army of the Cumberland in securing the Western Theater.

His brother Henry H. Cardwell continued to serve in the same regiment and survived the war. Both men's service stands as testimony to the loyalty and sacrifice of East Tennessee Unionists, who risked their lives for a country they refused to abandon—even when their home state had seceded. <u>Cardwell Line I - Predicted</u>. Photo Credit[70]

West Virginia
Cardwell Union Soldier

WEST VIRGINIA WAS UNIQUE AMONG THE STATES INVOLVED IN THE Civil War. When Virginia seceded from the Union in 1861, the western counties, which were largely pro-Union, chose to break away and form the new state of West Virginia in 1863. The state became a crucial battleground, with significant action in guerrilla warfare, mountain skirmishes, and strategic raids aimed at controlling key transportation routes through the Appalachian region.

West Virginia provided more Union troops per capita than any other state, with thousands of men enlisting in both infantry and cavalry regiments. Many of these regiments were tasked with defending railroads, mountain passes, and Union supply lines, ensuring that Confederate forces could not take control of the region.

Only one Cardwell man, Monaoh N. Cardwell, served in West Virginia regiments during the Civil War. His service in two units—the 1st West Virginia Veteran Infantry and the 5th West Virginia Infantry—places him among the many soldiers who fought to keep the new state in Union hands.

Though Monaoh N. Cardwell was the only Cardwell to serve from West Virginia, his dual service in both an early war infantry regiment and a veteran unit demonstrates his commitment to the Union cause. His service helped secure West Virginia's independence from Confederate Virginia, ensuring that the new state remained loyal to the Union.

This chapter honors the Cardwell soldier of West Virginia, preserving his contributions to the Cardwell Family history.

* * *

Monoah Nathan Cardwell (1822-1898) - *Private - Company K, 1st West Virginia Veteran Infantry & 5th West Virginia Infantry, USA*

Monoah Nathan Cardwell was born on 01 May 1822 in Cabell County, Virginia (now West Virginia), the son of Nathan Cardwell and Eleanor "Nelly" (McGinnis) Cardwell. He married Sarah Ann Hollenback around 1843, based on the birth of their first child the following year. Together they had nine children: Olivia Elen Cardwell (1844–1891), Nancy E. Cardwell (1845–), Amanda Cardwell (1847–), Edmonia Cardwell (1849–), Samantha Cardwell (1850–1928), William N. Cardwell (1854–1942), Melville Cardwell (1854–1931), Henry Hampton Cardwell (1856–1920), and Susan Cardwell (1862–). The Cardwell family is documented in the 1850, 1870, and 1880 census records for Cabell County.[1,2,3]

Monoah enlisted as a Private in Company K of the 1st West Virginia Veteran Infantry, USA, on 01 December 1862 at Charleston, West Virginia. His enlistment records indicate he was 45 years old at the time, though his birth year was recorded as approximately 1817. The discrepancy may have been a clerical error or the result of enlistment conventions of the time.

The 1st West Virginia Veteran Infantry was formed in late 1864 from the reenlisted veterans of several original West Virginia units, including the 5th West Virginia Infantry. That regiment had been one of the earliest Union formations raised in western Virginia, organized in 1861. It saw active service across the western counties of Virginia and the Shenandoah Valley. Its men participated in engagements such as Carnifex Ferry, Fayetteville, and the First Battle of Winchester, helping to secure vital territory for the Union in the border state of Virginia. The 5th West Virginia was involved in patrolling mountain passes, guarding railroads, and repelling Confederate raids throughout the region. By the end of 1864, the remaining experienced men were consolidated into the 1st West Virginia Veteran Infantry to continue service in the final campaigns of the war. Monoah's unit likely remained involved in occupation duties and the suppression of guerrilla activity until the war's close.

It is unclear when Monoah was discharged from service, but he did apply for and receive a federal pension, confirming that his service was recognized and sustained. No medical or disability information appears to have survived from his application, but the granting of a pension indicates he met the criteria established for Union veterans following the war.

Monoah Nathan Cardwell died on 19 December 1898 in Cabell County, West Virginia. The location of his burial has not been identified. Like many veterans of the war from that region, he appears to have returned to agricultural life and spent his remaining years with his extended family near his place of birth. <u>Cardwell Line I - Predicted</u>.

U.S. Colored Troops
The Cardwell Union Soldiers

THE ESTABLISHMENT OF THE UNITED STATES COLORED TROOPS (USCT) was one of the most significant developments in the Civil War, allowing formerly enslaved and free Black men to take up arms for the Union cause. Authorized by the Emancipation Proclamation in 1863, the USCT grew to nearly 180,000 soldiers, comprising more than 160 regiments of infantry, cavalry, and artillery.

These troops fought with distinction and valor, often facing not only the Confederate enemy but also racial discrimination within their own army. Many were assigned to guard strategic locations, participate in key battles, and ensure the enforcement of Union control in occupied Southern territory.

The Cardwell soldiers who served in the United States Colored Troops were part of a historic effort that helped turn the tide of the Civil War. Their contributions ensured the preservation of the Union and laid the foundation for African American military service in the decades to come. Despite facing prejudice and harsher conditions than their white counterparts, these men proved their dedication and courage in battle.

This chapter honors the Cardwell soldiers of the United States Colored Troops, preserving their service as a pivotal part of Cardwell Family history.

* * *

Aaron Cardwell (1815-1900) - *Private - Company B, 123rd US Colored Infantry, US Army & 13th US Colored Heavy Artillery, USA*

Aaron Cardwell was born about 1815, likely in or near Shelby County, Kentucky, where he later enlisted in the Union Army. On 07 April 1865, just days before General Lee's surrender at Appomattox, Aaron joined the United States Colored Troops in Shelby County. At the time of his enlistment, he was listed as fifty years old, with black eyes, black hair, and a height of 5 feet, 6 ¾ inches. He enlisted for a term of three years. His occupation was not recorded, but given his age and the time period, it is likely he had worked as a laborer for most of his life.

The details of Aaron's early life are largely undocumented, but census and military records offer some valuable clues. A review of the 1860 U.S. Federal Census – Slave Schedules for Shelby County reveals that Drucilla (Swearingen) Cardwell, the widow of Jesse James Cardwell, owned seven slaves at that time.[1] Among them was a fifty-five-year-old Black male, unnamed like all others in the schedule, but of a matching age and location. While no direct evidence confirms the identity of this man, it raises the strong possibility that Aaron had once been enslaved by the Cardwell family and later adopted their surname—a common practice among formerly enslaved individuals after emancipation. Though the connection cannot be proven definitively, it is a compelling lead for future researchers.

Aaron appears in the 1870 U.S. Census for Shelby County, Kentucky, living with his wife, Mary LNU (1813-), and two children: Letitia Cardwell (1855-) and Legrand Cardwell (1859-). This postwar record confirms that he survived the conflict and had returned to civilian life with his family. No additional census records have been located for Aaron or his immediate family in later years.

His widow, Mary, filed for a U.S. military pension on 10 January 1900, which confirms Aaron's service in the Union Army. Unfortunately, the application does not specify his regiment or provide additional personal details, and no burial record has been found. The location of Aaron Cardwell's grave remains unknown.

Though many questions about Aaron's life remain unanswered, his enlistment in the Union army at the close of the Civil War underscores a quiet but profound commitment to the cause of emancipation and the preservation of the Union. His story represents the experience of many Black Americans who emerged from enslavement and risked everything for freedom and a better future. <u>Ancestry Undetermined</u>.

* * *

Frank Cardwell (1836-) - *Private - Unassigned U.S. Colored Troops, USA*

Frank Cardwell was born around 1836 in Jackson County, Tennessee, according to his enlistment records. He entered service with the Union Army on 19 September 1864 in Milwaukee, Wisconsin, agreeing to serve for one year. Frank reported his occupation as a laborer and was described in his service record as 5 feet 6 inches tall, with black eyes, black hair, and a black complexion.

At the time of Frank's enlistment, African American recruits who had not yet been assigned to specific units were processed and trained in provisional regiments. These men were generally distributed across established U.S. Colored Troops regiments as manpower needs arose. While Wisconsin did not raise its own regiment of United States Colored Troops (USCT), African American men who enlisted there were often sent to regiments active in the Mississippi Valley, Louisiana, or the Eastern Theater. Frank's service record does not indicate a unit assignment, which suggests that he may have served in a support or holding capacity before being assigned elsewhere. The brevity of his service file leaves many questions unanswered.

To better understand Frank's possible origins, the 1860 U.S. Federal Census – Slave Schedules for Jackson County, Tennessee, was examined. No slaveholders named Cardwell were found in that county. However, nearby Smith County, Tennessee, listed Buckner Strum Cardwell as the owner of twelve enslaved individuals. Among them was a black male whose age aligns with Frank's birth year. Given the geographic proximity, surname, and matching age, it is plausible that Frank may have been formerly enslaved by Buckner S. Cardwell. While no definitive proof exists, the circumstantial evidence points strongly to this connection.

Despite extensive efforts, no post-war census, pension, marriage, or death records for Frank Cardwell have been found. His date and place of death remain unknown, and he may have died shortly after his service or lived in obscurity beyond the reach of current records.

Note: Frank Cardwell's enlistment in Wisconsin is notable, as relatively few African American men from Tennessee appear in Union records from that state. His story reflects both the dispersion of formerly enslaved individuals seeking freedom and the varied enlistment patterns of African American soldiers during the final year of the Civil War. <u>Ancestry Undetermined.</u>

* * *

Harrison Cardwell (1840-1865) - *Private - Company G, 107th U.S. Colored Infantry, USA* - **Died of Disease**

Harrison enlisted on 23 August 1864 in Louisville, Jefferson County, Kentucky. According to that record, he was born in 1840 in Shelby County, Kentucky. He was 5 feet and 10.5 inches tall, dark complexion, dark eyes, and dark hair. His occupation was Laborer.

Organized in 1864, the 107th USCT Infantry was stationed in Kentucky and Tennessee, primarily tasked with garrison duty, supply protection, and occupation of key Southern territories. These men played an essential role in maintaining order and ensuring the security of newly freed Black communities in the South.

Records show that Harrison died on 24 July 1865 in Morehead City, North Carolina at a Regimental Hospital of dropsy/edema. Searches of census records have not provided any additional details. Harrison was married, but her name is unknown. She applied for a Widow's Pension after his death. The location of his grave is unknown, but likely in Morehead City, North Carolina. <u>Ancestry Undetermined.</u>

* * *

Henry Cardwell (1845-) - *Private - Company K, 5th United States Colored Heavy Artillery, USA*

Henry Cardwell was born about 1845 in Warren County, Tennessee, according to his enlistment papers. He enlisted on 24 February 1865 in Cincinnati, Ohio. Henry was 5 feet and 4 1/2 inches in height, dark complexion, dark eyes, dark hair, and his occupation was farmer. Henry enlisted for one year of service and records show he was discharged at the end of that term.

The 5th USCT Heavy Artillery was a specialized unit responsible for manning large-caliber cannons at Union fortifications. Raised in 1863, it was stationed along the Mississippi River, protecting supply lines and assisting in the defense of key cities such as Memphis and Vicksburg.

Searches on census, death, marriage, etc., records all provided no additional information. The year of his death and location are not known. The 1860 U.S. Federal Census – Slave Schedules for Warren County, Tennessee lists Henry Jefferson Cardwell (His biography is recorded in the Confederate Cardwell Veterans under the State of Tennessee.) The record states that Henry Jefferson Cardwell owned five slave and more importantly, one black male that was born about 1845. It is highly likely that is Henry Cardwell, the freed slave that enlisted with Company K of the 5th Regiment of U.S. Colored Artillery. <u>Ancestry Undetermined</u>.

* * *

Isham Cardwell (1819-) - *Private - Company L, 8th Colored Heavy Artillery, USA*

Isham Cardwell was born about 1819 in Tennessee, according to his enlistment records. He joined the Union Army as a Private in Paducah, McCracken County, Kentucky, on 19 December 1864. At the time of his enlistment, he was described as standing 5 feet 6 inches tall, with a dark complexion, black eyes, and black hair. His occupation was listed as laborer.

Isham served in the 8th United States Colored Heavy Artillery (USCT), a regiment organized in 1864 that played an essential role in the defense of Union strongholds in the Western Theater. The 8th USCT was tasked with guarding strategic locations along the Mississippi River, manning forts, and patrolling river crossings in Louisiana and Mississippi. These duties, while often away from major battlefield engagements, were crucial to the Union's ability to hold territory and supply lines throughout the Deep South. Units such as the 8th USCT frequently faced harsh conditions, logistical challenges, and the constant threat of Confederate raids, particularly in contested regions where control shifted rapidly. Although details of Isham's individual service are limited, regimental records indicate that the 8th USCT remained active through the closing months of the war and during Reconstruction efforts in Texas.

Isham Cardwell was ultimately discharged on 10 February 1866 in Victoria, Texas, suggesting that he remained in service through the early postwar occupation period. No further records have been found regarding Isham's life after his discharge. His name does not appear in subsequent federal censuses, and no documentation has been located concerning a marriage, children, or the date and location of his death.

In seeking to understand Isham's origins, the 1860 U.S. Federal Census – Slave Schedules for McCracken County, Kentucky, was reviewed, but found no slaveholders with the Cardwell surname listed in that county. However, neighboring Graves County was home to Lafayette Cardwell, an English-born resident who owned eight slaves.[2] While none of those individuals match Isham's recorded birth year, the presence of a Cardwell slaveowner in the immediate region suggests a possible connection. As was common after emancipation, formerly enslaved individuals often adopted the surname of their previous enslaver, particularly if no legal surname had previously been recorded. This connection remains speculative, and further documentation would be required to confirm a direct link between Isham Cardwell and Lafayette Cardwell or his household.

Despite the fragmentary nature of the records, Isham Cardwell's brief appearance in the historical record reflects the courage and commitment of thousands of African American men who served in the United States Colored Troops. Many, like Isham, served quietly, returned home without recognition, and disappeared from official documentation. Their contributions, however, remain essential to understanding the full human cost and complex legacy of the Civil War. <u>Ancestry Undetermined.</u>

* * *

William Cardwell (1841-1864) - Private - *Company H, 61st United States Colored Infantry, USA* - **Died of Disease**

William Cardwell was born around 1841 in Fairfax County, Virginia, according to his military enlistment records. His physical description notes that he stood six feet tall, with a Black complexion, black eyes, and black hair. At the time of his enlistment, his occupation was listed as "farmer," a common designation for formerly enslaved or free Black laborers working in agriculture across the South and border states.

The 61st USCT Infantry was formed in 1864 and saw combat in Tennessee, Mississippi, and Arkansas. It was often tasked with guarding supply depots, suppressing Confederate resistance, and reinforcing Union outposts in the South. It is unknown to what level that William participated in any of these activities, if at all.

No information has yet been uncovered regarding William's early life or family. The 1860 U.S. Federal Census – Slave Schedules for Fairfax County, Virginia, do not list any Cardwell slaveholders in the area, making it difficult to determine whether William was once enslaved by a family of that name or had adopted the surname through other associations. It remains possible that he was enslaved by a non-Cardwell family or had relocated to Fairfax County from another region before the war.

William's service with the Union army during the Civil War ended tragically. He died on 08 June 1864 in a Regimental Hospital in Memphis, Shelby County, Tennessee. The cause of death was recorded as "intermittent fever," a term commonly used during the period to describe recurring fevers, often associated with diseases such as malaria. No burial location has been identified for William, though it is possible he was interred near Memphis in a military cemetery or hospital burial ground. Without a specific regimental designation in the surviving record, additional research may be necessary to determine the exact unit in which he served.

Although the available records on William Cardwell are limited, his enlistment and death in federal service underscore the personal risks taken by many former slaves during the Civil War. His sacrifice—like that of thousands of Black soldiers—deserves recognition as part of the larger narrative of Union service and the struggle for freedom during the conflict. Ancestry Undetermined.

* * *

Photo 13.1: *William P. Cardwell (1845-1865) Headstone. Camp Nelson National Cemetery, Nicholasville, Jessamine County, Kentucky.*

William P. Cardwell (1845-1865) - *Private - Company C, 5th United States Colored Cavalry, USA -* **Died of Disease**

William P. Cardwell was born around 1845 in Shelby County, Kentucky. His early life remains largely undocumented, but by the final years of the Civil War, he had joined the ranks of the United States Colored Troops (USCT), enlisting on 27 August 1864 in Louisville, Kentucky. At the time of his enlistment, William was described as 5 feet 4 ½ inches tall, with a dark complexion, dark eyes, and dark hair. His occupation was recorded as laborer.

He served as a Private in Company C of the 5th Regiment, United States Colored Cavalry. This unit was part of a broader effort by the Union Army to recruit African-American soldiers following the Emancipation Proclamation. The 5th USCC was organized in Kentucky and comprised formerly enslaved and free Black men who were eager to fight for their freedom and that of others. The regiment saw service in Kentucky and Virginia, often tasked with challenging assignments such as guarding supply lines, performing picket duty, and engaging in raids against Confederate guerrilla forces. Though their contributions were often overlooked in official histories, the men of the USCT played a crucial role in the Union's final push toward victory.

Although William's service was brief, it came during a pivotal period of the war. The winter and early spring of 1865 were marked by harsh conditions and heavy disease outbreaks in army camps. On 20 March 1865, William died of pleurisy while stationed at Camp Nelson in Jessamine County, Kentucky. Camp Nelson was one of the most important recruitment and training centers for African American troops in the Western Theater. It also served as a refugee center for freed slaves, providing food, shelter, and a path to freedom for thousands.

The details of William's background are not fully known. However, a review of the 1860 U.S. Federal Census – Slave Schedules suggests a possible connection to Harmon Greathouse Cardwell, who owned four slaves in Shelby County at the time.[3] Two of those individuals were twenty-year-old males, raising the possibility—though not a certainty—that William had once been enslaved by Harmon Cardwell. It was common for formerly enslaved individuals to adopt the surname of their previous owners, a practice that complicates but also sometimes aids genealogical research. While no direct documentation confirms this link, the coincidence in location and surname suggests a possible connection worth further exploration.

William P. Cardwell's sacrifice is memorialized at Camp Nelson National Cemetery in Nicholasville, Jessamine County, Kentucky, where he was buried.[4] His service in the Union Army, particularly in a regiment of the United States Colored Troops, reflects the courage and determination of thousands of Black Americans who fought not only for the Union cause but for their own liberation and the hope of a better future. William's short life and military career stand as a testament to the price paid by many during this tumultuous chapter in American history. Ancestry Undetermined. Photo Credit[5]

Miscellaneous
Cardwell Union Soldier

As the Civil War entered its final phase, the Union Army sought to maintain experienced, battle-hardened soldiers in active service. In 1864, the War Department authorized the creation of Veteran Volunteer Infantry Regiments, composed of reenlisted soldiers who had already served honorably in previous Union regiments. These units were offered incentives such as higher pay and shorter enlistment terms to encourage veterans to continue their service. Their role was vital in ensuring the Union Army remained well-manned for the final campaigns of the war and post-war occupation duties.

This chapter honors the Cardwell soldier who served in the 1st U.S. Veteran Volunteer Infantry, ensuring his contributions to the Union cause are preserved in the historical record of the Civil War. It also includes several individuals whose connection to the Cardwell name remains unresolved—those incorrectly indexed under the surname, as well as others whose claimed participation in the conflict has not been substantiated through available research.

* * *

Photo 14.1: *Patrick H. Cardwell (1839-1908) Headstone. Greenlawn Memorial Park, Newport News, Newport News City, Virginia.*

Patrick Henry Cardwell (1843-1908) - Private - *Company E, 1st Regiment, US Veteran Volunteer Infantry, USA.*

Patrick Henry Cardwell was born about 1839 in Virginia to George W. Cardwell and Ann E. LNU Cardwell. He is listed in their home in the 1850 James City, Virginia census records.[1] In 1860, Patrick is living with Patrick Jordan in Henrico County, Virginia. [2] Their relationship is unknown, but could indicate a relative or his employer. Patrick has the distinction of having served in both the Confederacy and Union armies.

Patrick enlisted as a Private with Company D, 1st Virginia Artillery, CSA on 20 May 1861 at Williamsburg, James City County, Virginia. His records indicate he was transferred or detached to Company G, 32nd Virginia Infantry, CSA, but it appears he served the majority of his service with the 1st Virginia Artillery, CSA. Patrick was captured at Waterloo, Pennsylvania during the Battle of Gettysburg on 05 July 1863. He was sent to the Union POW Camp at Point Lookout, Maryland. On 17 February 1864, he took an oath of allegiance and enlisted with Company E, 1st Regiment, US Veteran Volunteer Infantry, USA.

Organized in 1864, the 1st U.S. Veteran Volunteer Infantry was assigned to garrison duty, occupation duties in Southern states, and reinforcement operations during the final Union offensives. Many of its soldiers had previously served in some of the most intense battles of the war, making them among the most seasoned fighters in the Union ranks. The regiment helped enforce Reconstruction policies and maintained security in formerly Confederate-controlled areas.

The Veteran Volunteer Infantry regiments were composed of soldiers who had already endured years of war, and their continued service played a crucial role in securing final Union victories. Patrick Henry Cardwell's service in the 1st U.S. Veteran Volunteer Infantry reflects the commitment and sacrifice of seasoned Union soldiers who remained in the fight even after their original enlistments had expired. He was discharged on 27 November 1865, location unknown. Patrick has the distinction of being one of only three Cardwell men that fought in both the Union and Confederacy.

Patrick married Roselia Alice Chandler on 21 Jun 1866 in James City County, Virginia. They had the following children; Saint George Cardwell (1867-1940), Charles Edward Cardwell (1870-), Nellie Josephine Cardwell (1873-1962), Susan Elizabeth Cardwell (1875-1960), Mary Lucy Cardwell (1878-1954), and Franklin Henry Cardwell (1881-1954). The family is listed in the 1870 York County, Virginia and 1880 James City County, Virginia census records.[3,4]

He was admitted to the Home for Disabled Volunteer Soldiers in Hampton, Virginia on 23 October 1900 for reason of Paralysis. That record states that he was 57 years of age (born 1843), 5 feet and 6 inches in height, fair complexion, grey eyes, grey hair, and a farmer. Patrick died on 18 April 1908 in Newport News, Virginia. He is buried at Greenlawn Memorial Park, Newport News, Newport News City, Virginia.[5] Note: He also has a biography in the Confederate Cardwell Veterans of Virginia chapter. Cardwell Line I - Predicted. Photo Credit[6]

* * *

UNRESOLVED & INCORRECT LISTINGS

Running a comprehensive list of men named Cardwell who served during the Civil War results in numerous duplicate entries, alternate initials, and several individuals mistakenly indexed under the Cardwell surname. In some cases, clerical errors, phonetic similarities, or misread handwriting have led to incorrect listings.

Despite extensive research, a few of these names remain unresolved. For example, no definitive family connections or verifiable personal records could be established for men such as Leon and Thomas, both of whom are listed as having served from Michigan. Multiple hours of investigation—including reviews of census records, marriage licenses, death certificates, and other genealogical resources—produced no evidence to link these individuals to known Cardwell families. Furthermore, the Civil War service records for each of these men are limited to a single file entry, with no supporting documents to clarify identity or background.

These unresolved cases are noted here for the sake of completeness and transparency in the historical record.

* * *

Francis Cardwell - *Private - Company L and D, 1st Vermont Cavalry, USA*

A case of mistaken identity involves Francis Cardwell. In military records, his surname appears interchangeably as Cardwell and Cardinell. Upon examining the complete set of documents associated with this individual, it is evident that his correct surname was Cardinell. Only a single Civil War document mistakenly lists his name as Cardwell.

Subsequent searches across census records, military databases, and genealogical sources yielded no connection between this man and any Cardwell family. Nevertheless, because his name appears once in official Civil War records under the Cardwell spelling, he has occasionally been included in broader indexes of Cardwell veterans.

Based on the totality of the evidence, it is clear that Francis was not a Cardwell by name, and his inclusion under that surname resulted from a clerical or transcription error. As such, this record should be excluded from the confirmed roster of Cardwell Civil War veterans.

* * *

Frank Cardwell (-1865)—*Company G, 15th Connecticut Infantry, USA* - **Killed in Action**

The origins of Frank Cardwell remain unknown. No definitive record has been found to establish his date of birth, parentage, or family background. He does not appear in census records under the Cardwell name, and no birth or family documentation has yet been linked to him. Despite these uncertainties, Frank is listed in the official military rolls as having served during the Civil War and is included in this volume due to his indexing under the Cardwell surname.

Frank enlisted on 08 December 1864 from East Haven, Connecticut, and was mustered in as a Private with Company G, 15th Regiment, Connecticut Infantry. The regiment had originally been formed in August 1862 for three years of service and had seen significant action in North Carolina and Virginia. By the time of Frank's enlistment, the 15th Connecticut was serving in eastern North Carolina, attached to the 2nd Brigade, 2nd Division, 23rd Army Corps.

In March 1865, Union forces under General Jacob D. Cox launched a campaign to seize control of the railroad junction at Goldsboro, North Carolina. As part of this effort, Frank and the 15th Connecticut Infantry participated in the o), which took place from 7 to 10 March 1865. On 09 March 1865, Frank Cardwell was killed in action during the heavy fighting near Southwest Creek. He had been in the army for just three months.

Military documents associated with Frank's service include alternate spellings of his surname, such as "Cardnell" and "Caldwell," complicating efforts to trace his personal history. No pension records, burial location, or post-war documentation have been found, and it remains uncertain whether he was actually a member of the Cardwell family or if the similarity in surname was coincidental or the result of a clerical error.

Nevertheless, Frank's inclusion in this work honors his brief but ultimate sacrifice in the service of the Union. His story stands as a reminder of the many soldiers whose identities remain only partially known, and whose contributions, though undocumented in full, are no less worthy of remembrance. Further genealogical research is encouraged to determine if Frank Cardwell belonged to the broader Cardwell lineage. Ancestry Undetermined.

* * *

Leon Cardwell (1837 -) - *Private - Company L, 10th Michigan Infantry, USA*

In the case of Leon Cardwell, the only service record associated with this name is noted as having originally been filed under "Levi Cardnell." Examination of that file confirms that there is just one record, with no additional documentation. A review of the official online rosters for the 10th Michigan Infantry indicates that the name listed under the unassigned men is either "Levi Cardnell" or "Levi Cardinal." This individual was recorded as 25 years old, with an estimated enlistment in 1862, which would place his birth around 1837.

Despite these details, no census, military, or family records could be located for any man named Leon or Levi Cardwell in Michigan during that period. Based on all available evidence, it appears highly likely that this individual was not a Cardwell by name, and the listing resulted from a transcription or indexing error.

It is therefore my conclusion that this record should not be included in the roster of confirmed Cardwell veterans.

* * *

Thomas Cardwell (-) - *Private - 6th Michigan Cavalry, USA*

In a separate instance, I conducted several hours of research attempting to identify a Thomas Cardwell reported as having served from Michigan during the Civil War. Like the case of Leon/Levi, this entry is problematic. According to the limited records available, Thomas served in one of the Michigan cavalry regiments attached to the command of General George Armstrong Custer, a prominent and aggressive Union cavalry leader in the Eastern Theater, later known for his death at the Battle of Little Bighorn.

Thomas Cardwell's entire military record consists of a single service index card, with no accompanying documents in pension files, compiled service records, or regimental histories. Despite targeted searches across census listings, marriage and death records, Michigan military rosters, and historical accounts of Custer's regiments, I was unable to uncover any further information about this man.

Given the absence of corroborating records and the common occurrence of name transcription errors during the period, I conclude that this individual was either misidentified or mistakenly indexed as a Cardwell. Accordingly, this record should not be included among confirmed Civil War veterans bearing the Cardwell surname. It is noted here for the sake of completeness and transparency in the historical record.

* * *

William H. Cardwell (1823-) - *Private - Company I, 57th Massachusetts Infantry & Company I, 59th Massachusetts Infantry & 2nd Battalion, Veteran Reserve Corps, USA*

William H. Cardwell was born around 1823 in Athlone, Ireland, according to his Civil War enlistment record. He enlisted on 21 March 1864 at Cambridge, Massachusetts, and was mustered in as a Private in Company I of the 57th Massachusetts Infantry. He was later transferred to Company I of the 59th Massachusetts Infantry and eventually to the 2nd Battalion of the Veteran Reserve Corps.

Military records describe William as 5 feet 9 inches tall, with blue eyes, brown hair, and a light complexion. His occupation was listed as blacksmith. His service file notes that he suffered from a "hernia of right side," and he was reported as sick during his term of service. No discharge date has been located, but he received a pension on 05 January 1865.

There is some uncertainty regarding his postwar life. A man named William H. Cardwell appears in the 1870 census in Philadelphia, Pennsylvania, and may be the same individual, though the commonality of the name among the Cardwell family makes confirmation difficult. There is also a separate Pennsylvania service record for a William H. Cardwell, which could refer to the same man or a different individual entirely.

In the absence of a confirmed postwar record, the date and location of this William H. Cardwell's death and burial remain unknown. Hopefully, future research will provide some clarification.

Photo 14.2: *William Henry Cardwell (1834-1874) - Australia - circa 1861*

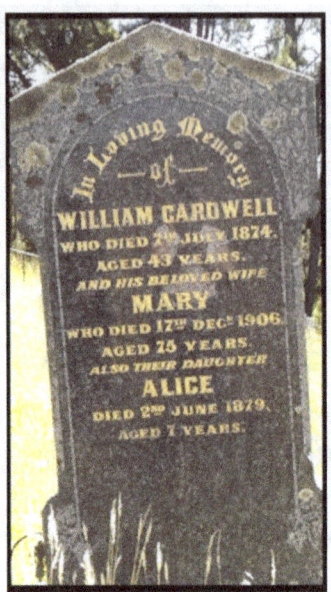

Photo 14.3: *William Henry Cardwell (1834-1874) - Mitta Mitta Cemetery, Towong Shire, Victoria, Australia*

William Henry Cardwell (1834-1874) - *Unknown Rank - Unknown Unit, USA*

William Henry Cardwell was born about 1837 in County Armagh, Ireland, to Thomas Cardwell and Anne (Payne) Cardwell. His father and several of his siblings immigrated to Australia in 1855 from Dublin aboard the *Rienzi*. William, however, remained behind and traveled to the United States sometime in the late 1850s. He was married on 26 September 1859 in Manhattan, New York, to Mary Cardwell, the daughter of Henry Cardwell and Alice (Leiman) Cardwell. Although she shared the same surname, no definitive family connection between the two has been established.[7]

The couple initially settled in Hartford, Connecticut, where William was employed as a painter. They are enumerated in Connecticut for the 1860 U.S. Federal Census.[8] According to his obituary, William claimed to have served in the American Civil War prior to emigrating to Australia. The couple had a total of nine children, with the eldest born in the United States and the remaining children born in Australia. Their children were: Thomas Cardwell (1861–1934), Ann Eliza Cardwell (1863–1904), William Henry Cardwell Jr. (1866–1942), James "Jim" Cardwell (1866–1942), Mary Cardwell (1868–1948), Margaret Ellen Cardwell (1869–1956), Robert Cardwell

(1871–1952), Alice Cardwell (1872–1879), and John Cardwell (1875–1935).

William departed New York for Australia and arrived in Melbourne, Victoria, aboard the *Continent* on 17 January 1862.[9] Given that transoceanic voyages from New York to Australia typically took between three to four months during that period, it is estimated that he left the United States sometime between mid-September and early November of 1861. This narrow window limits the number of military units in which he could have plausibly served during the early months of the Civil War.

If William Henry Cardwell did indeed serve, the most probable service would have been in one of the three-month regiments mustered in Connecticut during the early days of the war. The 1st Connecticut Infantry was organized in Hartford and mustered into service on 22 April 1861. This regiment participated in the First Battle of Bull Run in July and mustered out shortly afterward, which aligns with William's likely departure window. Two other Connecticut units, the 5th and 8th Connecticut Infantry Regiments, were mustered in July and September 1861, respectively, but enlistment in either of these units would have required William to desert in order to leave for Australia by November. He is found in neither of their records.

Although he lived in Hartford, it is possible—but less likely—that he may have enlisted with a New York unit. If so, the most plausible option would be the 71st New York State Militia, which mustered in on 10 April 1861 and mustered out in July. However, despite exhaustive research into the relevant service records, no definitive match for William Henry Cardwell has been located in any of these units or in broader federal military records. If he served at all, it was in a capacity that has since been lost to history, or the story was embellished or misremembered by family or later sources.

William Henry Cardwell and his new family settled in the Mitta Mitta District of Victoria, Australia upon their arrival. It is recorded the his wife Mary and oldest child, Thomas, traveled with him to Australia.

After settling in Australia, William and his family took up residence in the Mitta Mitta district of Victoria. His wife Mary and their eldest child, Thomas, are documented as having accompanied him on the voyage aboard the *Continent*. Tragically, William drowned in a flood on the Mitta Mitta River on 07 July 1874. He was buried in the Mitta Mitta Cemetery in Towong Shire, Victoria.[10] Mary remained in the area for the rest of her life, passing away in 1906.[11]

William Henry Cardwell has been the subject of considerable genealogical and historical research in Australia. He is profiled in *Civil War Veterans in Australia* by Roy Parker (2000), which confirms the enduring uncertainty regarding his exact unit of service. Additional research was contributed by Barry Crompton of Melbourne, Len Traynor of Sydney, and Bob Simpson of Beechworth, Victoria. The book was edited by Parker's daughter, Mrs. Virginia Crocker, with immigration data further clarified by researcher Terry Foenander. Robert Till did an excellent job researching William Henry Cardwell's descendants. He work, accessed through Ancestry.com, provided many missing pieces to this biography. Ancestry Undetermined - Predicted Line II. Photo Credits[12,13]

Appendix

Cardwell Statistics

THE CIVIL WAR WAS NOT ONLY A CLASH OF ARMIES AND IDEOLOGIES—IT was a personal ordeal that left its mark on every family it touched. For the Cardwell family, whose descendants served in both the Union and Confederate armies, the war became a defining crucible. Their collective service spanned nearly every major branch of the military—infantry, cavalry, artillery, and support roles—and their outcomes mirror the conflict's vast human cost. By analyzing compiled service records, unit affiliations, and known fates, this chapter provides a statistical portrait of the Cardwell surname in wartime, offering a unique microcosm of the Civil War's reach.

The four sections that follow explore these statistics in depth. First, we examine branch distribution among Confederate Cardwell veterans, revealing a stark divergence from traditional Confederate service ratios—particularly an outsized preference for cavalry service. Next, we assess the Union Cardwell service by branch, discovering a surprising symmetry with their Confederate counterparts despite the two armies' vastly different structures and strategies.

Following these branch-focused analyses, the chapter turns to the combat outcomes of both Confederate and Union Cardwell men. Here, we trace the lasting toll of the war through wounds, deaths, imprisonment, and disease. Each category—Killed in Action, Wounded, Died in Captivity, and others— places individual names into a broader statistical framework, showing not only how many were lost but also how they were lost.

Together, these four lenses—Confederate Branch, Union Branch,

Confederate Outcome, and Union Outcome—form a detailed statistical account of one family's Civil War experience. Though numbers alone can never tell the full story, they reveal patterns of allegiance, hardship, and sacrifice that deepen our understanding of the Cardwell legacy in America's defining conflict.

Confederate Statistics by Branch

The Cardwell men who served in the Confederate States Army represent a fascinating microcosm of service trends across the Civil War South. After analyzing the compiled data of Confederate Cardwell veterans from eleven states, a notable pattern emerges: a significantly higher-than-average proportion of these men served in cavalry units compared to the standard Confederate military branch distribution. This chapter examines the numbers, the underlying reasons for this anomaly, and how certain artillery units tied to cavalry operations further shift the statistics in favor of mounted service.

The Confederate military was composed primarily of three principal branches: infantry, cavalry, and artillery. By most historical estimates, the breakdown of Confederate service by branch was roughly as follows: 75% Infantry, 20% Cavalry, and 5% Artillery. This structure mirrored the practical needs of the Confederate war effort. Infantry units formed the backbone of both offensive and defensive operations. Cavalry units provided mobility, reconnaissance, and strategic harassment, while artillery units, though fewer, played key roles in fortifications and battlefield support.

In contrast, the compiled records of the Cardwell Confederate veterans yield a markedly different composition. Out of 224 men documented, 102 served in cavalry units (45.5%), 104 served in infantry units (46.4%), and 18 served in artillery units (8.0%). These numbers alone suggest a disproportionate preference or selection for cavalry service among the Cardwell family compared to the general Confederate soldier population. Whereas the

Confederate average for cavalry service was about 20%, the Cardwell men participated at more than double that rate.

The reasons behind this anomaly are multifaceted. First, geography and culture play a prominent role. Many of the Cardwell men hailed from rural counties in states such as Kentucky, Tennessee, Alabama, and Texas—regions known for their rugged terrain, reliance on livestock, and long-standing equestrian culture. In such places, young men were typically skilled horsemen from an early age. Riding was not only a common form of transportation but also a marker of independence, status, and identity. This familiarity with horses naturally predisposed many to prefer cavalry service, which promised greater autonomy, movement, and prestige than the slower-paced, foot-bound infantry.

Secondly, the guerrilla nature of the war in certain border states like Kentucky, Missouri, and Tennessee made cavalry operations especially appealing—and often more practical. Confederate cavalry units operating under leaders such as John Hunt Morgan, Nathan Bedford Forrest, and Joseph Wheeler were known for their daring raids, rapid movement, and loose hierarchical structures. Men from these areas often joined such cavalry bands as a matter of local loyalty, regional identity, or resistance to Union occupation. For example, several Cardwell men from Kentucky served in Morgan's Cavalry, a celebrated and romanticized unit that conducted high-profile raids deep into Union territory. The allure of joining a famed mounted unit cannot be underestimated in explaining enlistment patterns.

There is also a socioeconomic aspect to consider. Infantry service was often associated with conscripts and those of lower economic status who lacked the resources to outfit themselves for cavalry duty. Cavalrymen were generally expected to furnish their own horses and some basic equipment. Therefore, the ability to serve in cavalry often indicated a certain level of material comfort or family support. While the Cardwell family did not uniformly belong to the Southern planter aristocracy, many appear to have come from stable, land-owning backgrounds that may have allowed them the resources necessary for mounted service.

The involvement of Cardwell men in artillery units also reflects unique characteristics worth analyzing. While artillery accounted for only 5% of general Confederate service, 8% of the Cardwell men served in such units. More striking, however, is that several of these artillery units were light or horse artillery, which functioned as mobile support units for cavalry formations. Examples include Shoemaker's Horse Artillery, McGregor's Battery of Stuart's Horse Artillery, and Paris's Staunton Hill Artillery. These units were attached to cavalry corps and operated with high mobility, providing artillery support during raids and fast-paced engagements.

If we were to reclassify these light artillery units under the cavalry umbrella due to their operational alignment, the number of Cardwell men involved in mounted or cavalry-adjacent service rises significantly. Of the 18 artillerymen, at least 6 served in such horse artillery units, raising the effective cavalry-aligned total from 102 to 108—or 48.2% of all Cardwell Confederate veterans. This nearly equals the total number who served in infantry, which stands at 104 men.

This near-parity in infantry and cavalry service among the Cardwells presents a stark contrast to the broader Confederate military population, where infantry outnumbered cavalry nearly 4 to 1. Such disparity reinforces the hypothesis that familial culture, local recruitment patterns, regional conflicts, and individual skillsets played powerful roles in shaping the enlistment decisions of the Cardwell men.

Additional factors should also be acknowledged. The fluid nature of Civil War unit organization, especially late in the war, saw many cavalry and infantry units consolidated or transformed. Some infantrymen became dismounted cavalry. Others, such as those in state guard or militia roles, shifted between roles depending on local needs. This administrative flexibility can sometimes blur the clarity of branch distinctions in the historical record, though the original unit designations still offer useful insight.

In some states, the cavalry presence among the Cardwell men is particularly striking. For example, in Tennessee, 57% of all Cardwell Confederate veterans served in cavalry units. Kentucky followed with 56%, while Arkansas saw 62.5% in cavalry. These states, all either border or western theater states, were hubs of guerrilla warfare, mounted raiding, and partisan operations—further confirming the regional correlation.

It is important to consider that the high rate of cavalry enlistment may also reflect survivorship in records and traditions. Cavalry units, known for their flair and independence, were often well-remembered by local communities and families. Their exploits were frequently recorded in memoirs, newspaper stories, and oral tradition, contributing to a better preservation of their names in the historical record.

In conclusion, the data surrounding the Confederate service of the Cardwell men illustrates a meaningful deviation from average Confederate enlistment patterns. While infantry dominated the Confederate Army broadly, the Cardwell men exhibited an unusually high representation in cavalry and mobile artillery service. These trends are best explained by geographic origin, cultural values, economic capacity, and the nature of conflict in their regions. When factoring in horse artillery units that functioned as cavalry adjuncts, the overall Cardwell alignment toward mounted service becomes even more pronounced.

This analysis contributes to our understanding not just of one family's Civil War experience, but of the broader interplay between social, regional, and strategic factors that influenced how men chose (or were assigned to) their roles in the Confederate military machine.

Cardwell_Confederate_Branch_Percentages

State	Infantry %	Cavalry %	Artillery %
Confederate Average	75.0	20.0	5.0
Cardwell Combined	44.0	46.9	9.0
Alabama	48.3	31.0	20.7
Arkansas	37.5	62.5	0.0
Kentucky	0.0	100.0	0.0
Louisiana	75.0	25.0	0.0
Mississippi	100.0	0.0	0.0
Missouri	0.0	100.0	0.0
North Carolina	84.6	0.0	15.4
South Carolina	0.0	100.0	0.0
Tennessee	42.9	50.0	7.1
Texas	50.0	16.7	33.3
Virginia	46.2	30.8	23.1

Union Statistics by Branch

The Cardwell men who served in the Union Army during the American Civil War reflect a fascinating symmetry when compared to their Confederate counterparts. After analyzing the compiled data of Union Cardwell veterans from thirteen states, a striking pattern emerges: these men distributed themselves among the military branches in proportions that nearly mirror those of the Cardwell men who fought for the Confederacy. This paper explores these statistics, draws comparisons, and considers what factors may have influenced the Cardwells' remarkably balanced military representation on both sides of the conflict.

The structure of the Union Army closely mirrored that of the Confederate Army, comprising three principal combat branches: infantry, cavalry, and artillery, along with a range of other roles such as engineers, musicians, and medical personnel. According to most estimates, the Union Army as a whole was approximately composed of 80% infantry, 14% cavalry, and 6% artillery. These numbers reflect the Union's strategic emphasis on large-scale infantry operations supported by smaller cavalry and artillery forces.

In contrast, the Cardwell men who served the Union demonstrate an unusual divergence from this national trend, while simultaneously aligning closely with the distribution found among the Confederate Cardwell men. Of the Union Cardwell veterans documented, 47.4% served in the infantry, 39.7% in cavalry units, 5.1% in artillery, and 7.7% in other roles or staff positions. These percentages bear a close resemblance to the Confederate Cardwell breakdown: 44.0% infantry, 46.9% cavalry, and 9.0% artillery. Such similarities suggest that factors influencing branch selection among the Cardwell men transcended the Union-Confederate divide.

The elevated rate of cavalry service, nearly three times the national average of 14%, is particularly noteworthy. As with the Confederate side, geography likely played a central role. Many Union Cardwells hailed from border or western states such as Kentucky, Missouri, and Tennessee—regions where mounted service was common, especially given the demands of scouting, raiding, and rapid response to guerrilla threats. These states also fielded irregular cavalry and state militia units that blurred the lines between conventional and partisan warfare. For a young man with equestrian experience, cavalry duty offered mobility, perceived prestige, and a form of military service well-suited to rural life.

Another factor contributing to this distribution is family tradition and local recruitment patterns. In tight-knit communities where Cardwell families resided, enlistment often occurred in groups, and young men followed the paths of friends, neighbors, or older siblings. If a local regiment was mounted or artillery-based, that could sway the balance toward a particular branch. Such patterns often led to regional clustering by service type, which is observable in states like Missouri and Kentucky, where cavalry service predominated among Union Cardwell men.

The 5.1% of Union Cardwells in artillery roles closely matches both the Confederate Cardwell artillery rate (9.0%) and the overall Union average (6%). These men often served in batteries that supported larger infantry or cavalry formations. Some also served in coastal defenses or garrisoned fortifications—duties that required discipline, technical aptitude, and long hours of maintenance. While fewer in number, artillery service carried its own hazards, particularly in major engagements such as Petersburg, Vicksburg, and Chattanooga.

The remaining 7.7% of Union Cardwells served in other capacities, including the U.S. Colored Troops (USCT), and specialized units such as engineers or musicians. These roles, though smaller in number, highlight the diverse nature of Union military operations and the need for a wide range of support and specialty services.

The similarity in branch percentages between Union and Confederate Cardwell men suggests that underlying cultural, regional, and familial influences played a consistent role regardless of allegiance. This is particularly compelling when considered against the backdrop of dramatically different national recruitment strategies and wartime objectives. While the Union prioritized large infantry corps and extensive rail-based logistics, and the Confederacy leaned on cavalry for mobility and communication, the Cardwell men in both armies pursued service paths that reflect shared values and capabilities.

It is also worth noting the potential role of survivorship bias and memory in shaping our records. Cavalry and artillery units, often celebrated in postwar accounts and community histories, may be overrepresented in family lore and pension records. However, the documented evidence from muster rolls and service files confirms that the Cardwell men's service in these branches was both substantial and real.

In conclusion, the Cardwell men who served in the Union Army defy the standard expectations of Civil War military demographics. Their distribution among the branches—47.4% infantry, 39.7% cavalry, 5.1% artillery, and 7.7% in other roles—closely aligns with their Confederate kin. This unexpected symmetry speaks to the enduring influence of geography, culture, family, and personal aptitude in shaping the military experience of this single surname group. Whether in blue or gray, the Cardwell legacy reveals a family deeply engaged in every aspect of the Civil War, across every branch, and on both sides of the great national conflict.

Cardwell Union Branch Percentages

	Infantry	Cavalry	Artillery	Other
Union Average	80.0	14.0	6.0	1.0
Cardwell Combined	47.4	39.7	5.1	7.7
Delaware	100.0	0.0	0.0	0.0
Iowa	100.0	0.0	0.0	0.0
Illinois	50.0	50.0	0.0	0.0
Indiana	100.0	0.0	0.0	0.0
Kansas	50.0	50.0	0.0	0.0
Kentucky	60.0	20.0	10.0	10.0
Missouri	23.1	61.5	0.0	15.4
Nebraska	0.0	100.0	0.0	0.0
New York	50.0	50.0	0.0	0.0
Oregon	0.0	100.0	0.0	0.0
Pennsylvania	75.0	0.0	12.5	12.5
Tennessee	50.0	50.0	0.0	0.0
US Colored Troops	42.9	14.3	28.6	14.3

Confederate Combat Outcomes

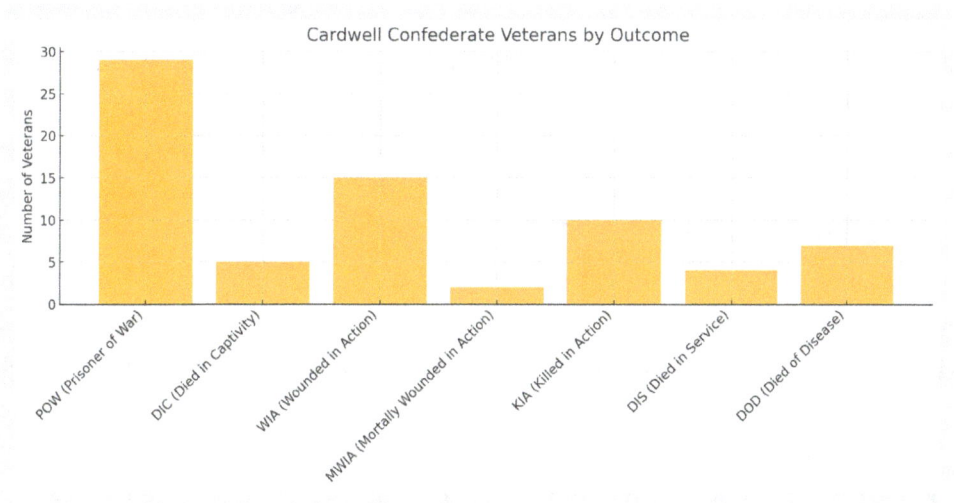

Analysis of Combat Outcomes Among Cardwell Confederate Veterans

The compiled data on the service outcomes of Confederate veterans bearing the Cardwell surname provides a valuable window into the sacrifices endured by this extended family during the American Civil War. By categorizing their fates into standard military outcomes—Prisoner of War (POW), Died in Captivity (DIC), Wounded in Action (WIA), Mortally Wounded in Action (MWIA), Killed in Action (KIA), Died in Service (DIS), and Died of

Disease (DOD)—we gain a clearer understanding of how the war impacted not just armies, but individual families.

Prisoners of War (POW): 29 Veterans

With 29 Cardwell veterans captured during the course of the war, the POW category stands as the most populated. This high number may reflect both the extensive participation of Cardwell men in front-line units and the increasingly desperate final years of the Confederacy, during which surrenders became more common. Some of these prisoners would later die in Union camps, while others endured captivity only to return home. The POW experience was often brutal, with overcrowded conditions, meager rations, and psychological strain leaving lasting scars.

Died in Captivity (DIC): 5 Veterans

Of those captured, five Cardwell men died in Union captivity. These men represent a tragic subset—individuals who survived the battlefield only to succumb in the hardship of Northern prisons such as Point Lookout, Elmira, or Camp Chase. Their deaths reflect the poor sanitary conditions, malnutrition, and exposure that characterized Confederate prisoner experiences, especially in the last two years of the war. The mortality rate among Cardwell POWs thus stood at over 17%, aligning with the broader historical averages for Confederate prisoners of war.

Wounded in Action (WIA): 13 Veterans

Thirteen Cardwell men are recorded as having been wounded in action and surviving their injuries. This number highlights the frequency with which these soldiers were placed in harm's way—likely reflecting high rates of enlistment in infantry and cavalry units that saw direct combat. These wounds would have left many with long-term disabilities in a period before modern medicine and rehabilitation. The WIA figure also underscores the resilience of these veterans, many of whom returned to service even after sustaining serious injuries.

Mortally Wounded in Action (MWIA): 4 Veterans

Four Cardwell veterans were mortally wounded—meaning they were injured in combat and later died from those wounds. This figure is significant because it highlights not just those killed instantly (recorded separately as KIA), but also those who lingered for hours, days, or even weeks before death. The separation of MWIA from WIA allows for a clearer understanding of battlefield lethality and also reflects the painful reality of Civil War medicine, where many died due to infection or lack of surgical expertise.

Killed in Action (KIA): 10 Veterans

Ten Cardwell men were killed outright in battle. These soldiers represent the ultimate sacrifice and underscore the violence and deadly nature of Civil War combat. Many of these deaths occurred in well-documented engagements such as Bull Run, Chickamauga, or the Overland Campaign, where Confederate casualties were staggeringly high. This figure makes KIA the third-largest category among fatal outcomes, following POW and DOD when combined with MWIA.

Died in Service (DIS): 4 Veterans

Four Cardwell men died while in service, but not directly from combat wounds or disease. This category typically includes deaths from accidents, exhaustion, or other non-combat causes while on active duty. It represents another angle of wartime hazard—showing that simply being enlisted exposed soldiers to fatal risks even outside the battlefield. It also suggests that these men were performing continuous and hazardous duties, such as construction, fortification, or logistical work, where exposure and fatigue could prove fatal.

Died of Disease (DOD): 7 Veterans

Seven Cardwell men died of disease—long recognized as the number one killer of soldiers in the Civil War. This number reinforces the historical pattern: more soldiers died from illness than from bullets. Poor camp hygiene, lack of clean water, contaminated food, and minimal access to trained medical personnel all contributed to these losses. That nearly one in ten Cardwell veterans died this way reflects how disease often spread unchecked through encampments, particularly during the winter months and siege conditions.

Broader Implications

Taken together, this analysis reveals a striking level of sacrifice and endurance. Nearly 40% of the known Confederate Cardwell veterans experienced either death, injury, or imprisonment—a sobering statistic. The variety of causes—combat, disease, and imprisonment—illustrates the multifaceted dangers of military service in the Confederacy.

Moreover, these figures give personal weight to broader Civil War history. Each number represents a family who suffered a loss, a community that lost a contributor, and a name that carried forward memory, often in silence or sorrow. The patterns also reflect geographic trends, with high POW and DOD rates likely resulting from men captured or stationed in theaters like

Virginia, Tennessee, and Georgia—regions with notorious prisons and poor living conditions.

When compared to the broader statistics of Confederate military service, the outcomes observed among the Cardwell veterans largely mirror the general trends experienced across the Confederate States Army. Historically, around 1 in 4 Confederate soldiers were wounded, and roughly 1 in 10 died from disease—figures closely echoed in the Cardwell data. The proportion of Cardwell men taken prisoner, approximately 24%, is consistent with Confederate surrender rates, especially in the latter half of the war when large numbers of troops were captured en masse during failed campaigns and final capitulations. Likewise, the ratio of those killed or mortally wounded in action —about 10% of the total sample—aligns with battlefield mortality rates seen in high-casualty units. These similarities suggest that the Cardwell family's wartime experiences were not exceptional but rather emblematic of the widespread suffering, danger, and attrition that characterized service in the Confederate army. Their collective history stands as a microcosm of the broader Confederate military experience.

By documenting these outcomes and analyzing them, the Cardwell Confederate veterans are given their due in historical memory—not simply as soldiers in a vast war, but as individuals whose service, suffering, and death shaped the lives of their descendants and the history of the American South.

Union Combat Outcomes

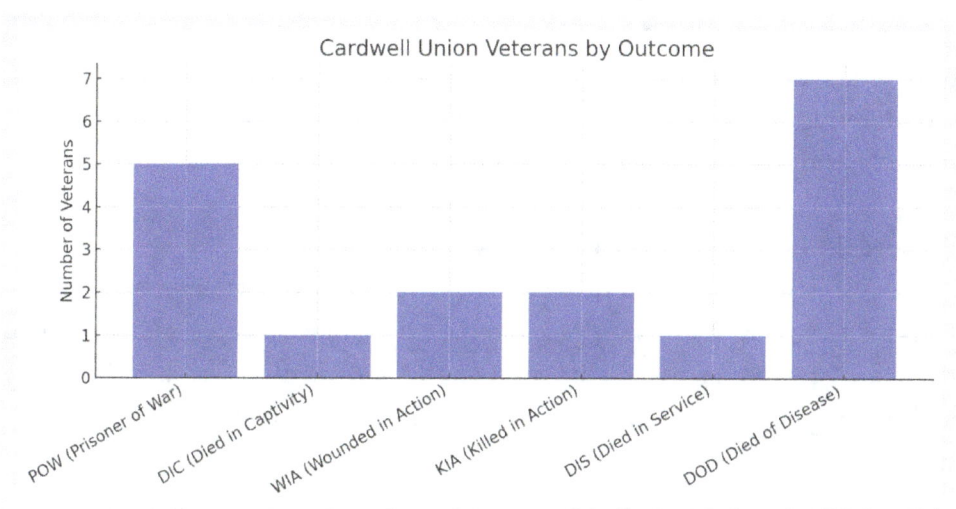

Cardwell Union Veterans by Outcome

Analysis of Combat Outcomes Among Cardwell Union Veterans

The compiled data on the service outcomes of Union veterans bearing the Cardwell surname provides a meaningful lens through which we can examine the toll of the Civil War on this extended family. By sorting the fates of these men into recognized military outcome categories—Prisoner of War (POW), Died in Captivity (DIC), Wounded in Action (WIA), Mortally Wounded in Action (MWIA), Killed in Action (KIA), Died in Service (DIS), and Died of

Disease (DOD)—we gain insight into the personal cost of war on a single surname group. For the 66 Cardwell men who served in Union blue, their recorded outcomes reflect a spectrum of sacrifice and endurance.

Prisoners of War (POW): 5 Veterans

Only five Cardwell men serving in the Union Army were recorded as having been taken prisoner. This relatively low number may reflect either the nature of their service assignments or the overall difference in risk exposure between Union and Confederate forces. Unlike their Confederate counterparts, Union soldiers who were captured had a somewhat better chance of survival in Southern prisons, though harsh conditions still prevailed.

Died in Captivity (DIC): 1 Veteran

Of those five captured, one Union Cardwell died while held in captivity. This individual adds a poignant dimension to the data—having survived combat only to perish in confinement. While Union prisoners often fared better than Confederate ones due to exchange programs and supply access, the suffering endured by those who died in Southern prisons remains a solemn testament to the war's grim realities.

Wounded in Action (WIA): 2 Veterans

Two Cardwell men were recorded as having been wounded in action. This relatively low figure may point to the roles or locations in which many of these men served, or to gaps in surviving records. Still, these injuries likely had lifelong effects, especially in an era before modern surgery and rehabilitation.

Killed in Action (KIA): 2 Veterans

Two Union Cardwell soldiers were killed outright in battle. These deaths represent the ultimate sacrifice and are solemn reminders of the brutal combat conditions faced in battles across places like Chickamauga, Stones River, and Vicksburg. These men died in service to the Union cause and remain among the most direct symbols of wartime loss.

Died in Service (DIS): 1 Veteran

One Union Cardwell died during his term of service due to non-combat causes not specifically linked to disease or wounds. Such deaths often resulted from accidents, overwork, or environmental exposure, especially during construction, logistics, or other military support duties.

Died of Disease (DOD): 7 Veterans

Seven Cardwell Union veterans died of disease—a figure that reinforces the historical truth that illness claimed more Civil War lives than bullets. Despite the Union's better resources and medical infrastructure, unsanitary camp conditions, contaminated water, and infectious diseases such as dysentery, typhoid, and pneumonia took their toll. These deaths underscore how vulnerable soldiers were, regardless of their combat exposure.

Broader Implications

Together, these outcomes reveal that 18 of the 66 Union Cardwell veterans—over 27%—either died, were wounded, or were taken prisoner during their service. Though smaller in scale than their Confederate kin, this subset of the Cardwell family still experienced significant loss. Compared to national Union averages, the proportion of POWs and disease deaths among the Cardwell men aligns closely with broader patterns seen across the Federal Army.

The relatively small number of combat deaths and injuries may be due to several factors, including service in less exposed units, timing of enlistment, or simply good fortune. However, the high percentage of disease deaths is consistent with known mortality causes during the war, where even in the best-equipped camps, sanitation remained poor and medical knowledge limited.

In documenting these outcomes, the Union Cardwell veterans emerge not just as names on a roster, but as men whose lives were shaped—and often shortened—by the defining conflict of 19th-century America. Their sacrifices mirror those of countless soldiers and serve as a reminder that victory in war carries with it an undeniable human cost. Whether wounded, imprisoned, or lost to disease, these men contributed to the Union cause and left a legacy that endures in both national history and family memory.

Union POW Camps

THE AMERICAN CIVIL WAR WITNESSED NOT ONLY BATTLEFIELD LOSSES but also immense suffering within prison walls. Among the thousands of Confederate and Union soldiers who endured imprisonment, several men bearing the surname Cardwell were captured, confined, and in some cases, perished in Federal prisoner of war camps. This report examines that small but significant group, using available historical data to explore patterns of confinement, survival, and death. Drawing from a compiled database of Civil War veterans with the Cardwell surname, this analysis identifies 19 men who were held in Federal POW camps. Of those, 7—over one-third—died in captivity.

This report includes detailed breakdowns of each prison where Cardwell men were confined, individual service data, survival outcomes, and historical background on each camp. Supporting charts provide visual clarity on these trends.

Overall Mortality in Federal Camps: A Cardwell Perspective

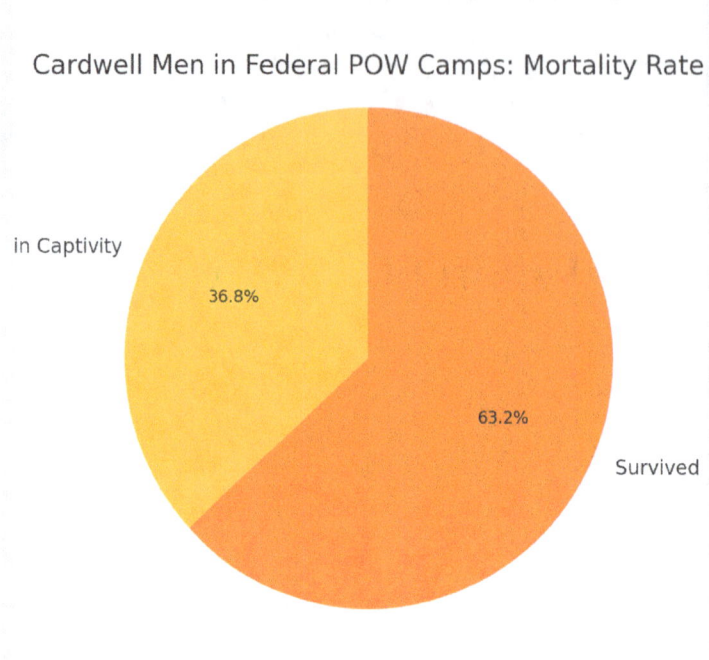

Cardwell Men in Federal POW Camps: Mortality Rate

in Captivity

36.8%

63.2%

Survived

Out of 19 Cardwell men held in Federal prisoner-of-war camps:
- **7 died in captivity** (36.84%)
- **12 survived captivity** (63.16%)

This mortality rate is notably higher than the overall Confederate death rate in Union camps, which hovered around 12–15% in most scholarly estimates. The Cardwell men thus serve as a microcosm of the brutal toll exacted on prisoners—especially at camps with poor sanitation, overcrowding, and harsh climates.

Analysis and Observations

1 Elmira and Alton: These two camps accounted for four of the seven Cardwell deaths—highlighting how environment and neglect significantly impacted mortality.

2 Douglas: The single most deadly camp for the Cardwells, with three deaths, matches historical records of poor conditions.

3 Point Lookout: All six men survived, making it an anomaly among the larger, overcrowded facilities. This may speak to capture timing or unit assignment.

4 Virginia and Tennessee: The states most represented among imprisoned Cardwells were Virginia and Tennessee, reflecting Confederate enlistment trends and the strategic locations of capture.

5 Units and Captures: Several men belonged to the same units or brigades, suggesting they were likely captured together—perhaps at battles like Fort Donelson, Missionary Ridge, or Petersburg.

Conclusion

The fate of the 19 Cardwell men imprisoned in Federal camps during the Civil War reveals a profound story of suffering, endurance, and loss. The 36.8% death rate among them exceeds national averages and reflects the brutal conditions endured by Confederate prisoners. Each name—etched in historical records—adds a personal face to the impersonal statistics of war.

The diversity in outcomes between camps also reflects the uneven treatment and support prisoners received. From the deadly cold of Elmira to the relative survivability of Point Lookout, these camps became defining experiences for the Cardwell men who survived—and the final chapter for those who did not.

As researchers, genealogists, and descendants continue to explore these histories, this record serves as a memorial and a resource—one that honors the lives of all who served, suffered, and endured.

Alton Military Prison
Alton, Madison County, Illinois

Photo UPA.1: *Alton Military Prison - photograph taken in 1861 - The large white building in the foreground is the main blockhouse. A small portion of Smallpox Island is in the upper right.*

Photo UPA.2: *Alton Prison Confederate Monument - North Alton Confederate Cemetery, Alton, Madison County, Illinois - The 58-foot granite obelisk to honor 1,354 Confederate soldiers who died while imprisoned at the Alton Military Prison during the Civil War. Their names are inscribed on six bronze plaques affixed to the monument.*

Photo UPA.3: *Smallpox Island Confederate Memorial - Lincoln Shields Recreation Area, West Alton, Missouri. It honors 222 Confederate soldiers that died of smallpox at the Smallpox Island, a quarantine facility of Alton Federal Military Prison across the Mississippi River. Among those honored are William Thomas Dobson Cardwell of Arkansas and William Y. Cardwell of Tennessee.*

Camp Alton Military Prison

During the American Civil War, the war effort was not limited to battlefields. The struggle extended into cities, railways, hospitals, and perhaps most grimly, prison camps. Among the numerous Union-run prisons that held Confederate soldiers, Alton Military Prison in Illinois occupies a distinctive place in Civil War history. Once a state penitentiary, Alton became one of the first—and most overcrowded—Federal military prisons in operation. It housed not only Confederate soldiers but also Union deserters, political prisoners, and civilians caught in the shifting loyalties of a divided nation.

In examining the conditions and legacy of Alton, we gain a better understanding of the war's human cost, particularly in relation to those who were removed from combat but not from hardship. This is especially meaningful for genealogical and historical studies of families like the Cardwells, two of whom perished behind its walls.

The Alton State Penitentiary was originally constructed in 1833 and began operation in 1835 as Illinois's first state prison. Built from locally quarried limestone, its imposing stone walls and stark cell blocks stood along the Mississippi River, near the border with Missouri. The prison was closed in 1860 due to concerns over its deteriorating condition and overcrowding. Ironically, those very problems would soon be exacerbated.

When the Civil War broke out in 1861, the Union faced an unforeseen logistical crisis: where to house the increasing number of Confederate prisoners of war. After the battles of Fort Donelson and Island No. 10 resulted in thousands of Confederate captures in early 1862, the Federal government reopened Alton as a military prison, despite its previous closure.

The prison reopened officially in February 1862. Quickly, it began to receive Confederate prisoners from battles in Missouri, Tennessee, Arkansas, and Mississippi. Within weeks, hundreds of men were crowded into the decaying cell blocks. The prison, designed for perhaps 800 inmates at most, soon held over 1,400, and at times as many as 1,900. The facility was also used to detain Union deserters, civilians accused of disloyalty, and even women—an unusual detail among Civil War prisons.

Alton's facilities were wholly inadequate for the sudden demand. The masonry had crumbled, drainage was poor, and there was limited fresh water. The Mississippi River, though nearby, was not a clean water source, and dysentery and diarrhea became widespread. Ventilation was minimal, especially in the lower levels, where prisoners languished in suffocating heat during summer and bitter cold during winter.

Alton became infamous for its appalling conditions. Overcrowding, inadequate sanitation, insufficient food, and lack of medical care contributed to high mortality rates. A smallpox epidemic swept through the prison in late 1862 and early 1863, killing hundreds of inmates and guards alike. The situation became so dire that a separate "smallpox island" was designated across the river, where infected prisoners were sent to isolate and die.

Guards were often cruel or indifferent. Rations were poor and sometimes spoiled. Blankets were scarce, and prisoners slept on stone floors or narrow bunks. The mortality rate at Alton is estimated at around 10–15% for Confederate prisoners—a significant figure considering many men were held for only months at a time. Over 11,700 Confederate prisoners passed through the gates of Alton, and 1,534 are believed to have died there. Disease was the leading cause, particularly smallpox, typhoid fever, and pneumonia.

The Cardwell family's experience at Alton highlights this grim toll. Two men—**William Thomas Dobson Cardwell** of the 37th Arkansas Infantry and **William Y. Cardwell** of Forrest's Alabama Cavalry—were confined at Alton and died there.

Though Alton was not an escape-proof facility, relatively few successful escapes were recorded. The prison's stone walls and river location deterred most attempts. Guards, often drawn from Illinois or nearby states, were armed and stationed around the perimeter. Discipline was strict, and punishments for escape attempts or disobedience were harsh.

Prisoners passed the time by carving objects from bone, writing letters (if materials were available), or playing cards. Confederate chaplains or literate prisoners occasionally held prayer meetings. For most, however, the days passed in dull routine marked by roll calls, poor meals, and the constant threat of illness.

The prison was initially under the jurisdiction of the Union Army's Department of the Mississippi, and later the Department of the Missouri. Its commandants were typically junior officers tasked with maintaining order and accountability. The structure of Alton was more rigidly enforced than some of the ad hoc prison camps that arose later in the war, but this did not translate to better conditions.

Reports of abuse and neglect eventually reached military officials and journalists. Inspections were made, but little was done. Alton was a low priority for reform, especially compared to camps like Andersonville in the South, which drew national attention for their horrors.

Alton Military Prison ceased its role as a prison of war facility in July 1865, shortly after the end of the war. The surviving Confederate prisoners were paroled or exchanged. The prison itself was permanently closed soon afterward, and the structure fell into disrepair.

In the years following the war, the site remained a potent symbol of Civil War suffering. In the early 20th century, parts of the prison were dismantled, though some sections of the limestone walls remain. The site is now maintained by the Illinois State Historic Preservation Agency, and interpretive plaques honor both Union and Confederate dead. Today, visitors can see remnants of the old prison and a memorial to the Confederate soldiers who died at Alton.

In 1909, the United Daughters of the Confederacy erected a 58-foot granite obelisk at the site of the official Confederate Cemetery in Alton, Illinois. This striking memorial marks the collective graves of 1,354 Confederate soldiers who died while imprisoned at the nearby Alton Federal Military Prison during the Civil War. Their names are inscribed on six bronze plaques mounted on the monument, which now stands within the North Alton Confederate Cemetery.

Among the those memorialized were William Thomas Dobson Cardwell of Arkansas and William Y. Cardwell of Tennessee. While both men are remembered at the Alton cemetery as part of the collective memorial, their names also appear on the Smallpox Island Confederate Memorial located at Lincoln Shields Recreation Area in West Alton, Missouri. It honors the Confederate prisoners of war who died a smallpox outbreak between 01 August 1863, and 31 March 1865, at the Alton Federal Military Prison across the Mississippi River in Illinois, but were quarantined at Smallpox Island. The memorial lists the names of 222 Confederate soldiers who succumbed to the disease during their imprisonment.

The memorial stands near the former site of Smallpox Island, where infected prisoners were quarantined. Those prisoners confined to the hospital on Smallpox Island were buried there on the island. Over time, the island was eroded by the Mississippi River, and its exact location is now submerged beneath the waters of the Melvin Price Locks and Dam. The Lincoln Shields Recreation Area provides a place for reflection and remembrance of those who perished during this tragic chapter of the Civil War.

The legacy of Alton is not just in its stones or its statistics, but in the silent testimony of those who endured its harsh conditions. As historians and descendants continue to investigate the past, the memory of Alton lives on— not as a monument to victory or defeat, but as a symbol of the enduring human consequences of war. Photo Credits[1,2,3]

Camp Butler Military Prison
Springfield, Sangamon County, Illinois

Photo UPB.1: *Camp Butler, Springfield, Illinois. Circa 1862.*

Located just a few miles northeast of Springfield, Illinois, near the town of Riverton, Camp Butler began as a Union military installation but evolved into a site of confinement, hardship, and quiet suffering during the Civil War. Though smaller and less infamous than prisons like Camp Douglas or Elmira, Camp Butler nonetheless bore witness to disease, deprivation, and death on a large scale. Its story is one of improvisation under pressure—marked by inadequate planning, overwhelming need, and the tragic consequences that followed. For William Dudley Cardwell of the 30th Tennessee Infantry, Camp Butler was a place of danger, uncertainty, and ultimately, survival.

Camp Butler was officially established in August 1861, designated as one of Illinois's primary training and mustering centers by Governor Richard Yates and Senator Stephen A. Douglas. Its location—just seven miles from Springfield and adjacent to the Chicago and Alton Railroad—made it ideal for mobilizing and provisioning Union forces destined for the Western and Eastern Theaters. Named after William Butler, a respected Springfield resident and Illinois State Treasurer, the camp initially served as a staging ground for thousands of volunteers. At this stage, there was no indication that it would soon be pressed into service as a prison.

The camp's transformation began in February 1862, following the Union victory at Fort Donelson, Tennessee. The surrender of over 12,000 Confederate soldiers in that engagement created an immediate crisis for the Union Army: where to house so many prisoners. Camp Butler was one of several facilities hastily repurposed to receive them. Within weeks, over 2,000 Confederate soldiers—many ill, wounded, or exhausted—were shipped north and unloaded at Springfield. The existing infrastructure at Camp Butler, suited for temporary military housing, proved grossly inadequate for long-term confinement.

There were no formal prison barracks at first—only tents or quickly assembled wooden sheds. Sanitary arrangements were minimal, and drinking water was often drawn from unsafe sources. The Illinois winter was already underway, and the sudden influx of weakened Southern prisoners, many wearing threadbare uniforms, created a humanitarian crisis. Measles, pneumonia, dysentery, typhoid, and smallpox swept through the camp. The death toll mounted rapidly. By the summer of 1862, it became necessary to create a new burial ground near the camp. That cemetery—now part of Camp Butler National Cemetery—ultimately held the remains of 866 Confederate prisoners who died at the site, many within mere weeks of arrival.

Among those captured at Fort Donelson and sent to Camp Butler was Private **William Dudley Cardwell** of the 30th Tennessee Infantry. Like many of his fellow Confederates, he arrived in poor condition—fatigued, undernourished, and vulnerable to disease. Though official records do not detail the specifics of his confinement, his presence is confirmed through prisoner registers. His survival is also confirmed—thanks to a prisoner exchange at Vicksburg, Mississippi, on 23 September 1862, William was released after roughly seven months of captivity. The timing of his exchange spared him from the worst mortality period at Camp Butler, which extended into 1863.

No further military records have been located for William after his parole, but he survived the war, returning to Sumner County, Tennessee, where he married and raised a large family. By 1880, he had moved west and settled in Kansas, where he lived until his death in 1926. His experience at Camp Butler, though not as dramatic as some, reflects the quiet endurance of many Confederate soldiers who lived through the war's harshest detainment conditions. His biography appears in full in the chapter on Confederate Veterans of Tennessee in Brothers in Grey.

As Camp Butler continued to operate as a POW camp, the initial chaos was never fully resolved. The camp remained under the command of various Union officers, most of whom had little experience in managing a prison population. Supplies were limited, medical staffing was stretched thin, and basic logistical needs often went unmet. While later improvements included wooden barracks and a more stable hospital, these came too late for many of the earliest detainees.

Newspapers in Springfield and military inspectors commented critically on the camp's poor preparation. Reports from clergymen and civilians led to public concern, prompting some reform, but the core issues—overcrowding, inadequate facilities, and the sheer unpredictability of war—could not be easily resolved. Unlike Camp Douglas, which became notorious for intentional cruelty, Camp Butler's failures stemmed more from logistical collapse than deliberate neglect. Nevertheless, the consequences were severe: by war's end, over 20,000 Confederate POWs had passed through, and nearly one-third of them died in custody—figures comparable to Elmira and higher than those at Point Lookout or Camp Chase.

By 1865, the prison function of Camp Butler was winding down. The camp resumed its earlier role as a mustering-out station for returning Union troops. It was officially closed in 1866, but the cemetery remained. Over time, this burial ground evolved into Camp Butler National Cemetery, now a peaceful and well-maintained site that honors veterans of all American conflicts. Among the 19,000 graves, a clearly marked Confederate section preserves the memory of those who died far from their homes—men who were soldiers, prisoners, and, in many cases, victims of disease and circumstance.

Today, few physical traces of Camp Butler's prison infrastructure remain, but its legacy endures through stone and soil. The cemetery stands as one of the few places in the United States where Union and Confederate dead lie side by side, a quiet reminder of war's human toll and the strange fraternity that can arise from shared suffering.

For the Cardwell family, William Dudley Cardwell's survival at Camp Butler stands as a rare story of endurance during a war that claimed so many lives on and off the battlefield. His time there situates him within the quiet tragedy of a prison camp that remains overshadowed by more notorious sites—but which deserves remembrance. Photo Credit[1]

Camp Chase Military Prison
Columbus, Franklin County, Ohio

Photo UPC.1: *Camp Chase Confederate Memorial in Columbus, Ohio.*

Tucked into the western outskirts of Columbus, Ohio, Camp Chase began as a training ground for Union soldiers and evolved into a major prisoner-of-war camp during the American Civil War. While less infamous than sites like Elmira or Andersonville, Camp Chase housed over 26,000 Confederate prisoners during its years of operation, and roughly 2,200 of them died while in captivity.

The camp was marked by a strange duality. On one hand, its death rate was significantly lower than other Union camps, and many prisoners recalled fair treatment. On the other, it suffered from the same problems that plagued nearly all wartime prisons: overcrowding, disease, supply shortages, and harsh winters. The legacy of Camp Chase is preserved today through the Camp

Chase Confederate Cemetery, one of the largest Confederate burial grounds in the North.

Among the Confederate soldiers confined here was **George H. Cardwell** of the 13th Kentucky Cavalry. George was a captured later in the war at Marshall County, Alabama, near Huntsville, on 15 January 1865. He was transported to Camp Chase, arriving there on 25 January 1865. George was paroled on 25 March 1865, just a few weeks before the end of the conflict. He returned to his family in Kentucky and lived out his life among his family and friends.

Camp Chase was established in May 1861, just weeks after the outbreak of war. It was named in honor of Salmon P. Chase, then Treasury Secretary under Abraham Lincoln and later Chief Justice of the U.S. Supreme Court.

Located on farmland just west of Columbus, the camp initially served as a training and muster site for Ohio volunteers. Thousands of Union recruits passed through its gates en route to the front. The camp also became a transit hub for new regiments and a supply depot.

However, by late 1861, with the war intensifying and large numbers of Confederate soldiers captured in early engagements like Fort Donelson and Mill Springs, the Union government needed additional places to confine prisoners of war. Thus, Camp Chase was retooled as a prison, and its role shifted drastically.

The conversion of Camp Chase into a prison began in earnest in early 1862. Wooden barracks and stockades were constructed to accommodate thousands of prisoners. At its peak, the camp held up to 9,400 Confederate soldiers, although it was originally intended to house far fewer.

The camp was divided into two principal areas: one for Union troops and one for prisoners. The prison section was enclosed by a high wooden fence, with watchtowers positioned at regular intervals. Guards patrolled the perimeter, though escape attempts were uncommon and rarely successful.

Compared to the horrors of Elmira or Camp Douglas, conditions at Camp Chase were relatively more humane. The climate in Ohio was less severe than that of New York or Illinois, and the camp's administrators were somewhat more diligent about providing rations, medical care, and shelter.

That said, the camp was far from comfortable. Prisoners lived in overcrowded wooden barracks, which were poorly insulated in winter and stiflingly hot in summer. Sanitation was a persistent issue, and outbreaks of disease—including smallpox, typhoid, and dysentery—occurred regularly.

Food rations were minimal, and clothing was often inadequate. Some prisoners arrived with nothing more than the tattered uniforms they wore at the time of capture. The mortality rate hovered between 8 and 10 percent, relatively low by Civil War standards, but still significant when applied to thousands of confined men.

Camp Chase was commanded at various times by both seasoned officers and political appointees. Some commanders, such as Colonel William P. Richardson, were known for maintaining firm but fair discipline. Inspections by the War Department occasionally led to improvements, especially in sanitation and rations.

Unlike many camps, Camp Chase was not plagued by extensive reports of abuse or cruelty. While prisoners certainly endured hardship, many later wrote that guards were professional, and some reported even friendly relations. Civilians from Columbus occasionally visited or provided food and supplies to prisoners, especially during the Christmas season.

Despite their confinement, Confederate prisoners at Camp Chase attempted to maintain morale and a semblance of normalcy. They organized musical performances, religious services, and even debates. Those with literacy skills wrote letters home, though censorship was common. Small-scale commerce sometimes occurred among prisoners, trading rations or crafts.

Some prisoners earned money or favors by carving items from wood or bone—such as rings, figurines, or utensils—often sold to guards or civilians. Religious observance was important to many; chaplains held services when allowed, and copies of the Bible were distributed by Northern charities.

However, conditions remained grim in many respects. Burial details worked constantly, and many prisoners died without ever knowing the outcome of the war.

Camp Chase operated as a prison until 05 July 1865, when the last prisoners were released following the official end of hostilities. The camp itself was dismantled soon afterward. Nothing of the original prison remains today, as the land was absorbed into the expanding city of Columbus.

What endures is the Camp Chase Confederate Cemetery, one of the most poignant and historically significant Civil War burial sites in the North. It holds the remains of 2,260 Confederate soldiers, most of whom died from disease during captivity.

The cemetery features a granite arch gateway, added in 1902, and a central monument honoring the unknown dead. It is listed on the National

Register of Historic Places and maintained by the U.S. Department of Veterans Affairs.

The annual Camp Chase Memorial Service, once hosted by the United Daughters of the Confederacy and now maintained by heritage and veterans' groups, pays tribute to the men who died there—regardless of political cause.

While Camp Chase does not carry the same infamy as some Civil War prisons, it holds a meaningful place in Union and Confederate memory. Its relatively lower death rate and reputation for humane treatment mark it as an example of what wartime imprisonment could have been, had resources and leadership been more consistent elsewhere.

Camp Chase's story is one of transformation—from a peaceful Ohio farm, to a bustling Union training ground, to a crowded prison camp, and finally to a solemn cemetery. It is a place of layered memory, where both the tragedy of war and the hope of reconciliation are etched into the landscape.

For the Cardwell family, Camp Chase represents a rare chapter of survival amid hardship. George H. Cardwell, like so many others, suffered the uncertainty of capture, the discomfort of barracks life, and the threat of disease. Yet he lived, and through his survival, we are offered a glimpse into one of the more humane, though still sobering, Civil War prison experiences. Photo Credit[1]

Camp Douglas Military Prison
Chicago, Cook County, Illinois

Photo UPD.1: *Confederate prisoners at Camp Douglas Military Prison - Chicago, Illinois. Circa 1863. By Courtesy of the Chicago Historical Society.*

Photo UPD.2: *Confederate Mound Memorial - Camp Douglas POW Dead - Oak Woods Cemetery, Chicago, Cook County, Illinois.*

Often overshadowed in the popular imagination by Andersonville in the South or Elmira in the North, Camp Douglas in Chicago, Illinois, was in reality one of the most lethal and notorious Union prisoner-of-war camps of the Civil War. Known for its deplorable conditions, rampant disease, and overcrowding, the camp claimed the lives of thousands of Confederate prisoners. Some historians have labeled it "the Andersonville of the North," and rightly so—by war's end, as many as 6,000 Confederate soldiers had died within its walls. By early 1865, the camp was severely overcrowded, with over 12,000 prisoners crammed into space originally meant for half that number. Over the length of the conflict, roughly 26,000 Confederate soldiers were imprisoned at Camp Douglas.

Camp Douglas serves as a stark testament to how logistical failure, mismanagement, and apathy can turn confinement into death. Its history is vital not only to understanding the Union's role in Civil War imprisonment but also to honoring the memory of those Cardwell men who died behind its fences.

Camp Douglas was originally established in August 1861 as a training camp for Union recruits, named in honor of Illinois Senator Stephen A. Douglas. Located on the southern outskirts of Chicago, it occupied approximately 60 acres of poorly drained land near Lake Michigan. Although its location made sense for transport and supply purposes, the terrain quickly proved disastrous—it was flat, low-lying, and swampy, with frequent standing water and little natural drainage.

Initially designed to house only about 6,000 men, the camp would eventually be pressed into service as a prisoner-of-war facility after the Union victories at Fort Donelson and Shiloh in early 1862, which resulted in the capture of thousands of Confederate soldiers. Thus began the camp's transformation from a temporary training ground into one of the largest and deadliest Union prisons of the war.

The first Confederate prisoners arrived at Camp Douglas in February 1862, and from the start, it was clear the facility was unprepared. The camp's barracks were poorly insulated, latrines overflowed, and drinking water often came from polluted wells or nearby creeks contaminated by human waste. Disease spread quickly.

The living conditions at Camp Douglas were some of the worst in the Union prison system. Exposure to Chicago's frigid winters, unsanitary facilities, poor nutrition, and frequent outbreaks of smallpox, pneumonia, and dysentery created a perfect storm of suffering.

Guard brutality also contributed to the camp's harsh reputation. Prisoners described being beaten or shot for minor infractions, and multiple escape attempts were met with disproportionate punishment.

According to official reports and modern estimates, between 4,000 and 6,000 Confederate soldiers died at Camp Douglas—many of them buried in mass graves at nearby Oak Woods Cemetery. The Union government did not initially keep detailed burial records, and many deaths went undocumented or were poorly recorded.

For the Cardwell family, Camp Douglas was particularly tragic. A total of five Cardwell men are known to have been imprisoned there. Of these, three—**William T. Cardwell**, **William H. Cardwell**, and **Achilles E. Cardwell**—died in captivity, while three others—**Thomas Logan Cardwell**, **William L. Cardwell** and **James R. Cardwell**—survived.

Brothers James R. Cardwell and William T. Cardwell, along with Achilles E. Cardwell, were captured during the fall of Fort Donelson on 16 February 1862, when their Confederate units surrendered en masse to Union forces.

All three were transported to Camp Douglas in Chicago, one of the primary destinations for Confederate prisoners taken at Donelson. James R. Cardwell was fortunate—he was included in a prisoner exchange that occurred on 05 April 1862 at Vicksburg, Mississippi, and he survived the war. His brother, William T. Cardwell, and Achilles E. Cardwell, were not so fortunate. Both died in captivity at Camp Douglas within just a few months of their arrival, victims of the disease and harsh conditions that defined early operations at the prison.

William L. Cardwell was captured near Nashville, Tennessee, on 10 December 1864, during the closing campaigns of the war. He was sent to Camp Douglas and remained there until his release on 10 May 1865, shortly after the Confederate surrender.

William H. Cardwell, a member of the 9th Tennessee Cavalry, took part in General John Hunt Morgan's Raid into Indiana and Ohio during the summer of 1863. He was captured at the Battle of Buffington Island on 19 July 1863 and sent with hundreds of Morgan's troopers to Camp Douglas. After approximately 250 days in captivity, William H. Cardwell died from disease on 25 March 1864, one of many who perished during the camp's peak overcrowding and periods of rampant disease.

One of the most compelling individual stories associated with Camp Douglas is that of Private Thomas Logan Cardwell, a Confederate cavalryman in Company C, 8th Regiment Kentucky Cavalry, CSA. Thomas, along with William H. Cardwell, were among the hundreds of troopers under the legendary General John Hunt Morgan, whose daring 1863 cavalry raid swept through Kentucky, Indiana, and into the far reaches of Ohio, extending deeper into Union territory than any other major Confederate force during the war. Morgan's Raid captured national attention, not just for its audacity, but for the chaos and panic it created across several Northern states. It ultimately ended in disaster for the raiders.

Cardwell was captured at the Battle of Salineville, Ohio, on 26 July 1863, during the final engagement of Morgan's Raid. Salineville marked the official collapse of the expedition, with Morgan and over 700 of his men either killed, wounded, or captured. Thomas Logan Cardwell was among the captured, and according to official records, he was transferred to Camp Douglas and listed as present there by 22 August 1863. Like many of Morgan's men, he faced months of confinement far from the war's Southern theaters, held in one of the Union's harshest prison environments.

What makes Cardwell's imprisonment at Camp Douglas especially notable is that his likeness—along with those of several of his captured comrades—was preserved in a remarkable photographic album created during their imprisonment. This album, attributed to the photographer D.F. Brandon of Camp Douglas, includes 25 *carte de visite* portraits, 22 of which are identified members of the 8th Kentucky Cavalry, CSA. Nearly all of the men featured had been captured in Ohio on 19 July and 26 July 1863, and were imprisoned at Camp Douglas together. Among those documented in the collection was Thomas Logan Cardwell, which is his only known photograph.

The album is believed to have been compiled and owned by Private Caleb Doyle of Shelbyville, Shelby County, Kentucky, a fellow soldier in Company C of the 8th Kentucky Cavalry. Each portrait is labeled in the same distinctive handwriting, likely Doyle's, and most of the images are studio back-marked with "D.F. Brandon, Camp Douglas, Illinois," confirming the place and period of imprisonment. In 2016, this extraordinary collection was acquired by the Hayes Presidential Library and Museums, where it remains a poignant visual testament to the men of Morgan's Raid and the grim aftermath of their capture.

Cardwell's journey did not end at Camp Douglas. On February 10, 1865, after more than 18 months of confinement, he was transferred to Point Lookout, Maryland, another major Union POW camp. There, he was released just two weeks later, on 24 February, after taking the Oath of Allegiance to the United States. But freedom was fleeting. As the war neared its end, Thomas was captured a second time in Knoxville, Tennessee, on 26 April 1865, just days after Johnston's surrender in North Carolina. This time, he was sent to a Union military facility in Nashville, where he was held until 11 May 1865, likely one of the last Cardwell men to be released from Union custody. Note: All of their biographies are in the Confederate Tennessee and Kentucky chapters in the companion book.

The 50% mortality rate among Cardwell men held at Camp Douglas underscores its reputation as one of the most lethal sites in the Union POW system.

Camp Douglas ceased operations in May 1865, shortly after the Confederate surrender. The camp was dismantled, and the grounds were eventually sold off for residential development. Nothing of the original camp remains today.

However, the memory of its victims endures in Oak Woods Cemetery, where a 46-foot monument—the Confederate Mound—marks the site of a mass grave holding thousands of Camp Douglas dead. The monument, erected by the United Confederate Veterans and later maintained by the federal government, stands as one of the largest Confederate memorials in the North.

Historians have continued to debate the camp's legacy. While some argue that Camp Douglas was simply a victim of circumstance and limited wartime resources, others assert that the Union's neglect was both systematic and avoidable. The truth likely lies somewhere in between.

Camp Douglas remains one of the darkest chapters of the Union's wartime imprisonment policy. For the Cardwell family, its legacy is deeply personal. Three sons—William T., William H., and Achilles E.—entered the camp never to return. Their names, alongside thousands of others, stand as quiet rebukes to a system that failed its captives.

As historians and descendants seek to honor those who lived and died at Camp Douglas, the lessons of the camp remain clear: war is not only fought on battlefields, and its victims are not always armed. In remembering Camp Douglas, we remember those who endured—and those who did not—within the cold, disease-ridden confines of one of America's most tragic wartime facilities. Photo Credit[1,2]

Elmira Prison Camp
Elmira, Chemung County, New York

Photo UPE.1: *Elmira Prison Camp - 1861*

Photo UPE.2: *The Confederate Monument at Woodlawn National Cemetery, Elmira, Chemung County, New York.*

Among the Civil War's grim ledger of suffering, Elmira Prison stands out as a symbol of the North's own capacity for neglect and human misery. Located in upstate New York, the camp was originally built as a Union training depot and depot for Army supplies, but it was hastily converted into a prisoner-of-war facility in mid-1864. In just over a year of operation, Elmira would earn a fearsome reputation for overcrowding, disease, inadequate shelter, and a brutally cold winter—conditions that led to the deaths of nearly 25% of its inmates.

Known informally as "Hellmira" by its Confederate prisoners, Elmira was one of the most lethal Federal prison camps of the war. It holds particular relevance in the history of the Cardwell family, as two Cardwell men—James Upshur Cardwell and Joseph B. Cardwell, both of the 26th Virginia Infantry—were imprisoned at Elmira and died there. Their tragic fates offer a window into the suffering endured by thousands and mark Elmira as a vital chapter in any study of Civil War imprisonment.

Elmira, New York, had already played a significant role in the Union war effort by 1861. It served as the site of a large military depot and as a staging ground for thousands of Union recruits heading to the front. Situated on the Chemung River, with rail access and abundant farmland, Elmira was ideally located for military logistics. However, it was not originally designed or intended to hold prisoners of war.

This changed in mid-1864, as Union forces captured thousands of Confederate soldiers following the Overland Campaign and the battles of Cold Harbor, Petersburg, and the Shenandoah Valley. With prison facilities in places like Camp Douglas and Point Lookout at or near capacity, the War Department authorized the conversion of the Elmira depot into a military prison in July 1864.

The transformation was swift and insufficient. Within weeks, prisoners began arriving by train, many of them wounded or sick from previous engagements or long marches. Over 12,000 Confederate soldiers would be processed through Elmira in its short but catastrophic existence.

Elmira Prison was located on a low-lying tract of land adjacent to Foster's Pond, a stagnant marsh that contributed to the prison's poor drainage and became a breeding ground for mosquitoes and disease. The camp was surrounded by a twelve-foot-high wooden stockade and featured guard towers and a perimeter patrol system, but it lacked basic infrastructure for sanitation and shelter.

The prison was designed to hold roughly 5,000 men, but within months it exceeded 10,000. Barracks were hastily constructed, and many prisoners were housed in tents well into the winter of 1864–65. When temperatures dropped, many of the tented prisoners froze, literally dying from exposure.

Food rations were technically in line with War Department regulations, but in practice, they were often inadequate. Contaminated drinking water and spoiled meat were frequently reported. The diet lacked sufficient vegetables, leading to scurvy and other nutritional deficiencies. Medical care was likewise lacking. The camp's hospital was understaffed and overwhelmed by illness ranging from dysentery and typhoid to pneumonia and measles.

The winter of 1864–65 was exceptionally brutal. Snow piled against the prison walls. The Chemung River froze, and many men housed in tents perished from exposure. Frostbite and hypothermia became common causes of death. The prison lacked sufficient blankets, wood, and heating for its inmates. Reports from surviving prisoners describe wearing rags, sleeping on bare ground, and watching fellow inmates die in their sleep overnight.

Elmira's mortality rate reached nearly 25%, one of the highest among Union-run prison camps. Of the 12,123 Confederate soldiers held there, over 2,900 died. Many of them were buried in nearby Woodlawn National Cemetery, in mass graves or small plots marked by simple stones.

Two of those buried there were **James Upshur Cardwell** and **Joseph B. Cardwell**, both Virginians from the same regiment—the 26th Virginia Infantry. Their deaths at Elmira reflect not only personal tragedy but the larger suffering inflicted by institutional neglect.

The camp's commandant was Major Henry V. Colt, a cousin of firearm inventor Samuel Colt. He had no previous experience managing a large military facility and struggled to enforce order or improve conditions. While some officials blamed Colt for the excessive death toll, most historians believe he was simply overwhelmed by the scale of the crisis and constrained by bureaucracy.

The Surgeon General of the United States, Joseph K. Barnes, conducted inspections of Elmira and found its conditions abysmal. He noted overcrowding, medical shortages, and disease—but systemic change was slow to arrive. Some historians have debated whether Elmira's conditions constituted deliberate neglect. Edwin M. Stanton, the Secretary of War, received numerous reports detailing the misery within the camp but took little action to alleviate it.

There is no definitive proof that Elmira's high death rate was intentional, but in practice, the failure to act amounts to criminal negligence by modern standards. The Confederacy's infamous Andersonville Prison—known for its even higher death rate—often receives more attention, but Elmira's suffering was not far removed in scale or cause.

Despite the harshness of the environment, prisoners attempted to maintain morale. Some wrote letters to loved ones—if they could obtain paper. Others carved wooden trinkets, created playing cards, or formed makeshift bands. Chaplains occasionally held religious services. Still, the monotony and despair of daily existence in a freezing, disease-ridden enclosure wore down most inmates.

The psychological impact was lasting. Men who survived Elmira often suffered from lingering health problems. Diaries from prisoners describe the horror of watching bunkmates die nightly and the trauma of surviving conditions worse than many battlefields.

Elmira closed in July 1865, shortly after the end of the war. The surviving prisoners were released, and the camp was dismantled. The site of the prison itself is now a residential neighborhood, but its memory endures thanks to the work of local historians and the preservation of Woodlawn National Cemetery, where thousands of Confederate dead—including the two Cardwell men —are interred.

The cemetery features a monument erected in 1937 by the United Daughters of the Confederacy. Each year, memorial events are held to honor the dead. While debates about the Confederacy continue in American cultural memory, these graves are widely regarded as sites of solemn reflection rather than political statement.

Elmira stands as one of the most tragic Union-run prisons of the Civil War. Hastily constructed, poorly maintained, and fatally mismanaged, it became a place of torment for thousands of Confederate soldiers, including two members of the Cardwell family. Their deaths—like those of nearly 3,000 others—are a sobering reminder of how war can crush not only armies but the individuals caught in their path.

In remembering Elmira, we honor more than the victims—we acknowledge the failures that led to their suffering and recommit to preserving the dignity of those who, even in captivity, endured the harshest consequences of a nation divided. Photo Credits[1,2]

Camp Morton Military Prison
Indianapolis, Marion County, Indiana

Photo UPM.1: *Prisoners at Camp Morton, Indianapolis, Indiana.*
Circa 1863

During the American Civil War, the rapid and overwhelming capture of thousands of Confederate soldiers forced the Union Army to convert existing civilian and military sites into improvised prison camps. One such site was Camp Morton, located in Indianapolis, Indiana. Originally constructed as the Indiana State Fairgrounds, and later used as a training ground for Union volunteers, Camp Morton became a prisoner-of-war camp in early 1862. Over the course of the war, more than 15,000 Confederate soldiers were confined there.

Though not as notorious as Andersonville or Elmira, Camp Morton came to embody the harsh, often hastily arranged, and poorly supplied reality of Civil War imprisonment. For the Cardwell family, the site holds particular significance: William C. Cardwell and John Ray Cardwell both endured incarceration there. Their survival offers a human window into one of the North's most active—but often overlooked—POW camps.

Camp Morton was named for Oliver P. Morton, Indiana's wartime governor and a staunch supporter of the Union. In 1861, he designated the Indianapolis fairgrounds as a military training facility. But that use changed abruptly after the Union victory at Fort Donelson in February 1862. With more than 12,000 Confederate soldiers captured in a single campaign, Camp Morton was hastily repurposed to house the influx of POWs.

The site was enclosed by a twelve-foot wooden stockade, and inside were rows of wooden barracks, latrines, a hospital, and mess halls. Originally intended to house around 3,000 men, the camp frequently held twice that number. The Union command struggled with overcrowding, disease prevention, and the basic logistics of feeding and sheltering thousands of prisoners.

Life inside Camp Morton was grim. Confederate inmates suffered through cold Indiana winters, poor sanitation, and limited medical care. Especially during the winter of 1862–63, illnesses such as pneumonia, smallpox, typhoid fever, and dysentery spread quickly. By the end of the war, approximately 1,700 Confederate prisoners had died within the camp's walls.

Despite these conditions, Camp Morton was sometimes regarded as less brutal than other Union prisons. Civic organizations—including Indianapolis churches and women's relief societies—occasionally provided blankets, food, and spiritual support. Prisoners organized worship services, carved wooden crafts, and played music to pass the time. A small number performed light labor or worked in prison shops.

Two men bearing the Cardwell surname were confined at Camp Morton —**William C. Cardwell** and **John Ray Cardwell**—both of whom survived. Though they were captured at different times and places, their experiences reflect the broader range of challenges faced by Confederate prisoners in Northern custody.

William C. Cardwell, a soldier in Company B, 53rd Tennessee Infantry, was captured at the fall of Fort Donelson on 16 February 1862. He was among the first wave of Confederate prisoners sent to Camp Morton during its earliest and deadliest phase of operation, when the camp was overcrowded and poorly equipped to handle mass incarceration. While many of his fellow Tennesseans succumbed to disease or exposure, William survived. After several months in captivity, he was exchanged on 28 August 1862 at Vicksburg, Mississippi, under a formal prisoner exchange agreement. He returned to Smith County, Tennessee by 1870. After that, his trail goes cold; no further military or burial records have been found.

John Ray Cardwell, of Company H, 6th Kentucky Mounted Infantry, was captured during Morgan's Raid—a bold Confederate cavalry incursion into Indiana and Ohio during the summer of 1863. On 19 July 1863, during the Battle of Buffington Island, Union forces surrounded and overwhelmed Morgan's command as it attempted to retreat across the Ohio River. Over half of the 1,900 Confederate raiders were captured, including Private John Ray Cardwell. He was briefly imprisoned at Camp Douglas in Chicago before being transferred to Camp Morton, where he remained until his release in 1865. After the war, he returned to Hopkins County, Kentucky, where he lived out the remainder of his life.

Camp Morton was administered by the Department of the Ohio, and throughout the war, its command changed hands multiple times. Several officers had little or no experience in running a detention facility, though conditions at the camp were often deemed better than those at other sites due to local oversight and public attention. Still, overcrowding and disease remained chronic problems.

After the war, Camp Morton was decommissioned and the wooden barracks were dismantled. The grounds were eventually developed into a residential neighborhood. No physical trace of the camp remains today. The Confederate dead, originally buried at Greenlawn Cemetery, were later moved to Crown Hill Cemetery in Indianapolis. There, beneath a simple monument known as the Confederate Mound, lie the remains of over 1,600 Confederate prisoners who died in captivity. The inscription reads:

"In memory of the Confederate soldiers who died at Camp Morton and lie buried here."

Though less well-known than larger or more controversial Union prison camps, Camp Morton was a central part of the Midwest's wartime infrastructure. For William C. Cardwell and John Ray Cardwell, it was a place of suffering—but also survival. Their experiences highlight not only the physical hardships of imprisonment but also the resilience and endurance of men caught in the machinery of war far from home.

Their names, preserved in military registers and family memory, offer a glimpse into the quiet toll that war exacted behind prison walls. For every man who perished in confinement, others survived—often through a mixture of chance, toughness, and timely release. Let their stories, especially those like the Cardwell brothers in arms, remain part of the Civil War's enduring human narrative. Photo Credit[1]

Point Lookout POW Camp
St. Mary's County, Maryland

Photo UPL.1: *Point Lookout POW Camp, St. Mary's County, Maryland. The rectangular area in the upper right shows the POW Camp with structors and tents. The Union hospital is at the lower left.*

On a narrow peninsula at the confluence of the Chesapeake Bay and the Potomac River, Point Lookout, Maryland, served as one of the largest and most crowded Union prison camps during the American Civil War. From 1863 to 1865, the Point Lookout Prisoner-of-War Camp held more than 50,000 Confederate soldiers, more than any other Federal prison.

Despite its size and notorious overcrowding, Point Lookout's mortality rate was lower than other Union camps like Elmira and Camp Douglas. For the Cardwell family, Point Lookout stands out as a rare chapter of survival. Six Cardwell men were imprisoned here, all of whom endured harsh conditions and lived to see the war's end. Their experiences offer a compelling contrast to the high death tolls seen at other sites like Alton and Elmira.

Point Lookout had long served as a strategic location for both military and medical purposes. Located in St. Mary's County, Maryland, it was a site of Union operations early in the war due to its location at the southern tip of the state and its access to waterways. In 1862, the Union Army established Hammond General Hospital on the peninsula to treat wounded Union soldiers.

Following the Battle of Gettysburg in July 1863 and other large-scale engagements, the number of captured Confederate soldiers dramatically increased. To accommodate the influx, the Union converted land adjacent to the hospital into a prisoner-of-war camp. The first group of Confederate POWs arrived in July 1863, and over the next two years, Point Lookout would become one of the largest military prisons in the North.

Point Lookout was unique among Civil War prison camps in that it had no permanent wooden stockade at first. Instead, the camp was an open-air enclosure surrounded by a 12-foot-high wooden fence and patrolled by sentries. The prison camp occupied about 30 acres of the peninsula and was bounded by Chesapeake Bay on one side and the Potomac River on the other, limiting escape routes.

The camp was designed to hold 10,000 prisoners, but by the end of 1864, it held nearly 20,000 men. The overcrowding was extreme. Most prisoners lived in tents year-round, exposed to the sweltering summer heat and freezing winter winds coming off the water. Shelter was inadequate, and many tents were overcrowded, with four to five men squeezed into spaces designed for two.

Though Point Lookout did not match the shocking mortality rates of Elmira or Camp Douglas, conditions were still extremely harsh. Disease, exposure, malnutrition, and sanitation issues plagued the camp.

Food rations were insufficient and poorly prepared. Many prisoners suffered from scurvy, dysentery, and chronic diarrhea. Medical facilities were limited, and Confederate prisoners were not given access to the nearby Union hospital.

Perhaps the most notorious issue was exposure to the elements. The Chesapeake climate could be brutal. In the winter, the wind blew off the water and made even mild temperatures feel icy cold. Prisoners were denied adequate blankets or clothing, especially late in the war.

Despite these conditions, prisoner morale at Point Lookout varied. Some accounts describe prayer meetings, chess games, and writing letters home. Small black-market exchanges occurred between prisoners and guards, although these were forbidden. The psychological burden, however, was immense—especially for those held for months or even years.

Point Lookout's most notable distinction in the Cardwell family story is that all six Cardwell men held there survived. This sets it apart from camps like Elmira, Douglas, and Alton, where Cardwell deaths occurred.

Brothers Thomas Logan Cardwell and James Jesse Cardwell both served in the 8th Kentucky Cavalry, enlisting together on 10 September 1862. Their unit rode under the command of General John Hunt Morgan and participated in the famed Raid into Indiana and Ohio during the summer of 1863.

James Jesse Cardwell was captured at Wheeling, Ohio, on 20 July 1863. Initially sent to Fort McHenry, Maryland, he was later transferred to Point Lookout, arriving on 01 November 1863. According to his service records, James remained in captivity for over a year before being paroled on 10 February 1865.

His older brother, Thomas Logan Cardwell, was captured a few days later on 26 July 1863 at the Battle of Salineville, Ohio, the final engagement of Morgan's Raid. He was sent to Camp Douglas in Chicago, where he endured harsh conditions for over 18 months. On 10 February 1865—the very same day his brother James was paroled from Point Lookout—Thomas arrived there as a new transfer. In an ironic and involuntary coincidence, the brothers crossed paths at the camp, though under reversed circumstances. Thomas was released just two weeks later, on 24 February 1865, but was captured a second time near Knoxville, Tennessee, on 26 April 1865, and confined briefly in a Union holding facility at Nashville until his final release on 11 May 1865.

All other Cardwell men imprisoned at Point Lookout served in Virginia Confederate units. Their full biographies are detailed in the chapter on Confederate Veterans of Virginia in Brothers in Grey, but a brief overview is provided here to illustrate their collective experience at this notorious federal prison.

Patrick Henry Cardwell, a private in Company D, 1st Virginia Artillery, enlisted on 20 May 1861, one of the earliest enlistments among the Cardwells. He was captured the day after the Battle of Gettysburg, on 05 July 1863, and sent to Point Lookout, arriving during what many historians consider the prison's worst period. In a surprising turn of events, Patrick took the Oath of Allegiance to the United States on 17 February 1864 and, on that same day, enlisted in the 1st Regiment, United States Veteran Volunteer Infantry (U.S.V.V.I.), Company E. This regiment, composed of former Confederate soldiers who had pledged loyalty to the Union, served primarily in non-combat, garrison, and security roles, often guarding prisons and federal installations. Patrick survived the war and is one of the rare Cardwell men who served in both the Confederacy and the Union.

Josephus A. Cardwell, a private in the Virginia Heavy Artillery (Campbell Battery), was captured on 05 April 1865 at the Battle of Amelia Springs, part of the final retreat from Richmond. He arrived at Point Lookout on 13 April 1865 and was paroled 69 days later, on 21 June 1865—one of the shortest documented imprisonments among the Cardwell men.

George Drinker Cardwell, a veteran of the Goochland Light Artillery, had already served over two years before being captured at the Battle of Sailer's Creek on 06 April 1865, just days before Lee's surrender. Like thousands of Confederate soldiers taken during that final week, he was sent to Point Lookout, where he remained until 26 June 1865, when he took the Oath of Allegiance and was paroled.

Charles Wesley Cardwell, later known nationally as the Last Surviving Confederate Veteran of Virginia in the 1940s, enlisted in the 20th Battalion, Virginia Heavy Artillery shortly after turning seventeen in February 1865. He saw combat only once, at the Battle of Farmville on 06 April 1865, where he was captured. He was sent to Point Lookout, like so many of Lee's retreating forces, and was paroled on 24 June 1865. His youth at the time of capture and his later public identity as a Confederate veteran added symbolic weight to his survival and long postwar life.

Together, these narratives offer a unique window into the role Point Lookout Prisoner-of-War Camp played in the final chapters of Confederate military service. The Kentucky brothers—captured in 1863 and converging at the same facility in 1865—and the Virginians, taken in the waning days of the Confederacy, represent two distinct waves of Confederate incarceration: the early captures during bold raids and the mass surrenders that came with the Confederacy's collapse.

The relatively high survival rate for these men reflects not only the lesser lethality of Point Lookout compared to other camps, but also possibly the timing of their imprisonment—many arriving after the worst conditions of 1863 had passed.

The prison was guarded by Union troops stationed at Fort Lincoln, built nearby to oversee both the hospital and the POW camp. Accounts of brutality by guards exist, but they are less severe than in places like Camp Douglas. Union troops were rotated regularly, and though discipline was firm, there were fewer reports of arbitrary executions or severe punishments.

However, Point Lookout's reputation was far from gentle. Some prisoners alleged that guards shot men attempting to cross invisible lines or denied water as punishment. Others cited religious and racial discrimination. Many of these claims are difficult to verify, but they reflect the emotional and physical intensity of life within the camp.

Roughly 3,384 Confederate soldiers died at Point Lookout between 1863 and 1865. The mortality rate was about 8%, lower than the national average for Civil War POW camps, but still devastating.

Those who died were buried in the Confederate Cemetery near the camp, where the Point Lookout Confederate Memorial now stands—a 25-foot obelisk erected in the early 20th century. The names of the dead are inscribed on bronze plaques, a somber tribute to men far from home. Luckily, there are no Cardwell men buried there.

After the war ended in April 1865, Point Lookout continued operating for a few more months as prisoners were paroled or exchanged. By mid-1865, the site was decommissioned. The tents and barracks were removed, and the area returned to civilian use.

Today, the site is part of Point Lookout State Park, operated by the Maryland Park Service. Visitors can walk the grounds, view reconstructed Civil War-era buildings, and pay their respects at the Confederate cemetery. Interpretive signs and occasional living history events provide educational opportunities.

The legacy of Point Lookout is complex. While not as deadly as Elmira or Andersonville, it was still a place of suffering and deprivation. For the Cardwells who passed through its gates, it marked a crucible of endurance—a place they survived, but likely never forgot.

Point Lookout's role in the Civil War was vast and consequential. As the largest Union prison, it witnessed more human confinement than any other camp. While the conditions were harsh, and death a constant presence, its survival rate was relatively higher than some of its counterparts—offering a small measure of hope amidst the misery.

For the Cardwell family, Point Lookout holds a unique place in history. Six men entered, and six men emerged—a record unmatched in any other Union prison where their kin were held. Their resilience, perhaps bolstered by unit cohesion, timing of capture, or sheer luck, is a testament to their strength and endurance.

As historians continue to reassess Civil War memory and the treatment of prisoners on both sides, Point Lookout remains a symbol of both the cruelty and survivability of wartime imprisonment. For descendants and researchers alike, its story is essential. Photo Credit[1]

Surrendered vs. Captured
Understanding the Difference

As the American Civil War drew to its inevitable conclusion in the spring of 1865, Confederate armies across the Southern states were forced to surrender —not just individuals captured in battle, but entire commands, brigades, and armies. These surrenders were not isolated, spontaneous acts; they followed a pattern of formal negotiation, followed by disarmament, parole, and release. The distinction between being captured during active combat and being surrendered as part of a larger force at the war's end is a crucial one—both practically and symbolically. For many Southern soldiers, including numerous men of the Cardwell family, surrender meant returning home without imprisonment, but with the enduring weight of defeat and uncertainty.

This chapter explores the final Confederate surrenders of 1865, the terms and conditions imposed, the Union's procedures for handling surrendered men, and the criteria used for their release. It also examines how these events differed fundamentally from standard wartime captures and what this means for interpreting the service and postwar experiences of those Cardwell men who were paroled rather than imprisoned.

A War in Collapse: The Spring of 1865

By March 1865, the Confederate States of America was in visible decline. The Union Army had taken Richmond, Confederate supply lines were broken, and General William T. Sherman had devastated Georgia and the

Carolinas. The Confederate army—once a feared fighting force—was fragmented, underfed, and struggling with desertion.

Major surrenders occurred in waves:

• **09 April 1865**: General Robert E. Lee surrendered the Army of Northern Virginia to Ulysses S. Grant at Appomattox Court House, Virginia.

• **26 April 1865**: General Joseph E. Johnston surrendered the Army of Tennessee and associated commands to Sherman at Bennett Place, North Carolina.

• **04-26 May 1865**: Confederate forces in Alabama, Mississippi, Louisiana, Texas, and Indian Territory surrendered in turn, many under the command of Generals Richard Taylor, Edmund Kirby Smith, and others.

These surrenders were negotiated not as mass incarcerations but as honorable disbandments. Union leadership, particularly Grant and Sherman, emphasized magnanimity. The Confederates were not to be treated as criminals but as men defeated in battle, and allowed to return home, provided they agreed to the terms of surrender.

The Mechanics of Surrender: Disarmament and Documentation

When a Confederate force formally surrendered, the following steps generally took place:

1 Stacking of Arms:

Soldiers were ordered to form ranks and march to a designated site, often a road or field, where they were told to stack their rifles and deposit ammunition. Artillery pieces were also surrendered where applicable. Officers gave up their swords and revolvers, though some were permitted to retain sidearms as part of negotiated terms.

2 Issuance of Parole:

Each surrendered soldier was required to sign or receive a parole pass, typically on printed cards prepared by Union clerks. These parole documents served two purposes: to formally record that the soldier had surrendered, and to guarantee his safe passage home. A standard parole might read:

"The bearer, [Name], a soldier in the Army of the Confederate States, having surrendered to the United States forces, is hereby paroled and permitted to return to his home and remain undisturbed."

3 Record Keeping:

Union officers recorded names, ranks, units, and home counties. These lists were later transcribed and submitted to Washington to help track the demobilization of the Confederate armies and ensure compliance.

4 Non-Imprisonment:

Crucially, surrendered Confederate soldiers were not taken to prison camps on the most part. They were allowed to leave after surrendering arms and pledging not to take up arms against the United States again. In many cases, Union soldiers even shared rations with their former enemies.

Length of Detention and Return Home

Most surrendered soldiers were held only for a few days to two weeks at most. The delay depended on how fast Union officers could process parole papers and ensure security in the area. During this time, Confederate troops were confined to camp near the surrender site and quartered in makeshift bivouacs. Once paroled, many men walked hundreds of miles home, often in groups, lacking transportation and dependent on local civilians or Union relief stations for food and shelter.

In contrast, captured soldiers—those taken during combat operations—were marched under guard, placed in rail transport, and sent to established POW camps such as Camp Douglas, Elmira, or Point Lookout. These men were held for months to years, often in deplorable conditions, and many died in captivity.

Criteria for Release

The primary requirement for release was compliance with the terms of surrender, namely:

- Surrender of arms and equipment
- Swearing or accepting the parole terms
- Promise not to bear arms against the United States

There was no loyalty oath required at this stage (those came later during Reconstruction). Instead, parole was based on the honor system, and most Confederate soldiers accepted it. Officers and enlisted men alike were released under similar conditions, though some higher-ranking officers were required to report to Union authorities at designated intervals.

Those who refused parole or were captured outside of the surrender agreements were treated as standard POWs and sometimes imprisoned until late 1865.

Units vs. Individuals: How Surrender Happened

Surrender at the end of the war was almost always by unit, not by individual choice. When a commander agreed to terms, his entire brigade, division, or army followed. Soldiers had no say in the matter and could not opt out. In rare cases, men fled prior to the official surrender, hoping to avoid Union custody, or joined guerrilla bands.

Surrendered Cardwell Men: A Distinct Pattern

It is clear that a majority of the Cardwell men recorded as POWs were not captured in battle, but rather surrendered as part of their units at war's end, typically in April or May 1865.

These surrenders were formal, non-combative, and part of mass demobilizations. In contrast, Cardwell men like Joseph B. Cardwell and James Upshur Cardwell, captured earlier in the war and held at Elmira, died in prison—a fate avoided by those surrendered late in the conflict. Surrendered men returned home, demoralized but alive.

Post-Surrender Realities

Many surrendered soldiers faced hardships upon returning home. Their lands were often ruined, their families displaced, and their political rights uncertain. Yet, their ability to return directly home—without enduring long imprisonment—meant that surrendered men often re-entered civilian life more quickly than those released from Northern prison camps months or years later.

Some faced harassment during Reconstruction, especially in areas with strong Unionist presence. However, their parole papers often protected them from arbitrary arrest, at least initially. In time, former Confederate soldiers were required to take additional oaths of allegiance if they wished to vote or hold office.

Conclusion

The closing months of the Civil War were marked not by chaos, but by a relatively orderly surrender of Confederate forces—a process that spared thousands of men from extended imprisonment. For many Cardwell men, this meant a peaceful laying down of arms and an honorable return to civilian life. Their names appear not in the death registers of Northern prisons, but in the lists of paroled veterans—men who had fought, endured, and accepted defeat with dignity.

The distinction between capture and surrender is crucial to understanding the final chapter of their military service. While captured Cardwells died in places like Elmira, the surrendered Cardwells survived, rebuilt their lives, and left descendants who today preserve their legacy.

This duality—between suffering and death in prison and release on parole—marks a powerful distinction between the Confederate Cardwell men that became Prisoners of War, and a poignant reminder of how war's end was not the same for every man.

Confederate POW Camps

Several Union Cardwell veterans were taken prisoner during the Civil War, yet the details of their confinement remain murky. This ambiguity highlights a broader issue with Confederate prisoner-of-war (POW) facilities: a widespread lack of standardized recordkeeping, especially in the war's later years.

Unlike the more centralized and bureaucratically managed Union prisons, many Confederate camps operated with minimal documentation, inconsistent oversight, and little regard for future accountability. Furthermore, some prisoners were held only temporarily in makeshift facilities—rural stockades, local jails, or captured supply depots—before being transferred or exchanged. Others simply disappeared into the decentralized prison network, with no definitive account of their location or fate. These record gaps make it difficult to trace the exact circumstances faced by some Union Cardwells who were captured in combat. What is known, however, is that any time spent in Confederate captivity came with significant risk.

Poor sanitation, inadequate food, overcrowding, and disease were common across prison sites like Andersonville, Danville, and Florence. Even those fortunate enough to survive captivity often returned home with lasting physical and emotional scars. Against this backdrop, the limited records of Cardwell Union POWs serve as both a research challenge and a stark reminder of the war's human toll.

Andersonville Prison

Photo CA.1: *A drawing of Andersonville Prison by Thomas O'Dea, former prisoner*

Photo CA.2: *Andersonville prisoners and tents, southwest view showing the dead-line,*
August 17, 1864

Located in the pine-covered hills of southwestern Georgia, Camp Sumter—
better known as Andersonville—emerged in 1864 as the Confederacy's
desperate answer to its growing prisoner problem. Conceived as a purpose-
built facility to relieve overcrowded prisons in Richmond, it quickly devolved
into one of the most infamous prison camps of the Civil War. Over its brief
14-month lifespan, Andersonville came to symbolize the extremes of wartime
suffering, disease, and death. For Union soldier Dennis A. Cardwell of
Kentucky, it was a place of hardship survived. For Confederate-turned-pris-
oner William C. Cardwell of Tennessee, it was where his life came to a
tragic end.

Andersonville was established in February 1864 on 26 acres of farmland
near the small Georgia town for which it would be named. Surrounded by a
fifteen-foot high stockade wall and patrolled from guard towers every few
dozen yards, the camp had no barracks or formal shelter for its inmates. The
interior was open ground, exposed to the elements. Prisoners slept on the
earth itself, often digging shallow "shebangs" or lean-tos made from scraps of
wood, blankets, and clothing. Designed to hold 10,000 men, the prison
swelled to over 32,000 by midsummer, turning it into a human sea of misery.

It was into this environment that Private William C. Cardwell arrived in early 1864. Born around 1840 in Grainger County, Tennessee, William had grew to age in Sevier County after his family relocated there from Grainger County, Tennessee. He and his younger brother Clisby Austin Cardwell both enlisted in the Union Army, serving with loyalty to their home state. On 10 May 1862, William enlisted as a private in Company G of the 6th Tennessee Infantry. The regiment served in various engagements across Tennessee and surrounding regions. However, William's service ended not in battle but in captivity. He was captured by Confederate forces near Knoxville on 05 February 1864—just weeks before Andersonville opened.

Transferred quickly to the new facility, William was admitted to the prison hospital shortly after his arrival. Like many others, he likely arrived already weakened by travel, poor rations, and exposure. Medical care at Andersonville was primitive at best: the "hospital" was a crude, overcrowded area with no real buildings—just tents or open ground, where the sick lay untreated, waiting for death or survival. On 27 March 1864, after only a short time in the camp, William succumbed to the conditions. His cause of death was not recorded, but it was likely due to the common afflictions that claimed thousands—scurvy, dysentery, or pneumonia. He was buried on the camp grounds, now part of Andersonville National Cemetery, one among the nearly 13,000 Union dead interred there. His name and service are preserved on his grave marker and in the records of the National Park Service.

While William's war ended in captivity, another Cardwell man—Dennis A. Cardwell of Kentucky—managed to survive. Born about 1842 in Oldham County, Dennis enlisted as a private in Company B of the 6th Kentucky Infantry. The regiment saw action in many major engagements of the Western Theater, including Stones River and Chickamauga. It was at the latter, during the brutal fighting near the Georgia-Tennessee border, that Dennis was captured on 20 September 1863.

Initially held at one of several temporary Confederate prison sites, Dennis was eventually transferred to Andersonville in early 1864, becoming one of the earliest waves of Union soldiers to enter the camp. By this time, Andersonville was already buckling under its own weight. The small stream that ran through the center of the compound was used for drinking, bathing, and waste disposal. The overcrowding worsened by the day. Rations consisted mostly of cornmeal and the occasional piece of rancid meat. Disease spread without resistance.

Survival often depended on a combination of physical health, mental resilience, and sometimes, simple luck. Prisoners who could band together in small groups had better chances—sharing food, digging shelters, and supporting one another. Dennis somehow endured the worst months of the camp's operation, including the deadly summer of 1864. In December of that year, a prisoner exchange was finally authorized, and Dennis was among the fortunate few paroled and returned to Union lines.

He returned to Kentucky a changed man but managed to rebuild a life in the postwar years. Settling in Jefferson County, he married, raised a family, and lived until 1885. His name is not carved on any prison monument, but his survival ensured that the memory of Andersonville was passed down through the quiet endurance of those who lived it.

Though vastly different in outcome, the fates of William and Dennis Cardwell intersect in the long shadow of Andersonville. They were not related by immediate family, but their experiences mirror the war's strange, often tragic symmetry—two men bearing the same surname, caught in the same vortex of war, yet entering the same infamous prison.

Andersonville's cruelty was not the product of malice alone. Captain Henry Wirz, the prison's commandant, repeatedly pleaded with Confederate authorities for more supplies and medical aid, but by 1864 the South was already collapsing. Trains could not deliver food. Medicine was scarce. Even lumber to build shelters was nearly exhausted. Inmates froze in winter and sweltered in summer, their bodies wasting away from malnutrition. In the end, Andersonville became more than a prison—it became a symbol of a war that had gone on too long and consumed too much.

Following the war, Wirz was tried by a military tribunal and executed for war crimes in one of the most controversial trials in U.S. history. The camp itself fell into ruin but was eventually preserved as a site of national remembrance. Today, the Andersonville National Historic Site includes not only the original cemetery but also the National Prisoner of War Museum, which honors American POWs from all conflicts.

Few physical remnants remain of the stockade that once held thousands of men, but the stories endure. For the Cardwell family, those stories are anchored in the very real lives of William and Dennis. One died far from home, buried under a Georgia sky; the other returned home and tried to move forward. Together, their experiences speak not just to the horrors of a single camp, but to the broader human cost of the Civil War.

Their biographies appear in full in the chapters on Union veterans of Kentucky and Tennessee, respectively. The legacy of their service—and the suffering they endured—remains an essential part of the larger Cardwell family history and the enduring memory of Andersonville itself. Photo Credits[1,2]

BATTLE CASE STUDIES

THIS SECTION OF THE APPENDIX—TITLED *BATTLE CASE STUDIES*—IS dedicated to a focused examination of key Civil War engagements in which members of the extended Cardwell family are known to have fought. While the primary biographies throughout this work have detailed individual military service, this chapter moves from the personal to the tactical, placing these men within the broader movements of their respective regiments on the battlefield.

The aim is not only to honor their participation but to reconstruct the likely circumstances they faced during the chaos of war. These reconstructions are based on an extensive review of official records, regimental histories, after-action reports, and battlefield maps. In most cases, the specific companies and regiments of each man are known. While the individual experiences of privates and noncommissioned officers often went unrecorded in the official archives, their broader actions can be reasonably inferred through the documented movements of their units.

Each case study identifies the known Cardwell men who fought in a particular battle, sorted by Union and Confederate service. We trace their assignments to specific brigades, divisions, and corps, examining how those formations were deployed and what roles they played during the battle's key phases. By understanding the terrain, command structure, timing of engagement, and known casualties, we can develop a grounded view of where each man likely stood—and how he may have fought or fallen.

It should be noted that this appendix does not offer a comprehensive treatment of every battle in which a Cardwell participated. Many served in lesser-known engagements or skirmishes for which detailed records are incomplete or nonexistent. Instead, this chapter highlights a select handful of major battles—those for which reliable unit histories and battlefield documentation allow for confident reconstruction. These entries represent a cross-section of the war's major theaters and give voice to the military experience of the Cardwell family through some of its most defining conflicts.

The first entry in this chapter focuses on the Battle of Shiloh, one of the war's bloodiest and most pivotal early encounters in the Western Theater. The actions of eight Cardwell men—four Confederate and four Union—are explored in the context of their respective regiments' roles during the two days of savage fighting in April 1862. Through these profiles, we seek to bring clarity to a murky battlefield, and to place individual sacrifice in its rightful place within the larger sweep of history.

The actions of each man featured in the case studies within this section are explored in greater detail than their individual biographies found throughout these two volumes.

Battle of Shiloh

The Battle of Shiloh, fought on April 06 and 07, 1862, near Pittsburg Landing in southwestern Tennessee, was the first major and bloody clash in the Western Theater of the American Civil War. Over two days of intense and chaotic fighting, Union forces under Major General Ulysses S. Grant withstood a surprise Confederate assault led by General Albert Sidney Johnston and General P.G.T. Beauregard. The engagement resulted in nearly 24,000 total casualties and shocked the nation with its ferocity. Among the tens of thousands who fought were several men bearing the surname Cardwell, serving on both sides of the conflict. Their presence on the battlefield provides a rare lens into the complex and personal nature of the Civil War, in which kinship and geography often split families between blue and gray.

This case study explores the likely placement and battlefield actions of Cardwell men known to have participated in the Battle of Shiloh. Each man is examined in the context of his unit's role in the battle, drawing from regimental reports, battlefield positions, and known service records.

* * *

CONFEDERATE

Sergeant Benjamin M. Cardwell - *Company K, 24th Regiment, Alabama Infantry (CSA)* **- Wounded in Action**

Benjamin M. Cardwell entered the Confederate Army as a seasoned veteran, having previously served as a non-commissioned officer during the War with Mexico. His enlistment on 13 August 1861 in Talladega County, Alabama, led to his appointment as 2nd Sergeant in Company K of the 24th Alabama Infantry, CSA—a regiment composed primarily of central Alabama men and mustered into service in the summer of 1861. His early leadership role likely stemmed from his prior military experience and reputation in the community.

When the 24th Alabama Infantry was committed to the field, it was quickly drawn into the Confederate push into Kentucky, although the real test of the regiment came at the Battle of Shiloh on April 06–07, 1862. Assigned to General Gladden's Brigade, the 24th Alabama was thrust into the fierce fighting on the morning of April 06 as part of the Confederate offensive that caught Union forces by surprise near Pittsburg Landing in Hardin County, Tennessee.

During the chaos of the early hours of Shiloh, Benjamin was wounded in action, though the precise nature of his injury is not recorded in surviving documents. The regiment saw bitter close-quarters fighting in the thick woods and fields as they attacked Union encampments and pushed Federal forces back toward the Tennessee River. With the loss of their brigade commander, General Adley Gladden, and mounting casualties, the brigade was tested to its limits. For Benjamin, the experience would have been one of the most harrowing of his life—a mixture of leadership responsibility and survival amid one of the bloodiest engagements of the war.

Despite the regiment's valor, the Confederate failure to secure a decisive victory at Shiloh marked a turning point in the Western Theater. Benjamin survived his wounds and returned to duty, continuing to serve in the grueling campaigns that followed. Later in the war, he was also associated with Company I of the 44th Mississippi Infantry, CSA, although the timeline and nature of that service remain unclear.

His company, like many others in the 24th Alabama, endured severe hardships throughout the war. Of the seventy-six original members of Company K, only seven returned home in good health. Many were lost to battle, disease, and deprivation, and those who did survive carried physical and emotional scars for the rest of their lives.

Benjamin lived until 16 August 1910, passing away at the age of eighty-nine in Shelby County, Alabama. He was laid to rest at Bay Springs Baptist Church Cemetery. His wartime service—particularly his wounding at Shiloh—stands as a testament to the endurance and sacrifice of those who served on the front lines of the Confederacy during its earliest and bloodiest campaigns.

* * *

Private Henry Jefferson Cardwell – *Company B, 35th Regiment, Tennessee Infantry (CSA)*

Henry Jefferson Cardwell was born around 1823 in Lone Mountain, Claiborne County, Tennessee, was the son of Francis G. Cardwell and Judah (Lebow) Cardwell. As a young man, he relocated with his family to Warren County, Tennessee, where they are listed in both the 1830 and 1840 U.S. Census records. On 06 September 1861, at the age of thirty-eight, Henry enlisted as a Private in Company B of the 35th Tennessee Infantry, CSA, near McMinnville. His enlistment came during the formative months of the Confederate Army of Tennessee, as units were rapidly organized to defend Southern interests in the Western Theater.

The 35th Tennessee was quickly drawn into one of the bloodiest engagements of the war: the Battle of Shiloh, fought on 06–07 April 1862 in Hardin County. The regiment was part of Brigadier General Patrick R. Cleburne's brigade, which played a central role in the early Confederate assault on the Union camps. Cleburne's men advanced through dense underbrush and swampy terrain under heavy fire, facing determined resistance from Union forces. Although there is no explicit mention of Henry's individual actions at Shiloh in his surviving service records, his enlistment date places him squarely within the ranks during the battle. The 35th suffered significant casualties during the two days of fighting, as Cleburne's brigade was repeatedly thrown into the thickest part of the engagement.

Just over a month later, on 24 May 1862, Henry was discharged from Confederate service. The reason for his discharge is not recorded, but there is no indication that he re-enlisted later in the war. He raised a large family in Warren County and was active in religious and educational institutions until his death in 1895.

* * *

Private James Wesley Cardwell - *Company E, 5th Tennessee Infantry (CSA)*

James Wesley Cardwell enlisted as a Private in Company E of the 5th Tennessee Infantry, CSA, on 13 June 1861 at Camp Brown in Obion County, Tennessee. At the time, the 5th Tennessee was organizing for Confederate service, and like many regiments raised in West Tennessee, it was soon thrust into the heart of early Western Theater campaigns. Company E, composed primarily of local volunteers, formed part of a regiment that would become heavily involved in the Battle of Shiloh less than a year later.

Although James's Confederate service records are limited, they do confirm his enlistment and later discharge at Camp Brown. The exact date and reason for his discharge remain unclear. However, the absence of evidence does not necessarily mean absence from battle. Given the timing of his enlistment and the fact that the 5th Tennessee Infantry was present and actively engaged at Shiloh on 06–07 April 1862, it is possible—if not probable—that James was still with his unit during the campaign.

At Shiloh, the 5th Tennessee fought under Brigadier General Alexander P. Stewart's Brigade within General John C. Breckinridge's Reserve Corps. On the first day of battle, Stewart's men were heavily engaged in the Confederate attacks against Union positions near the center and right of the Federal line. These engagements included brutal fighting in rugged terrain and dense woodland, often at close range and under confusing circumstances. The brigade played a crucial role in pushing back Union forces before nightfall halted the advance. On the second day, the 5th Tennessee held the line during the failed Confederate counterattacks, suffering significant casualties as Federal reinforcements pressed forward.

If James was present at Shiloh, as the timing of his enlistment suggests, he would have faced the ferocity of this large-scale conflict—one that claimed over 23,000 casualties in just two days and forever changed perceptions of the war's scope and brutality. The silence of his record after Camp Brown may reflect a common reality for many Confederate soldiers—lost paperwork, unrecorded furloughs, or discharge due to illness or injury that was never formally documented.

Following the war, James relocated to Kentucky, where he spent the remainder of his life. He died on 18 March 1893 in Owensboro, Muhlenberg County, and was buried in that region. Though little is known of his specific role at Shiloh, his enlistment and the known actions of his regiment place him in proximity to one of the war's most significant and devastating early battles. His likely participation deserves recognition as part of the broader story of the Cardwell family's sacrifices during the Civil War.

* * *

2nd Lieutenant Joseph Leonard Cardwell - *Company H, 24th Tennessee Infantry (CSA)*

Joseph Leonard Cardwell enlisted on 15 July 1861 as a Private in Company H of the 24th Tennessee Infantry, CSA, mustering in at Coffee County. Demonstrating leadership and local regard, he was elected 2nd Lieutenant on 24 March 1862.

The 24th Tennessee Infantry served in Brigadier General Patrick R. Cleburne's Brigade, one of the most respected and hard-fighting formations in the Confederate Army of Tennessee. At the Battle of Shiloh on 06–07 April 1862, Cleburne's brigade was thrust into the thick of combat early in the first day, advancing through swamps and underbrush under intense Union fire. The 24th Tennessee played a central role in the attack on the Union left, where Confederate forces sought to drive Grant's army from Pittsburg Landing. It was during these harrowing assaults that Cleburne's men—though aggressive and determined—suffered devastating losses. The brigade sustained the highest casualty rate of any Confederate brigade at Shiloh.

Although Joseph's compiled service records do not explicitly confirm his presence at Shiloh, the date of his promotion just days before the battle and the fact that he was still active in the regiment strongly suggest that he participated in the action. He would have entered Shiloh a newly elected officer, leading men from his home region through the chaos of one of the Civil War's most ferocious battles.

Just a few weeks after Shiloh, on 02 May 1862, the 24th Tennessee Infantry underwent a reorganization, part of a larger army-wide reshuffling following the passage of the Confederate Conscription Act. During this process, Joseph Leonard Cardwell was left without a command, a common outcome as officer positions were re-voted or reassigned. No further Confederate military records have been found for him, and it appears he returned home thereafter.

Following the war, Joseph resumed civilian life in Smith County, Tennessee, where he raised a large family and lived into the 20th century. In his later years, he resided with his daughter in Wilson County, where he passed away in 1925 at the age of ninety. His longevity and quiet postwar life stand in contrast to the fury of Shiloh in which he likely fought as a young officer. His service in Cleburne's brigade places him within one of the most storied units of the Army of Tennessee, and his early leadership role highlights the trusted position he held within his community during a time of national upheaval.

* * *

Private Lee Roy P. Cardwell - *Company F, 17th Tennessee Cavalry (CSA)* - **Wounded in Action**

Lee Roy P. Cardwell was born around 1840, in McNairy County, Tennessee, from a family with strong Confederate ties, as evidenced by the service of his brothers William Y. Cardwell and Thomas D. Cardwell in Forrest's cavalry. His Civil War service, while somewhat fragmented across several Confederate cavalry units, includes clear and compelling evidence that he participated in the Battle of Shiloh and was wounded there. According to Lee Roy's Confederate Pension Application, filed on 25 January 1900, he first entered Confederate service in the spring of 1861. His early involvement likely placed him within the mounted ranks of Company F, 17th Tennessee Cavalry (Newsome's), a precursor to other more formally organized units.

While his earliest muster rolls are elusive, official records confirm that he was formally enlisted as a Private on 01 June 1863 at Tuscumbia, Alabama, in Forrest's Alabama Cavalry. However, earlier service records from the Confederate War Department list him under Company G, 1st Confederate Cavalry, with an enlistment date of 09 January 1862 at Henderson, Tennessee. This timing and location strongly suggest his presence during the crucial months leading up to the Battle of Shiloh. By March 1862, Lee Roy was on detached duty at Corinth, Mississippi, under the orders of General P.G.T. Beauregard—an assignment that positioned him directly within the staging area of Confederate forces preparing for the assault at Pittsburg Landing.

Cavalry elements operating around Corinth, particularly under the command of General Nathan Bedford Forrest, were tasked with vital reconnaissance, screening, and flanking operations in advance of and during the

Battle of Shiloh on 06–07 April 1862. Lee Roy's detachment, working near Corinth, would have likely been swept into these maneuvers as Forrest's men harassed Union forces and scouted their positions along the Tennessee River. It was during the course of this engagement that Lee Roy suffered his first known wound—a gunshot injury to the foot that shattered three bones. According to his pension affidavit, the injury was severe enough to require a three-month furlough for recovery.

The wound not only affirms his presence at Shiloh but places him in the thick of the fighting, either during one of Forrest's aggressive cavalry actions on the flanks or in close-quarters engagements along the Union picket lines. Forrest's cavalry, though relatively small in number at Shiloh, played a bold and mobile role, conducting probing attacks and protecting the Confederate rear during their eventual withdrawal.

Following his return to duty, Lee Roy's cavalry service continued, including confirmed stints in Forrest's Alabama Cavalry and the 18th Tennessee Cavalry (Neal's), CSA. His commitment to the mounted arm of the Confederate service spanned much of the war, culminating in a second and more serious wound at the Battle of Harrisburg (Tupelo) in July 1864. He died in 1917 and was buried at Bells Chapel Cemetery in Gibson County.

Lee Roy P. Cardwell's presence at Shiloh, validated through his firsthand account and the documented wound he suffered, reflects the critical though often under-recognized contributions of cavalry troops in that battle. His life after the war—shaped by his wounds, his survival, and his devotion to duty—adds to the legacy of the Cardwell family's deep involvement in the Confederate cause.

* * *

Private Silas H. Cardwell - *Company H, 24th Tennessee Infantry (CSA)*

Silas H. Cardwell enlisted as a Private in Company H of the 24th Tennessee Infantry, Confederate States Army, on 27 June 1861 in Nashville, Tennessee. He joined alongside his older brother, William L. Cardwell, both volunteering for service as Tennessee aligned itself with the Confederacy. Silas was promoted to the rank of Corporal by January 1862, a reflection of his early conduct and reliability within the regiment, though the exact date of promotion is not noted in the surviving records.

The 24th Tennessee Infantry became part of the Army of Mississippi under General Albert Sidney Johnston and later General P.G.T. Beauregard. It was assigned to Brigadier General Patrick R. Cleburne's Brigade, a division noted for its strict discipline and combat effectiveness. By the spring of 1862, the 24th was positioned for action in one of the largest battles of the Western Theater—Shiloh.

At the Battle of Shiloh, fought on 06–07 April 1862 in Hardin County, Tennessee, the 24th Tennessee Infantry was heavily engaged on the first day of combat. Cleburne's Brigade was ordered to advance early on the morning of 06 April as part of the initial Confederate assault. Fighting through rough terrain and thick underbrush near the eastern sector of the battlefield, Cleburne's men encountered stiff Union resistance and suffered high casualties in their attempts to dislodge Federal troops. The 24th, positioned near the brigade's center, endured punishing artillery fire and musket volleys as it attempted to press the attack. Although the brigade made some gains, it was ultimately repulsed in several areas and incurred some of the heaviest losses of any Confederate formation on the field.

Though Silas's records do not explicitly state his presence at Shiloh, his continued service through April and his discharge in May 1862 strongly suggest that he took part in the battle. By that point, he had already served for nearly ten months and was likely among the many Tennesseans who fought on familiar soil against the advancing Union army.

Following the harrowing engagement at Shiloh, Silas was discharged for disability on 25 May 1862 near Corinth, Mississippi—then a major Confederate supply and hospital center. While the nature of his disability is not documented, the timing and location of his discharge—just weeks after Shiloh—raise the possibility that the condition stemmed from wounds or illness related to the battle or its aftermath.

After the war, Silas transitioned to civilian life and became a practicing physician. He appears as "Dr. S.H. Cardwell" in the 1870 U.S. Census for Jackson County, Tennessee, residing alone and working as a medical doctor. This postwar career suggests a man of intellect and purpose who found a new path of service after the conflict. He later moved to Arkansas, where he died on 01 August 1913 in Hot Springs, Garland County. The exact location of his burial remains unknown.

Silas H. Cardwell's service at Shiloh—though not directly confirmed—is supported by the timeline of his enlistment and discharge. His participation in one of the war's most brutal early battles, followed by a life dedicated to medicine, reflects a legacy of duty, resilience, and healing in the shadow of war.

* * *

Private William G. Cardwell - *Company K, 6th Tennessee Infantry (CSA)* - Killed in Action

William G. Cardwell enlisted as a Private in Company K of the 6th Tennessee Infantry on 15 May 1861 at Jackson, Tennessee, the seat of Madison County. His company, known locally as "The Danes," was formed from residents of the area and became part of the original makeup of the regiment. The 6th Tennessee Infantry was assigned to Brigadier General Patrick R. Cleburne's Brigade, a unit that quickly earned distinction for its discipline and performance in battle, and would go on to become one of the most reliable Confederate commands in the Western Theater.

Shortly after enlistment, William was placed on sick furlough as of 28 July 1861, likely due to illness during the harsh early months of encampment and drill. He returned to active duty by early 1862, just in time for the regiment's first major test—what would become one of the Civil War's most infamous engagements.

At the Battle of Shiloh, fought on 06–07 April 1862 in Hardin County, Tennessee, the 6th Tennessee Infantry was engaged in brutal fighting as part of Cleburne's Brigade. On the first day, Cleburne's men launched early attacks in difficult terrain, repeatedly clashing with Federal lines under heavy fire. This unit played a crucial role on the Confederate right flank, pushing toward the Hornet's Nest and the Peach Orchard. Though the brigade made some gains, they suffered severe losses and were unable to dislodge entrenched Union troops. By the second day, the Confederates' initial advantage had eroded. Union reinforcements under General Buell arrived during the night, and on the morning of 07 April the tide turned in favor of the Union.

It was during this second day of combat, amid chaotic attempts by Confederate units to stem the Union counteroffensive, that William G. Cardwell was killed in action. His precise circumstances remain unknown, but given the timing and movements of his regiment, he likely died during fierce resistance along the southern flank near Pittsburg Landing—one of the final

Confederate efforts to maintain their ground before being forced to retreat toward Corinth.

The immense number of casualties and the hurried nature of burials at Shiloh make it likely that William was interred in a mass grave, a fate shared by thousands of soldiers on both sides. His loss came in one of the most pivotal and deadly battles of the war, a turning point that shattered any remaining illusions of a short conflict.

William G. Cardwell's sacrifice at Shiloh reflects the harrowing cost borne by early Confederate volunteers who faced modern warfare on their own soil. He was one of many young Tennesseans who gave their lives in service to their state, dying not far from home in a battle that would echo through the remainder of the war.

* * *

UNION

Private William Benjamin Cardwell - *Company C, 11th Kentucky Infantry (USA)*

William Benjamin Cardwell enlisted as a Private in Company C of the 11th Kentucky Infantry (Union) on 23 September 1861 in Butler County, Kentucky. At age 20, he joined the ranks of a regiment that would go on to earn distinction in some of the hardest-fought campaigns of the Western Theater. The 11th Kentucky was composed primarily of volunteers from southern Kentucky, a region sharply divided in its loyalties, and its men were among those who fought to preserve the Union in a contested border state.

In early 1862, the 11th Kentucky Infantry was stationed at Calhoun and Camp Wickliffe before being ordered to join General Ulysses S. Grant's forces in preparation for an offensive into Tennessee. By late March, the regiment was in transit to the staging area at Pittsburg Landing. There, on 06–07 April 1862, they took part in the Battle of Shiloh, one of the war's first massive engagements and a brutal initiation for the young Kentucky regiment.

During the battle, the 11th Kentucky was attached to General Thomas L. Crittenden's Division under the command of General Alexander McCook. On the first day of fighting, the regiment was hurried into position to bolster the faltering Union lines. The suddenness of the Confederate assault threw many units into disarray, but the 11th Kentucky held firm despite intense fire and confusion. On the second day, with the arrival of Union reinforcements under General Buell, the 11th participated in the counteroffensive that ultimately drove the Confederates from the field. The regiment sustained casualties but earned praise for its steadiness under pressure.

Although William's personal service records do not mention a specific wound at Shiloh, it is noted that he fell ill and was hospitalized in Nashville just a month later, in May 1862. This may have resulted from the physical toll of the campaign and the poor conditions common in camp following major engagements. Nevertheless, he returned to duty and was promoted to Sergeant on 15 August 1862, a sign of his reliability and leadership potential.

Throughout the remainder of the war, William served with distinction, fighting at Stones River, Lookout Mountain, Kenesaw Mountain, and through the Atlanta Campaign. Despite another bout of illness in September 1863 that again sent him to a hospital in Nashville, he maintained continuous active service until his honorable discharge on 16 December 1864 at Bowling Green, Kentucky.

After the war, William returned to Butler County, Kentucky, and applied for a federal invalid pension in 1876, reflecting the lingering effects of his wartime illnesses. He raised fifteen children, with his first wife and later remarried after her passing. William became a successful farmer and merchant in Aberdeen, eventually acquiring 217 acres and entering the retail trade in 1884. Despite limited formal schooling, he was widely respected for his business sense, community leadership, and strong moral convictions.

William Benjamin Cardwell died on 01 May 1926 in Ohio County, Kentucky, at the age of 84. He was buried in Morgan-Smith Cemetery in Butler County. His enduring contributions on and off the battlefield reflect the steadfast spirit of Kentucky Unionists who helped turn the tide of the Civil War.

* * *

Conclusion

The Battle of Shiloh represents more than just a clash between two opposing armies—it epitomizes the divided nature of the Civil War itself. In this engagement, Cardwell men stood on both sides of the line, hailing from Tennessee, Kentucky, and Alabama.

These Cardwell men did not merely serve in units that happened to be at

Shiloh; they were present at some of the most pivotal and bloodiest moments of the battle. Whether advancing across Spain Field, holding the line at the Hornet's Nest, or relaying messages under fire, their experiences form a microcosm of the broader national conflict. In examining their actions, we see not only the historical facts of regimental movement and casualty reports but also the deeply human dimension of war: kin divided by ideology, drawn together by courage, and remembered through the places they stood and fell.

Battle of Stones River

Cardwell Men at the Battle of Stones River

The Battle of Stones River, fought from 31 December 1862, to 02 January 1863, near Murfreesboro, Tennessee, was one of the most brutal and strategically significant engagements of the Civil War's Western Theater. It pitted the Union's Army of the Cumberland, under Major General William S. Rosecrans, against General Braxton Bragg's Army of Tennessee. Though tactically inconclusive, the battle ended with Bragg's withdrawal and bolstered Northern morale following the disastrous Union defeat at Fredericksburg weeks earlier. President Abraham Lincoln later remarked that the Union's hard-won position at Stones River had been vital to sustaining the national cause during a critical moment.

Within this maelstrom of violence, nine Cardwell men—some brothers, others distant cousins—served on opposite sides of the battlefield. Their participation at Stones River reflects the broader national tragedy of a war that divided families and communities, especially in border states like Kentucky and Tennessee. These men fought in regiments that were heavily engaged in the battle's most intense fighting. Several served in front-line infantry units of the Army of the Cumberland or the Army of Tennessee, both of which sustained heavy losses.

For some, the battle would mark the end of their lives. For others, it was just one in a long series of punishing campaigns that defined their war experience. Whether Union or Confederate, the Cardwell soldiers at Stones River bore witness to the chaos, sacrifice, and endurance that characterized this pivotal winter clash. Their individual stories help humanize the scale of the battle, grounding its sweeping movements in the lived experiences of those who stood in its path.

* * *

UNION

Private Dennis A. Cardwell, Jr. - *Company B, 6th Kentucky Infantry (USA)*

Dennis A. Cardwell, Jr. enlisted in Company B of the 6th Kentucky Infantry (Union) on 26 October 1861 at Louisville, joining the ranks just weeks after his older brother, Henry C. Cardwell. Though administrative records offer little detail about his presence in the regiment through much of 1862, he was unquestionably active by the winter campaign of that year. The 6th Kentucky was part of the 1st Brigade, 1st Division, XXI Corps, a force that would play a critical role at the Battle of Stones River near Murfreesboro, Tennessee, fought from 31 December 1862 to 02 January 1863.

The regiment entered the battle as part of Colonel William B. Hazen's brigade, a unit that would earn lasting distinction for its stand in the area later known as "Hell's Half Acre." During the desperate fighting of the first day, Hazen's brigade was ordered to hold the center of the Union line as Confederate forces launched a massive assault aimed at rolling up the Union right flank. It was in this cauldron of battle that Dennis and his brother Henry took their places alongside the rest of the 6th Kentucky.

As wave after wave of Confederate attacks tore through the Union line, Hazen's brigade held firm around the Nashville Pike and the Round Forest, making it one of the few parts of the Federal line not to collapse under pressure. The cost was terrible: the brigade suffered hundreds of casualties. Among them was Henry C. Cardwell, who was killed in action on the battlefield. Dennis survived the engagement, though the trauma of the fight—and the loss of his brother—must have left an indelible mark.

Though Stones River was technically inconclusive, the Union Army held the field after Confederate General Braxton Bragg's withdrawal, turning the battle into a strategic victory. For Dennis, the ordeal was not over. Later in 1863, he was captured at the Battle of Chickamauga and endured imprisonment at the notorious Andersonville Prison. Remarkably, he survived both the battlefield and the horrors of captivity.

Following the war, Dennis returned to civilian life in Jefferson County, Kentucky. He married and had four children, but died relatively young in 1882. His widow later received a pension for his Union service. His final resting place remains unknown, but his record stands as testimony to the sacrifices endured by those who survived Stones River.

* * *

Corporal Henry C. Cardwell - *Company B, 6th Regiment, Kentucky Infantry (USA)* - Killed in Action

Henry C. Cardwell enlisted as a Private in Company B of the 6th Kentucky Infantry (Union) on 23 September 1861 in Louisville, Kentucky, at the age of nineteen. He was among the early recruits of the newly formed regiment and was later joined by his younger brother, Dennis A. Cardwell Jr., who enlisted the following month. Henry proved himself a capable soldier and was promoted to Corporal on 4 June 1862, serving with distinction through the unit's early campaigns.

By late December 1862, the 6th Kentucky Infantry had been assigned to Colonel William B. Hazen's brigade in the 1st Division of the XXI Corps, Army of the Cumberland. As the Union army moved toward Murfreesboro, Tennessee, Henry's regiment was positioned near the critical east-west corridor of the Nashville Pike—a focal point of the coming battle. On the morning of 31 December 1862, Confederate General Braxton Bragg launched a surprise assault on the Union right, attempting to rout the Federal forces before they could fully deploy.

In the midst of this chaos, Hazen's brigade was ordered to hold a key position at the Round Forest, an area that became one of the bloodiest fields of the battle. The 6th Kentucky Infantry fought tenaciously to repel repeated Confederate attacks. It was in this desperate struggle that Corporal Henry C. Cardwell was killed in action, one of the many Union soldiers who fell in the brutal fighting on the first day.

Though the Union army ultimately held the field, the cost was staggering.

Stones River would become one of the bloodiest battles of the war in terms of percentage of casualties. Henry's body was likely buried near the place where he fell. He does not appear on the roster of identified burials, and it is presumed he now lies among the unknown soldiers interred at Stones River National Cemetery in Rutherford County, Tennessee. His sacrifice, along with so many others, helped secure a crucial strategic victory for the Union in the Western Theater.

* * *

Sergeant William Benjamin Cardwell - *Company C, 11th Kentucky Infantry (USA)*

William Benjamin Cardwell enlisted as a Private in Company C of the 11th Kentucky Infantry (Union) on 23 September 1861 in Butler County, Kentucky. His regiment became part of the Army of the Cumberland and saw continuous service in the Western Theater. By the time of the Battle of Stones River, fought from 31 December 1862 to 02 January 1863, William had already been promoted to Sergeant and was serving in a regiment known for its resilience and reliability under fire.

The 11th Kentucky Infantry was assigned to Colonel Samuel Beatty's brigade in the 2nd Division of the Left Wing of the Union army. As the battle commenced, the Confederate army launched a powerful assault on the Union right, attempting to shatter the Federal line before it could fully form. Beatty's brigade, including William's regiment, was positioned on the Union left and initially avoided the early chaos. However, as the Union right crumbled, the 11th Kentucky was ordered forward to reinforce the collapsing line and help stabilize the center.

Over the next three days, the regiment fought in punishing engagements, holding defensive positions and repelling repeated attacks. On 02 January 1863, the 11th Kentucky participated in the Union counteroffensive that ultimately forced Bragg's army to retreat. Although William's personal service records do not detail his actions during the battle, his confirmed presence with the regiment and promotion status suggest that he played an active role in the campaign.

The Battle of Stones River was one of the bloodiest of the war, with casualties approaching 25% for both sides. It was a hard-fought but critical Union victory, securing Middle Tennessee and boosting morale following the disaster at Fredericksburg. William survived the battle and continued to serve with distinction in numerous campaigns through the end of his enlistment.

* * *

CONFEDERATE

Private Benjamin Jones Cardwell - *Company A, 33rd Alabama Infantry (CSA)*

Benjamin Jones Cardwell enlisted as a Private in Company A of the 33rd Alabama Infantry, CSA, on 25 December 1862 at the age of eighteen. His enlistment came during a critical phase of the war, as the Confederate Army of Tennessee prepared for renewed action against Union forces advancing into Middle Tennessee. The 33rd Alabama, organized earlier that year, had already been bloodied in combat and was part of Brigadier General Zachariah C. Deas's Brigade in Major General Benjamin F. Cheatham's Division.

Though a late December enlistee, Benjamin joined his regiment just days before the opening shots of the Battle of Stones River, fought from 31 December 1862 to 02 January 1863 near Murfreesboro, Tennessee. While it is possible he was still acclimating to camp life or undergoing limited training, it is more likely—given the urgency of Confederate preparations—that he was sent forward to reinforce the regiment in time for the fighting.

Deas's Brigade, including the 33rd Alabama, played a significant role in the initial Confederate assault on the morning of 31 December. The brigade helped spearhead the attack on the Union right flank, pushing back Federal forces in intense, close-quarters combat. As part of this push, the 33rd Alabama advanced across rough terrain and open fields under heavy fire. The regiment sustained severe casualties during the action, but its determined efforts contributed to the early Confederate gains.

For Benjamin, the battle would have been a baptism by fire. Whether positioned in reserve or directly engaged, he would have witnessed firsthand the chaos, noise, and terror of full-scale battle. Stones River marked his first major engagement, and the experience undoubtedly left a lasting impression on the young soldier.

He survived the bloody contest, which ended in a strategic Union victory, and continued to serve with the 33rd Alabama through the brutal campaigns that followed. His survival through nearly three years of continuous fighting is a testament to both his endurance and fortune. He died in 1927 in Coffee County, Alabama.

* * *

2nd Sergeant Benjamin M. Cardwell - *Company K, 24th Alabama Infantry (CSA)*

Benjamin M. Cardwell, a seasoned veteran of the Mexican-American War, entered Confederate service at the age of 41 and was quickly appointed 2nd Sergeant in Company K, 24th Alabama Infantry, CSA, upon his enlistment on 13 August 1861 in Talladega County. Drawing on prior military experience, Benjamin helped lead a newly formed regiment composed of men from across central Alabama. The 24th was soon attached to the Army of Tennessee and committed to the Western Theater's hardest campaigns.

By the end of 1862, Benjamin and the 24th had already seen combat at Shiloh—where he was wounded in action—and were engaged again in full force during the Battle of Stones River. As part of Brigadier General Zachariah Deas's Brigade in Withers' Division of Polk's Corps, the 24th Alabama played a central role in the Confederate assault on the Union right flank during the early morning hours of 31 December 1862.

The brigade advanced through thick woods and uneven terrain, driving Federal troops back in fierce and often hand-to-hand combat. The 24th Alabama was heavily engaged throughout the morning and early afternoon, suffering significant losses while pressing the attack. Benjamin, already a veteran of two wars, would have experienced the full measure of the chaos and brutality that characterized Stones River. His leadership role as a non-commissioned officer likely placed him close to the action, helping to rally his men under withering fire.

Although the Confederate assault achieved temporary gains, the battle ended in a costly stalemate that forced the Southern army to retreat. Benjamin survived the carnage, one of only a handful from his company who would see the war's end. The 24th Alabama remained in continuous service through the Atlanta Campaign and ultimately surrendered with the Army of Tennessee in 1865.

* * *

Private James R. Cardwell – *Company D, 26th Tennessee Infantry (CSA)*

James R. Cardwell enlisted as a Private in Company D, 26th Tennessee Infantry, CSA, on 04 July 1861 in Knoxville. After enduring capture and imprisonment at Camp Douglas following the surrender at Fort Donelson, he was exchanged in April 1862 and returned to active duty with his regiment. His brother, William , also captured at Fort Donelson, died in captivity in May 1862. By the time of the Battle of Stones River, James was a seasoned soldier, having already experienced combat and the brutal realities of a Northern prison.

At Stones River, the 26th Tennessee was part of General James Rains's Brigade within McCown's Division of Hardee's Corps. On the morning of 31 December 1862, the brigade was placed on the Confederate right, launching a furious assault against the Federal left. McCown's men, including the 26th Tennessee, struck with surprise and overwhelming force, breaking through Union lines and sending several brigades into retreat. Fighting was intense and sustained, marked by close combat in the wooded terrain and repeated Union counterattacks.

The 26th Tennessee Infantry sustained heavy losses—110 men killed, wounded, or missing—testament to the ferocity of their charge and the resistance they encountered. James was among those who survived the carnage, bearing witness to a battle that would prove to be one of the bloodiest of the war. Although the Confederates made significant early gains, they failed to achieve a decisive victory and ultimately withdrew from the field.

James continued to serve with his regiment through Chickamauga, where he was wounded in action, and remained in the ranks until the final Confederate surrender in North Carolina. He was promoted to 2nd Sergeant prior to Chickamuga. His endurance through multiple campaigns and the loss of his brother in captivity underscored the heavy personal toll of the war. He returned to Grainger County, Tennessee, after the conflict and lived there until his death in 1911.

* * *

Private John D. Cardwell - *Company A, 33rd Regiment, Alabama Infantry (CSA)*

John D. Cardwell enlisted as a Private in Company C of the 33rd

Alabama Infantry on 27 February 1862, just months before the regiment was thrust into some of the fiercest fighting in the Western Theater. His brother, Benjamin Jones Cardwell, enlisted with the 33rd in December 1862 and served with him. The 33rd was part of Brigadier General Zachariah C. Deas's Brigade, assigned to Withers' Division of Polk's Corps in the Army of Tennessee. After enduring their first major combat at Perryville, the men of the 33rd soon found themselves preparing for another brutal engagement— Stones River.

At the Battle of Stones River, fought from 31 December 1862 to 02 January 1863, the 33rd Alabama played a prominent role in the Confederate assault on the Union right flank during the early hours of the first day. Deas's Brigade moved forward across difficult terrain, launching a coordinated attack meant to drive the Union forces back toward Murfreesboro. The fighting was vicious and often at close quarters, as the Confederates attempted to exploit gaps in the Federal line.

The 33rd Alabama sustained heavy casualties during this operation. Although exact losses by company are not recorded, the regiment as a whole suffered significantly, reflective of the high cost of the early Confederate successes on the first day of the battle. Despite these gains, the Confederates were unable to secure a decisive victory, and the bloody stalemate ended with a strategic Union advantage.

John D. Cardwell survived the carnage of Stones River and went on to fight at Chickamauga and throughout the grueling Atlanta Campaign before falling ill in 1864. His combat record during Stones River places him among those who endured some of the most intense fighting of the early Western campaigns. Though his later life remains obscure, his presence at Stones River stands as part of the legacy of sacrifice borne by the 33rd Alabama Infantry.

* * *

Corporal John Henry Cardwell – *Company D, 2nd Tennessee Infantry (CSA)*

John Henry Cardwell enlisted on 14 May 1861 at the age of 19, joining Company D of the 2nd Tennessee Infantry, CSA, at Hartsville in Trousdale County. The regiment was mustered into Confederate service at Lynchburg, Virginia, and initially assigned to General Beauregard's Brigade. At the First Battle of Manassas, the unit came under fire while guarding a strategic bridge, though it was not fully drawn into the main action. After nearly a year of service in Virginia, the regiment returned to Tennessee in early 1862 and was soon thrown into the brutal fighting at Shiloh, where it suffered devastating casualties.

By December 1862, John and the 2nd Tennessee were seasoned veterans. They entered the Battle of Stones River as part of the Army of Tennessee, positioned under the right wing of General Braxton Bragg's forces. The regiment, by then placed within General Patrick Cleburne's Division, saw intense fighting throughout the multi-day battle. Confederate forces launched an aggressive assault on the Union right flank during the early hours of 31 December, achieving initial breakthroughs. However, the Union army held firm, and both sides endured staggering losses in a contest marked by cold weather, dense terrain, and ferocious artillery fire.

Although John's individual records offer no remarks about Stones River, he was marked Present at the time, and it is almost certain he fought with his regiment during the engagement. The 2nd Tennessee, already diminished from earlier battles, sustained further casualties in the fighting around Murfreesboro, contributing to the Confederacy's eventual withdrawal. For soldiers like John, Stones River represented one of the most grueling tests of endurance in the Western Theater.

Following the battle, John continued to serve in numerous campaigns, including Chickamauga and the Atlanta Campaign. He was hospitalized with illness in Macon, Georgia, in July 1864, and no further military or civilian records are known. He does not appear in the 1870 census, suggesting he died during or shortly after the war—possibly as a result of the illness for which he was treated in 1864. His burial site remains unknown.

* * *

Private William L. Cardwell – *Company H, 24th Regiment, Tennessee Infantry (CSA)*

William L. Cardwell enlisted as a Private in Company H of the 24th Tennessee Infantry on 27 June 1862 in Nashville, Tennessee, alongside his younger brother, Silas H. Cardwell. Though his formal enlistment occurred after the Battle of Shiloh, some Confederate records suggest the possibility of pre-enlistment presence for men who joined informally or served in local militias prior to muster. Regardless, by late 1862 William was officially part of a battle-hardened regiment.

The 24th Tennessee Infantry, at the time of Stones River, was assigned to Cleburne's Division, Hardee's Corps, in the Army of Tennessee. When the battle began on 31 December 1862, the 24th played a significant role in the Confederate assault on the Union right flank. At dawn, they advanced through thick underbrush and uneven terrain, contributing to the surprise and initial success that drove Union forces back several miles. The terrain, winter cold, and intensity of fire made the action particularly grueling. The 24th engaged in close-quarters combat and came under heavy Union counterattacks as the battle dragged into the new year.

While no personal remarks appear in William's service file for this engagement, regimental histories confirm that his unit was heavily engaged throughout the battle. The 24th suffered substantial casualties, and survivors of the engagement emerged bloodied but intact. Stones River marked a turning point in the Western Theater, and for William, it was the first of many major battles he would endure.

He continued to fight in subsequent campaigns, including Chickamauga, Missionary Ridge, and the Atlanta Campaign. He was captured near Granny White Bridge during the Battle of Nashville on 10 December 1864 and later sent to Camp Douglas, where he remained until the war's conclusion. He took the Oath of Allegiance on 10 May 1865. His name does not appear in any known postwar documents, and his family is listed without him in the 1870 census. His final fate remains unknown.

* * *

Conclusion

The Cardwell men who fought at Stones River left behind no sweeping manifestos or official after-action accounts, but their service reveals the quiet courage and deep personal cost that marked this campaign. One fell in the opening hours of the battle and now lies, most likely, in an unmarked grave among the thousands who perished on the frozen fields of Murfreesboro. Another would be wounded in future battles, survive prison camp, and carry the physical and emotional burdens of the war for decades after the final surrender. Still others simply disappeared from the record, casualties perhaps not of bullets, but of sickness, privation, and the long shadow of war.

This chapter serves not only to document their presence at Stones River but to remind readers of the interwoven fates of soldiers caught in the deadliest conflict in American history. In telling their stories, we preserve more than individual legacies—we honor the human dimensions of a battle too often summarized by statistics and strategic outcomes. The Cardwells at Stones River, in life and in death, were part of a struggle that defined their generation and reshaped the nation they left behind.

Morgan's Raid

Morgan's Raid, the daring 1863 cavalry incursion into Indiana and Ohio led by Confederate General John Hunt Morgan, remains one of the most ambitious Confederate operations behind Union lines. For a small group of Cardwell men—related through blood, marriage, and regional ties—the raid marked the pinnacle of their Civil War service. In all, nine men bearing the Cardwell surname took part in this legendary expedition, placing them among the most committed cavalrymen of the war. Their stories, recorded through service records, pension applications, and postwar testimony, offer a window into both the audacity of Morgan's command and the resilience of these Southern horsemen. This studies is included for the unusual high number of Cardwell men, from diverse families, taking part in this historic cavalry raid.

The cavalry was the elite, mobile arm of Civil War forces, often tasked with dangerous reconnaissance, hit-and-run attacks, and deep incursions. Cavalry life demanded physical toughness, superb riding skills, and a willingness to face high casualties. A remarkable trend emerges when examining the Civil War service of men with the Cardwell surname: they were overwhelmingly drawn to the cavalry. Analysis of compiled military data shows that 46.9% of Confederate Cardwells and 39.7% of Union Cardwells served in cavalry units. This is well above national averages, which hover around 20% for Confederate forces and just 14% for Union troops. The unusually high participation rate suggests that the Cardwells—many of whom came from rural, mountainous areas in Kentucky, Tennessee, and Virginia—were comfortable on horseback, accustomed to rugged terrain, and culturally inclined toward the independence and prestige associated with cavalry service.

In this context, it is particularly significant that nine Cardwell men took part in or provided support for Morgan's Raid—one of the most daring and perilous cavalry operations of the entire Civil War. Unlike typical cavalry engagements, which involved supporting infantry or defending key terrain, Morgan's Raid involved hundreds of miles of travel through enemy territory with minimal supply support. The raiders faced relentless pursuit, dangerous river crossings, and overwhelming odds. These men must have known the dangers. That they still joined the mission speaks to a high degree of bravery, or at the very least, fierce loyalty to the Confederate cause and to General Morgan himself. Their individual biographies appear in the chapters corresponding to their respective states.

* * *

Private James Alexander Cardwell - *Company E, 1st Tennessee Mounted Infantry (CSA)*

James Alexander Cardwell, a native of Smith County, Tennessee, served in Ward's Regiment, officially designated as the 1st Tennessee Mounted Infantry. His role as a scout placed him in a vital position within Morgan's operations. On 10 May 1863, shortly before Morgan's Raid commenced, James was severely wounded at the Battle of Greasy Creek in Kentucky. Though he did not participate in the full raid due to his injuries, his scouting duties and attachment to Morgan's forces qualify him as a supporting figure in the broader campaign. His testimony, preserved in a detailed pension application, attests to his contribution and suffering.

* * *

Sergeant James Madison Cardwell - *Company E, 2nd Kentucky Cavalry (CSA)*

The older brother of Thomas Mumford, James Madison Cardwell had a more extensive career with Morgan's Cavalry. He was first captured in 1862 while acting as a civilian scout, possibly spying or aiding Morgan's men under cover. Later formally enlisted, he participated in Morgan's Raid and evaded capture, returning to Confederate lines. He remained active under General Nathan Bedford Forrest and was killed in action at Bull's Gap, Tennessee, on 13 November 1864.

* * *

Private James Jesse Cardwell - *Company C, 8th Kentucky Cavalry (CSA)* - **Wounded in Action and Captured**

James Jesse Cardwell, a native of Shelby County, Kentucky, enlisted in 1862 with his brother, Thomas Logan Cardwell. Captured during Morgan's Raid at Wheeling, Ohio, on 20 July 1863, James was later transferred to Fort McHenry and then to Point Lookout, one of the largest and most infamous Union POW camps. His service record indicate that he was treated for wounds, probably related to action during the raid. He remained imprisoned until February 1865. His postwar life took him westward to Missouri and Kansas, but his Civil War experience remained a defining chapter.

* * *

Private John B. Cardwell - *Company F, 9th Tennessee Cavalry (CSA)*

John B. Cardwell, also of Smith County, Tennessee, served alongside William in Company F. According to his 1911 Confederate pension application, John took part in several actions under Morgan's command, including the Battle of Milton and skirmishes at Snow's Hill and Mann's Hill in Tennessee. Though his exact path during the raid is uncertain, his affiliation with the 9th Tennessee Cavalry places him squarely in the orbit of Morgan's 1863 campaign. Illness forced his discharge, and he later hired a substitute to continue in his place.

* * *

Private John Ray Cardwell - *Company E, 4th Kentucky Cavalry (CSA) - Captured*

John Ray Cardwell, of Hopkins County, Kentucky, was captured at Buffington Island on 19 July 1863, confirming his role in the raid. He was first imprisoned at Camp Douglas, then later transferred to Camp Morton, though his post-capture records are fragmentary. His biography highlights the fate of many of Morgan's men who were overwhelmed as Union forces closed in along the Ohio River.

* * *

Private Thomas Logan Cardwell - *Company C, 2nd Kentucky Cavalry (CSA)* - Captured

Thomas Logan Cardwell, also of Shelby County, was captured at the Battle of Salineville on 26 July 1863, the final engagement of Morgan's Raid. His service records were misfiled under "F.L. Cardwell," a clerical error that obscured his history until clarified through research. He was imprisoned at Camp Douglas, then Point Lookout, and was later recaptured near Knoxville in 1865. He survived the war and lived a long life in Kentucky.

* * *

Private Thomas Mumford Cardwell - *Company E, 2nd Kentucky Cavalry (CSA)*

Thomas Mumford Cardwell enlisted at the age of sixteen in Morgan's original cavalry regiment, which became the 2nd Kentucky Cavalry. However, he was discharged for disability just three months later in December 1862 and did not take part in the 1863 raid. His short service underscores the challenges many young soldiers faced when adapting to the physical rigors of war.

* * *

Private William H. Cardwell - *Company F, 9th Tennessee Cavalry (CSA)* - Captured and Died in Captivity

Another member of Company F was William H. Cardwell. His experience was perhaps the most tragic of the Cardwells who rode with Morgan. Captured at Buffington Island, Ohio—one of the key battles during Morgan's Raid—William was imprisoned at Camp Douglas, Illinois, where he died of chronic diarrhea on 04 November 1864. He was one of the many Confederate prisoners who perished in the harsh conditions of Northern prison camps and was later reinterred at Oak Woods Cemetery in Chicago.

* * *

Private William Mankin Cardwell - *Company F, 9th Tennessee Cavalry (CSA)*

William Mankin Cardwell of Smith County, Tennessee, enlisted in Company F of the 9th Tennessee Cavalry, part of Morgan's cavalry division. Though specific details of his participation are scant, family records and pension affidavits confirm that he served under Morgan and took part in the early stages of the raid. William fell ill during the campaign and was sidelined, a fate not uncommon given the grueling pace and primitive conditions faced by the raiders. He survived the war and died in Alvin, Texas, in 1922, remembered as one of the older veterans of Morgan's men.

* * *

Legacy of Risk and Resolve

The participation of these nine Cardwell men in Morgan's Raid stands as a powerful testament to both their daring and their resolve. The raid itself, while ultimately a strategic failure, succeeded in its short-term goals: spreading fear through the North, tying up Union resources, and inspiring Southern morale. For the Cardwells, it offered an outlet for valor—but also led to imprisonment, permanent injury, and death.

What makes their collective story so remarkable is not just their kinship, but the calculated risk they all undertook. They joined a mission widely understood to be dangerous, one that crossed hundreds of miles deep into enemy territory. These were not conscripts or reluctant draftees—they were volunteers, men drawn to cavalry service and ready to endure its perils. Their choice to serve in Morgan's command reflects both the traditions of their region and the personal qualities of audacity, mobility, and endurance that cavalry life demanded.

As historians continue to study Civil War family networks, the Cardwell men of Morgan's Raid stand as a striking example of how kinship, geography, and cultural affinity shaped not only enlistment patterns but battlefield outcomes. Their names—now preserved through detailed biographies and primary records—remain part of the legacy of one of the most unforgettable cavalry actions in American history.

Battle of Chickamauga

Cardwell Men at the Battle of Chickamauga

The Battle of Chickamauga, fought from September 18 to 20, 1863, in northwest Georgia, marked one of the bloodiest confrontations of the American Civil War and the most significant Union defeat in the Western Theater. The battle pitted the Union Army of the Cumberland, commanded by Major General William Rosecrans, against the Confederate Army of Tennessee under General Braxton Bragg. In this pivotal engagement, a number of Cardwell men—fighting on both sides—found themselves caught in the maelstrom. This case study chronicles their service, units, and likely movements during the battle, drawing from surviving records and regimental histories to provide a comprehensive account.

* * *

UNION

Sergeant Anthony Warren Cardwell – *Company D, 5th Tennessee Infantry (USA)*

Anthony Warren Cardwell was a Union loyalist born in Grainger County, Tennessee, on 20 November 1836. He was the son of John Wesley Cardwell and Sarah (Smith) Cardwell. Before the war, his family had relocated to Roane County, Tennessee, where Anthony settled with his wife, Sarena Ellen Carter, and their growing family. His enlistment in Company D of the 5th Tennessee Infantry (U.S.) on 26 February 1862 at Barboursville, Kentucky, placed him among the many East Tennesseans who rejected secession and crossed into Kentucky to join the Union cause. Shortly after enlistment, he was promoted to 5th Sergeant.

The 5th Tennessee Infantry, composed primarily of East Tennessee Unionists, was formed under Colonel James T. Shelley and became part of the Army of the Ohio. Anthony served actively through much of 1862, taking part in regional guard duties and reconnaissance missions aimed at securing key terrain in Kentucky and Tennessee. In September of that year, he was hospitalized in Bowling Green for illness, later transferred to a hospital at Cumberland Gap, and reduced in rank likely due to his absence from duty.

By early 1863, he had returned to his regiment and saw his rank of Sergeant restored in March. That summer, the 5th Tennessee Infantry took part in the Tullahoma Campaign and subsequently joined operations under General Rosecrans in the lead-up to the Battle of Chickamauga. When that battle unfolded on 19–20 September 1863, Anthony was among the Union defenders in Brigadier General James G. Spears's Brigade, part of Major General Gordon Granger's Reserve Corps.

On the second day of the battle, Spears's men were rushed to the southern end of the Union line to reinforce the faltering positions near Snodgrass Hill. The 5th Tennessee helped fortify the position held by General George H. Thomas, who would famously earn the nickname "The Rock of Chickamauga" for his steadfast defense. The brigade's timely arrival helped prevent a complete Confederate breakthrough and allowed Union forces to make an organized withdrawal to Chattanooga. While the Union army suffered a tactical defeat, Spears's Brigade—and the East Tennessee men within it—played a crucial role in salvaging the Union position.

Anthony survived the battle and continued his service into 1864, participating in the early phases of the Atlanta Campaign. He fell ill again in June of that year and was hospitalized in Altoona, Georgia, and later in Chattanooga. He ultimately recovered and remained with his regiment until his honorable discharge at Nashville on 30 June 1865.

Anthony Warren Cardwell's wartime service exemplifies the courage and resilience of East Tennessee's Unionists—men who endured social division and geographic isolation to support the preservation of the United States. His presence at Chickamauga places him among those who stood in one of the fiercest defensive actions of the war, where the loyalty of soldiers like him helped hold the line when it mattered most.

* * *

Private Dennis A. Cardwell – *Company B, 6th Kentucky Infantry (USA)* - Captured

Dennis A. Cardwell was born around 1837 in Kentucky, part of a family with deep roots in the state. By the time of the Civil War, he was residing in Hart County and enlisted on 25 December 1861 at Camp Hobson (Munfordville), Kentucky, as a Private in Company B, 6th Kentucky Infantry, a regiment that would serve with distinction in the Union Army of the Cumberland. The 6th Kentucky was part of the famed "Orphan Brigade," although it had remained loyal to the Union—a significant point given that many Kentucky units had Confederate leanings.

By September 1863, the 6th Kentucky Infantry was assigned to the 3rd Brigade, 3rd Division, 21st Army Corps under Major General Thomas L. Crittenden. As part of this formation, the regiment marched into northwestern Georgia with the Army of the Cumberland during the Chickamauga Campaign. In the days leading up to the battle, the regiment endured long marches and difficult terrain while maneuvering into position to support a major Union advance into Confederate-held territory.

At the Battle of Chickamauga, fought from 19–20 September 1863, the 6th Kentucky found itself engaged in heavy fighting on the second day of the conflict. On 20 September, following the surprise Confederate breakthrough led by General James Longstreet, the Union line was fractured, and intense, confused fighting took place throughout the wooded battlefield. During this chaos, large portions of the Union right were overwhelmed and isolated.

It was amid this confusion and collapse that Private Dennis A. Cardwell was captured by Confederate forces. He became one of thousands of Union soldiers taken prisoner during the battle, which ultimately ended in a costly Confederate victory. His capture reflects the disarray and danger experienced by the men of the 6th Kentucky, who fought with courage but were caught in one of the most devastating defeats for the Union in the Western Theater.

Dennis was one of the first wave of Union prisoners confined to the infamous Andersonville Prison in Georgia, after he was treated at a Confederate hospital for his wounds. He was luckily paroled in December 1864. His survival through imprisonment and the remainder of the war attests to his resilience and perseverance under extremely difficult circumstances.

Following the war, Dennis A. Cardwell returned to Kentucky and resumed civilian life. His participation in the Battle of Chickamauga—and his experience as a prisoner of war—places him among the many Union soldiers who endured not only the physical hardships of the battlefield but also the psychological trials of capture and imprisonment.

* * *

Private John Preston Cardwell – *Company D, 2nd Tennessee Cavalry (USA)*

John Preston Cardwell was born on 28 April 1832 in Grainger County, Tennessee. Before the Civil War, he and his family relocated to Sevier County, Tennessee, where strong Unionist sentiment prevailed despite the broader Confederate leanings of the state. On 15 August 1862, Cardwell enlisted in Company D of the 2nd Tennessee Cavalry (Union), a regiment composed largely of East Tennesseans committed to preserving the Union.

The 2nd Tennessee Cavalry was attached to the Cavalry Corps of the Army of the Cumberland, commanded by Brigadier General Robert B. Mitchell. Leading up to the Battle of Chickamauga, Cardwell's unit was tasked with vital duties—screening the Union advance through north Georgia, conducting reconnaissance, and defending critical wagon trains from Confederate raids. The terrain and dense forests of the region made mounted action difficult, but their knowledge of the Appalachian landscape gave them an edge.

On 18 September 1863, the day before the major engagement at Chickamauga, the 2nd Tennessee Cavalry engaged in skirmishes with Confederate cavalry units under General Nathan Bedford Forrest. During the battle itself (19–20 September), the regiment operated on the Union flanks and rear areas, repelling enemy probes and gathering intelligence for Union commanders. While they were not at the center of the infantry bloodbath, their mobility and disruption of Confederate operations were critical to the army's ability to maintain communication and execute a retreat when the lines began to break.

Cardwell's service during the Chickamauga Campaign typifies the role of loyal Tennesseans who defied the Confederacy and took up arms for the Union. As an East Tennessee Unionist, his enlistment represented both a political and personal stand in the most divided region of the divided nation.

After the war, John Preston Cardwell returned to Sevier County, where he resumed his life as a farmer and raised a large family. He died in 1902 and was buried locally, remembered by his descendants as a man of principle and perseverance who served in a conflict that tore his home state apart.

* * *

CONFEDERATE

Private Benjamin Jones Cardwell – *Company A, 33rd Alabama Infantry (CSA)*

Born in Coffee County, Alabama, Benjamin Jones Cardwell entered the ranks of the Confederate army at a pivotal time in the war. Just eighteen years old, he enlisted on 25 December 1862 as a private in Company A of the 33rd Alabama Infantry. He followed in the footsteps of his older brother, John D. Cardwell, who had joined the same regiment earlier that year. Organized under Colonel Samuel Adams, the 33rd Alabama was a battle-hardened regiment formed primarily from south-central Alabama counties and quickly attached to the Army of Tennessee. The unit participated in nearly every major campaign in the Western Theater, including the ferocious Battle of Chickamauga in September 1863.

At Chickamauga, the 33rd Alabama served in Deas's Brigade, part of Hindman's Division within Lieutenant General James Longstreet's Left Wing of Bragg's Army of Tennessee. On the second day of battle—20 September 1863—Deas's Brigade was part of Longstreet's massive assault that famously broke through the Union center near the Brotherton Farm. This breakthrough was a turning point in the battle and led to one of the worst defeats for the Union in the Western Theater. The 33rd Alabama, along with other regiments in the brigade, charged into the thick woods and smoke-choked fields, engaging in brutal close-range combat against Union troops attempting to rally around Snodgrass Hill.

Though specific details of Benjamin's actions that day are not recorded, his presence in Company A during the regiment's aggressive participation suggests he was directly involved in the attack. The regiment helped overrun Union positions and was part of the larger Confederate force that drove back Federal troops in one of the rare Southern victories of the war. However, the cost was high—Deas's Brigade suffered significant casualties, and the fighting left the field littered with the dead and wounded on both sides.

Benjamin remained with the 33rd through the Chickamauga aftermath and the continuing campaigns in Chattanooga, Atlanta, and the Carolinas. His service in a regiment that saw nearly constant combat speaks to the endurance and fortitude required of Confederate infantrymen in the Western Theater. Surviving the chaos of Chickamauga was itself a testament to his resilience.

After the war, Benjamin returned to civilian life in Coffee County, Alabama, where he married, raised a large family, and lived out the remainder of his years. He died in 1927 at the age of 83. His wartime service, especially at Chickamauga, placed him at the center of one of the Confederacy's most significant victories, and his story adds to the broader legacy of the Cardwell men who served with distinction under the most harrowing conditions of the Civil War.

* * *

Sergeant Benjamin M. Cardwell – *Company K, 24th Alabama Infantry (CSA)*

A veteran of two wars, Benjamin M. Cardwell brought previous military experience into the Civil War, having served during the Mexican-American War. Born on 22 November 1820 in Henry County, Georgia, Benjamin was already a seasoned man by the time he enlisted as a 2nd Sergeant in Company K of the 24th Alabama Infantry on 13 August 1861 in Talladega County. His leadership and maturity likely influenced his immediate appointment as a non-commissioned officer, and he entered service just as the Confederate army was organizing its defense of the Western Theater.

The 24th Alabama Infantry was quickly engaged in the war's most violent clashes. After suffering significant casualties at Shiloh, where Benjamin was wounded in action, the regiment recuperated and refitted before continuing its role in Bragg's Army of Tennessee. The men of the 24th participated in the Battle of Murfreesboro (Stones River) in late 1862, and by September 1863, they were hardened veterans, ready for what would become the second-bloodiest battle of the Civil War—Chickamauga.

At Chickamauga, the 24th Alabama was part of Deas's Brigade in Hindman's Division, attached to Lieutenant General James Longstreet's Left Wing. On 20 September, the second and decisive day of the battle, Deas's Brigade helped spearhead Longstreet's surprise assault that broke the Union line near the Brotherton Cabin. This breakthrough marked a turning point in the battle and set in motion a chaotic Union retreat. Company K, including Sergeant Cardwell, was likely involved in this aggressive push. The men advanced through dense woods, attacking Union troops defending their line along the southern flank, and engaging in brutal close-quarter combat.

Though details of Benjamin's personal actions at Chickamauga are not recorded, the service record of his regiment makes it clear that he would have faced intense fire, thick smoke, and near-continuous fighting throughout the day. Deas's Brigade, including the 24th Alabama, contributed significantly to the Confederate victory, though the cost was staggering in both lives lost and injuries sustained. It was one of the few clear Confederate tactical victories in the Western Theater.

Benjamin survived this horrific battle and remained with the regiment through the remainder of the war, serving in the Atlanta Campaign, the Franklin-Nashville Campaign, and at Bentonville. His endurance through four years of hard campaigning is remarkable, especially considering that out of the original 76 men in his company, only 7 would return home healthy.

Following the war, Benjamin returned to civilian life in Alabama, living in Shelby and Baker Counties, and raising a large family. He was granted a Confederate pension in 1908, recognition of his faithful service and sacrifices. He died in Shelby County in 1910 at the age of 89, a survivor of two American wars, and a representative of the generation that endured both the nation's expansion and its bloody fracture.

At Chickamauga, Benjamin M. Cardwell stood with one of the hardest-fighting units in the Confederate army. His participation in that battle is a testament to his fortitude and the experience of the Alabama soldiers who faced overwhelming odds and fought through some of the most difficult days of the Civil War.

* * *

Sergeant James Madison Cardwell – *Company E, 2nd Kentucky Cavalry (CSA)*

James Madison Cardwell was born on 03 December 1841 in Mercer County, Kentucky, and served in one of the most battle-hardened Confederate cavalry units of the Western Theater—the 2nd Kentucky Cavalry. Originally organized as the 1st Kentucky Cavalry under General John Hunt Morgan, the unit was later redesignated the 2nd and continued operations under various commanders, including Morgan himself and, later, the formidable General Nathan Bedford Forrest.

By September 1863, James Madison Cardwell had risen to the rank of Sergeant, a reflection of his skill and reliability during the prior year's demanding campaigns. In the months following Morgan's Raid, the 2nd Kentucky Cavalry became part of Forrest's cavalry division and took part in the Chickamauga campaign, fighting alongside the Army of Tennessee. Forrest's cavalry was used with remarkable flexibility by Confederate commanders, particularly General Braxton Bragg, who relied heavily on Forrest for reconnaissance, raids, and flanking maneuvers.

During the Battle of Chickamauga, fought from 19 to 20 September 1863, Forrest's cavalry—including James's regiment—played a critical role on the Confederate right flank. On the morning of 18 September, Forrest led a sweeping cavalry engagement at Reed's Bridge and Alexander's Bridge to drive off Union forces guarding those crossings over Chickamauga Creek. These actions allowed Bragg's infantry to advance into position, unimpeded.

As the battle commenced, Forrest's cavalry dismounted and fought as skirmishers in heavily wooded terrain. On 19 September, the 2nd Kentucky Cavalry helped blunt Union attempts to flank the Confederate right. On 20 September, Forrest's forces were among the first to detect the gap in the Union line that would eventually be exploited by General James Longstreet's devastating attack. Forrest urged Bragg to act decisively—warnings that went unheeded until it was nearly too late.

Sergeant James Madison Cardwell was likely engaged throughout this series of intense and fast-moving cavalry fights. Forrest's troopers were both scouts and shock troops, alternately mounting swift raids and holding defensive lines. By the end of the second day, Forrest's cavalry was part of the force that pushed the retreating Union army toward Chattanooga.

The Battle of Chickamauga marked one of the last major Confederate victories in the Western Theater, and it elevated Forrest's reputation as a tactical genius. James Madison Cardwell's participation in that pivotal campaign underscores the close involvement of Kentucky-born cavalrymen in the Confederacy's most ambitious efforts in 1863. He remained in the ranks following Chickamauga and would ultimately be Killed in Action the following year at the Battle of Bull's Gap. Though he did not survive the war, his valor at Chickamauga and in other campaigns helped cement the reputation of Kentucky's Confederate cavalry as among the best in the Western Theater.

* * *

Sergeant James R. Cardwell – *Company D, 26th Tennessee Infantry (CSA)* - **Wounded in Action**

James R. Cardwell, a Private in Company D of the 26th Tennessee Infantry, fought with distinction at Chickamauga, where he sustained a serious wound that left a permanent mark on his life. Born on 23 September 1837 in Rockingham County, North Carolina, he moved with his family to Union County, Tennessee, after the death of his father, a War of 1812 veteran. James enlisted at Knoxville on 4 July 1861, alongside his younger brother William, both joining the newly formed 26th Tennessee Infantry.

Prior to Chickamauga, James had already endured the loss of his brother, who died of pneumonia while they were both held as prisoners of war at Camp Douglas following their capture at Fort Donelson in February 1862. Exchanged in April 1862, James rejoined his regiment and continued service through the bitter campaigns that followed.

By September 1863, the 26th Tennessee had been folded into Bushrod Johnson's Brigade in Hood's Division of Longstreet's Corps, Army of Tennessee. As the Confederate Army maneuvered to retake Chattanooga, James and his comrades marched into the dense woodlands along Chickamauga Creek. On 19 September, the regiment was heavily engaged in a series of disjointed and brutal firefights, but it was the next day, 20 September, that proved most consequential.

On that Sunday morning, the Confederate army launched a coordinated assault against the Union right flank. Johnson's Brigade, including the 26th Tennessee, was at the center of the Confederate breakthrough. The dense undergrowth and rolling terrain of the Chickamauga forest turned the battlefield into a chaotic maze of smoke, gunfire, and confusion. It was amid this maelstrom that James R. Cardwell was struck in the left side by grape shot, the projectiles tearing into his ribcage and inflicting a wound that would never fully heal.

James was pulled from the line and sent to a field hospital. His wound was later documented in his 1902 Confederate pension application, supported by a physician's statement and a sworn affidavit from comrade William N. Waller, who had seen James fall in action during the charge. The injury not only ended his active combat role but left him with chronic pain that would last until his death nearly fifty years later.

Despite the personal cost, Chickamauga was considered a rare Confederate victory in the Western Theater. The 26th Tennessee played a decisive role in the breakthrough that nearly crushed the Union center. For soldiers like James, the win came at a steep price—lost comrades, physical ruin, and psychological scars.

James survived the war, surrendered with the remnants of the Army of Tennessee in North Carolina, and took the Oath of Allegiance on 01 May 1865. He returned to Grainger County, Tennessee, where he married Dicy Malissa Acuff in 1866 and resumed life as a farmer. He remained active in his community and applied for a Confederate pension in 1902, citing his wound at Chickamauga.

James R. Cardwell died on 29 October 1911 and was buried in the Cardwell Cemetery in Grainger County. His presence on the battlefield at Chickamauga—wounded during the largest Confederate assault in the West—marks him as one of the many Cardwell men whose sacrifices defined that bloody, pivotal struggle.

* * *

Private John D. Cardwell – *Company C, 33rd Alabama Infantry (CSA)*

John D. Cardwell enlisted in Company C of the 33rd Alabama Infantry on 27 February 1862 in Elba, Coffee County, Alabama. Born around 1843 in Coffee County, John was the son of Edmund and Nancy Cardwell and came of age in a region where support for the Confederacy ran deep. He was part of a tight-knit rural community that supplied a significant number of soldiers to the Confederate Army, including his younger brother, Benjamin Jones Cardwell, who would join the same regiment later that year.

The 33rd Alabama Infantry was quickly swept into some of the hardest fighting in the Western Theater. The regiment fought at Perryville in October 1862, where it endured a brutal trial-by-fire under Bragg's Heartland Offensive. Later that winter, the 33rd fought at the bloody Battle of Stones River near Murfreesboro, where it suffered heavy losses in a chaotic and inconclusive battle that nevertheless stalled Confederate momentum.

By September 1863, John D. Cardwell and his regiment were veterans of multiple engagements. At the Battle of Chickamauga, the 33rd Alabama was part of Deas's Brigade, Hindman's Division, in Longstreet's Left Wing. On the morning of 20 September, their sector played a pivotal role in executing Longstreet's breakthrough near the Brotherton Cabin—a moment that shattered the Union right flank and turned the tide of the battle in favor of the Confederacy. The brigade advanced through thick woods under heavy fire and helped push Union forces back toward Horseshoe Ridge. The terrain and confusion of battle were extreme, and regiments like the 33rd faced fierce resistance, particularly from Union units under General George Thomas, who earned his nickname "The Rock of Chickamauga" for holding the remaining line.

Company C would have seen its share of that struggle. As part of a coordinated assault, the men advanced amid smoke, shouting, and the deafening roar of musketry and artillery. The Confederate victory at Chickamauga came at a staggering cost—more than 34,000 casualties on both sides—and the 33rd suffered losses along with its brigade and division. Though the battle was a tactical Confederate success, the aftermath set the stage for the battles of Chattanooga just weeks later.

John survived Chickamauga and continued with the regiment into the Atlanta Campaign. However, the harsh realities of war soon caught up with him. On 21 May 1864, during the early phase of that campaign, he was admitted to Ocmulgee Hospital in Macon, Georgia, suffering from Typhoid Fever—a deadly and common disease among Civil War soldiers due to unsanitary conditions and poor water sources. He was furloughed on 07 June 1864, and no further military service is documented, suggesting he may not have returned to his regiment.

He reemerges briefly in postwar records, appearing on the 17 June 1867 Coffee County voter registration roll during Reconstruction. His inclusion verifies that he survived the war, at least into the late 1860s. After that, he disappears from the record. He does not appear in the 1870 census, and no burial site or death record has been found. It is likely that his health never fully recovered and that he died between 1867 and 1870, a casualty not of battle but of the long-term effects of wartime illness and hardship.

John D. Cardwell's presence at Chickamauga places him among the thousands of young Confederate soldiers who fought in one of the Civil War's most savage battles. His quiet postwar disappearance mirrors that of many Southern veterans whose lives were shortened by the aftereffects of disease and deprivation. His service, alongside his brother, reflects the local sacrifices made by families throughout the Wiregrass region of Alabama.

* * *

Corporal John Henry Cardwell – *Company D, 2nd Tennessee Infantry (CSA)*

At just nineteen years old, John Henry Cardwell enlisted on 14 May 1861 in Hartsville, Tennessee, joining Company D of the 2nd Tennessee Infantry, CSA. Drawn from Sumner County, John entered the Confederate ranks early, and his unit would become one of the most battle-tested regiments in the Army of Tennessee. Before ever setting foot on the fields of Chickamauga, Cardwell had already fought at First Manassas in Virginia, endured the chaos of Shiloh, and survived the carnage of Stones River. These early engagements forged a hardened soldier, and by the fall of 1863, John held the rank of Corporal.

The 2nd Tennessee Infantry entered the Battle of Chickamauga on 19 September 1863 as part of Brigadier General George Maney's Brigade within Cheatham's Division. On the second day of fighting, Maney's Brigade launched a fierce assault on Union positions near the Lafayette Road, engaging in some of the bloodiest and most confusing combat of the entire battle. The dense forest, tangled undergrowth, and the smoke of musket fire made visibility poor and coordination difficult. Amid this chaos, the 2nd Tennessee pressed forward under relentless fire, driving back elements of the Union line in the late morning hours of 20 September. The brigade's attack, although ultimately repulsed, helped sustain the Confederate pressure on the Union right flank and contributed to the overall Confederate victory.

As a corporal, John Henry Cardwell would have been responsible for maintaining the line under fire and rallying his fellow soldiers in moments of confusion and danger. His presence in this engagement places him in the center of a desperate and ferocious battle, remembered as the second bloodiest of the war. Although his service record does not detail any wounds, the physical and psychological toll of Chickamauga was heavy, and the fighting was far from over.

After Chickamauga, Cardwell continued with the 2nd Tennessee through the remainder of the war, seeing further action at Missionary Ridge, the Atlanta Campaign, and in the long series of defensive battles that followed. He reappears in the surviving records on 20 July 1864, when he was admitted to Ocmulgee Hospital in Macon, Georgia, suffering from syphilis. By then, the war had ground down many of its veterans, and disease often became as dangerous as enemy fire. That hospital record, listing him as a resident of Sumner County, Tennessee, is the last known documentation of his life.

No postwar records for John Henry Cardwell have been located. He does not appear in the 1870 census, and there are no pension files, burial markers, or probate documents to confirm his fate. It is likely that he died during or shortly after the war, either from illness or its lingering effects. His name stands among those Confederate soldiers whose service ended in obscurity, remembered only through the records of the regiment he served with and the battles he endured. At Chickamauga, however, his presence as part of the 2nd Tennessee Infantry ensured he took part in one of the most significant and savage confrontations of the Western Theater.

* * *

Sergeant John J. Cardwell - *Company D, 3rd Tennessee Infantry (CSA)* - Killed in Action

John J. Cardwell enlisted as a Private in Company D of the 3rd Tennessee Infantry (Clack's), CSA, on 22 May 1861 in Cheatham County, Tennessee. Just seventeen years old at the time, John joined the ranks alongside his older brother, Achilles. The 3rd Tennessee quickly became part of the Confederate forces defending the western reaches of the South and soon found itself thrown into the crucible of war.

The 3rd Tennessee Infantry saw its first major combat at the Battle of Fort Donelson in February 1862, where it suffered heavy losses. John and his brother Achilles were captured during the surrender and sent to Camp

Douglas in Chicago. Achilles died in captivity, but John survived and was exchanged in September 1862.

After returning to Confederate lines, John rejoined the reorganized regiment at Vicksburg. Promoted to Sergeant, he continued serving with the 3rd Tennessee as it reentered the fight in the Western Theater.

On 19 September 1863, the opening day of the Battle of Chickamauga, Sergeant John J. Cardwell was killed in action. His regiment, part of Brigadier General Seth M. Barton's Brigade under Breckinridge's Division, fought in the dense forests and tangled ravines of northern Georgia. The 3rd Tennessee was involved in aggressive assaults against Union lines, pushing through difficult terrain under intense fire. Fighting was often at close range, with visibility limited to yards in any direction. Amid this chaos, John was struck down during the brutal, back-and-forth combat that defined the early stages of the battle. He was killed during one of the few clear Confederate victories in the Western Theater, though the personal cost to his family was immense, having already lost another son earlier in the war.

As with many Confederate dead at Chickamauga, John J. Cardwell was likely buried near where he fell, in one of the mass graves hastily prepared after the battle. He was just nineteen years old. His service, marked by hardship, loss, and loyalty to his comrades, ended in one of the bloodiest encounters of the Civil War. His sacrifice remains a solemn testament to the youth who perished far from home in the tangled woods of Georgia.

* * *

Private William L. Cardwell - *Company H, 24th Tennessee Infantry (CSA)*

William L. Cardwell enlisted on 27 June 1862 in Nashville, Tennessee, joining Company H of the 24th Tennessee Infantry, CSA, alongside his younger brother, Silas H. Cardwell. The 24th was assigned to Cleburne's Brigade, a veteran Confederate force noted for its resilience and battlefield performance. By the time of the Battle of Chickamauga in September 1863, William had likely already fought at Perryville and Stones River, two major engagements that hardened the unit in preparation for what lay ahead.

At Chickamauga, the 24th Tennessee played a significant role in one of the most decisive Confederate victories in the Western Theater. Engaged in brutal, close-quarters fighting as part of General Patrick Cleburne's Division, the regiment helped to drive back Union forces in a series of coordinated assaults. Though details of William's personal experience at Chickamauga are not recorded, his presence with the regiment during this period suggests he endured the chaos and bloodshed of the battle firsthand.

Following Chickamauga, William continued in active service through numerous campaigns, including Missionary Ridge, the Atlanta Campaign, and the bloody Battle of Franklin. He was ultimately captured on 10 December 1864 near Granny White Bridge during the closing stages of the Battle of Nashville. Sent to Camp Douglas, a Union prisoner-of-war camp in Chicago known for its harsh conditions, William endured imprisonment during the final months of the war.

No definitive record of his release, death, or postwar life has been located. His absence from the 1870 census, where his wife and children are listed without him in Smith County, Tennessee, strongly suggests he died shortly after the war, either in captivity or soon after returning home. His final resting place remains unknown.

* * *

Conclusion

The Battle of Chickamauga stands as one of the Civil War's bloodiest and most consequential engagements in the Western Theater. For the Cardwell men—both Unionists and Confederates—it was a crucible that tested their convictions, endurance, and humanity. They served in a wide range of roles: some, like Anthony Warren Cardwell and John Preston Cardwell, were East Tennessee loyalists defending the Union in a deeply divided state; others, such as John J. Cardwell and Benjamin M. Cardwell, fought with the Confederate Army of Tennessee, charging into some of the fiercest assaults in the war.

Their experiences at Chickamauga reveal the depth of family divisions that marked the Civil War. Some Cardwells wore blue, others gray, and a few—like Dennis A. Cardwell and James R. Cardwell—suffered wounds and imprisonment that would mark them for life. Others, like John J. Cardwell, gave their lives on the battlefield. Though they served on opposing sides, what united these men was a shared resilience in the face of hardship and the brutal reality of war. Their presence at Chickamauga not only reflects the regional complexities of loyalty but also provides a deeply personal lens into the human cost of one of the Confederacy's last great triumphs.

Through these individual accounts, we glimpse how the war was experienced not in abstract terms of strategy or politics, but in muddy woods, scattered bodies, desperate charges, and long nights in field hospitals and prison camps. The Cardwell legacy at Chickamauga is not simply one of victory or defeat, but of sacrifice, survival, and the indelible marks left on a family caught up in the violent turning point of a nation's history.

Battle of the Wilderness

In May of 1864, the American Civil War entered a grim new phase. Union General Ulysses S. Grant, newly appointed General-in-Chief of all Union armies, launched his Overland Campaign—a brutal, unrelenting series of battles aimed at grinding down General Robert E. Lee's Confederate forces and forcing the war toward its end. The opening clash came in the tangled woods and scrub thickets of central Virginia, in a place that would earn its name not from any grand geography, but from the savage confusion and bloodshed that defined it: the Battle of the Wilderness.

Fought from 05 to 07 May 1864, the Wilderness was unlike any major battle that preceded it. Smoke from musket and cannon fire lingered in dense forest, fires broke out among the dry leaves, and men fought blindly at close quarters with little regard for formation or maneuver. Visibility was so poor and terrain so disorienting that entire regiments became lost or entangled with friend and foe alike. More than 29,000 soldiers were killed, wounded, or captured during the two days of fighting, with neither side gaining a decisive tactical victory—yet the campaign's strategic momentum would remain with Grant, who continued pressing Lee southward toward Richmond.

Among the thousands who fought in that crucible were eight men bearing the Cardwell name—six in Confederate gray and two in Union blue. Their presence on both sides of the line is a reflection of the war's deeply personal nature, especially in border states and among families with ties to both North and South. These men served in infantry, cavalry, and artillery units, each facing the terror of battle in their own corner of the Wilderness. Some would fall in the fighting or soon after from wounds. Others would endure, carrying the scars of that terrible forest for the rest of their lives.

This chapter recounts their experiences not simply as battlefield movements or regimental summaries, but as personal stories—lives marked by fire, loss, and perseverance during one of the war's most hellish encounters.

* * *

UNION

Private William Henry Cardwell - *Company E, 68th Pennsylvania Infantry (USA)*

By the spring of 1864, William Henry Cardwell was a veteran soldier serving with the 68th Pennsylvania Infantry, a regiment that had already seen hard fighting at Fredericksburg, Chancellorsville, and Gettysburg. Though well into his forties—possibly even his early fifties—William remained with his regiment as it joined the Army of the Potomac in General Ulysses S. Grant's bold new Overland Campaign, a series of relentless battles aimed at grinding down Robert E. Lee's Army of Northern Virginia.

At the Battle of the Wilderness, fought from 05 to 07 May 1864, the 68th Pennsylvania was assigned to the 3rd Brigade, 1st Division, II Corps, under the overall command of General Winfield Scott Hancock. On the morning of May 5th, the II Corps crossed the Rapidan River and advanced into the tangled thickets of the Wilderness, a dense, nearly impassable forest in Spotsylvania County, Virginia. As they moved forward, Union and Confederate forces collided in confused and brutal fighting, with lines of men often firing at enemies they couldn't see through the underbrush and smoke.

During this chaos, the 68th Pennsylvania took part in assaults and counterassaults near the Orange Plank Road and Brock Road intersections—key strategic positions contested by both sides. The heavy woods rendered artillery nearly useless, turning the battle into a series of savage infantry engagements. Despite the confusion, Union commanders managed to hold firm, and the men of the 68th stood their ground under extreme pressure. Although William's personal service record does not mention specific action at the Wilderness, he remained with his unit throughout the campaign and was likely present for the battle.

The Battle of the Wilderness marked the beginning of a new kind of war in the East—one of attrition and endurance. For older soldiers like William, the physical and mental strain of the fighting would have been immense. Yet he stayed with his unit until the final months of the war, surviving not only the Wilderness but also Spotsylvania, Cold Harbor, and the Siege of Petersburg.

William Henry Cardwell's participation in the Overland Campaign is a testament to his resilience. Despite his age, he stood alongside younger men in one of the most grueling series of engagements of the war. He survived the Battle of the Wilderness and continued to serve until his honorable discharge in June 1865. In later years, he was granted a federal pension, confirming the hardships he had endured. William died in 1887 and was laid to rest in Ivy Hill Cemetery in Philadelphia—his service remembered through both records and the recognition of his fellow veterans.

* * *

Private William John Cardwell - *Company G, 183rd Pennsylvania Infantry (USA)*

In the spring of 1864, William John Cardwell was just eighteen or nineteen years old when he found himself thrust into the chaos of the Overland Campaign as a private in Company G of the 183rd Pennsylvania Infantry. Born in Philadelphia to Irish immigrant parents, William had likely enlisted in late 1863 or early 1864, joining a regiment still in the final stages of formation. The 183rd Pennsylvania was one of many late-war units rapidly organized to bolster the Union army's strength as General Ulysses S. Grant prepared a relentless push against Confederate forces in Virginia.

Barely mustered and trained, the men of the 183rd were sent directly to the front lines and assigned to the 1st Brigade, 1st Division, II Corps, under General Winfield Scott Hancock. Their first major engagement came almost immediately at the Battle of the Wilderness, fought from May 05 to May 07, 1864. In this dense and tangled forest near Spotsylvania, Virginia, Union and Confederate forces collided in one of the war's most confusing and brutal confrontations. Visibility was low, movement was difficult, and the thick woods turned into a fiery trap as gunfire sparked forest fires that claimed the lives of wounded men.

Company G, alongside the rest of the 183rd, fought in the area of the

Orange Plank Road and Brock Road—ground that saw some of the battle's heaviest combat. With little combat experience and facing veterans of the Army of Northern Virginia, the new regiment held firm under intense pressure. The Wilderness battle was marked by disorganized attacks, fierce hand-to-hand fighting, and horrendous casualties. For a teenager like William, it was a grim initiation into warfare, made all the more punishing by the continuous marching and lack of rest that followed.

After the Wilderness, the 183rd Pennsylvania moved quickly into further action at Spotsylvania Court House, and from there, into the grinding meat of Cold Harbor and the Siege of Petersburg. Although William's personal military records do not confirm specific details of his role, his presence with Company G during this critical campaign strongly suggests that he experienced the full brutality of the Overland Campaign firsthand.

Sadly, William John Cardwell did not live long after the war. He died in Philadelphia on 08 May 1867, just two years after the fighting ended, at the age of twenty-two. Though the cause of death was not recorded, it is likely that his early passing was tied in some way to the hardship he endured during the war—whether through chronic illness, wounds, or psychological strain.

Though his grave is now lost to time, William John Cardwell's service is a reminder of the youth, sacrifice, and resilience of thousands of men who entered battle with little experience and gave everything they had. At the Wilderness, he stood with the Union Army at the beginning of its final, grinding campaign toward victory.

* * *

CONFEDERATE

Private David Adams Cardwell, Jr. - *McGregor's Battery, 2nd Stuart Horse Artillery (CSA)*

At the age of sixteen, David Adams Cardwell, Jr., joined the Confederate war effort as a private in McGregor's Battery of the 2nd Stuart Horse Artillery—a fast-moving, precision-striking unit that served alongside General J.E.B. Stuart's famed cavalry. By the spring of 1864, when Union forces under General Grant crossed the Rapidan River and initiated the Overland Campaign, Cardwell had already become part of a veteran outfit trained in mobile artillery warfare. Their task was both dangerous and vital: to bring firepower to rapidly changing cavalry engagements and to delay, disrupt, and confuse the larger movements of Federal troops.

As the Battle of the Wilderness erupted on 05 May 1864, McGregor's Battery was drawn into a hellish combat environment unlike any traditional field battle. The dense, tangled undergrowth of Spotsylvania County rendered cavalry charges nearly impossible and complicated the maneuverability of even the most mobile artillery. Yet for Confederate horse artillery units, these conditions demanded even greater speed, discipline, and adaptability—traits that defined McGregor's men. David Cardwell, riding with this elite battery, entered the Wilderness as part of a broader Confederate effort to screen and flank the Union advance through the thickets and ravines.

Though artillery had limited fields of fire in the Wilderness, McGregor's Battery was deployed at key chokepoints to pound enemy movements along the Orange Plank Road and Brock Road. The battery's mission was not only to deliver suppressive fire but also to disrupt Federal advances long enough for Confederate infantry to reinforce threatened positions. These engagements often required crews to unlimber their guns quickly, fire with minimal visibility, and then move again before becoming targets for counter-battery fire or infantry flanking maneuvers. For men like David Cardwell, these moments required sharp nerve and physical stamina under intense pressure.

At one point during the Wilderness battle, Stuart's cavalry and attached artillery—including McGregor's—clashed with Union cavalry under General Philip Sheridan in a series of fast-paced skirmishes that helped shape the course of the wider fight. Although outnumbered, the Confederate cavalry and its accompanying batteries played a crucial role in delaying Federal progress, buying time for Lee's infantry to establish defensive lines deeper in the tangled forest. It was in these chaotic moments that Cardwell's battery provided critical cover, its shots echoing through the thick smoke and pine.

While not wounded at the Wilderness, David Cardwell's later reflection that he was "under fire sixty-seven times" during the war likely includes this brutal engagement. The battery's endurance under fire in such restricted and unpredictable terrain was emblematic of the hardships faced by Confederate artillerymen in the final year of the war.

Following the Wilderness, Cardwell and McGregor's Battery continued through the rest of the Overland Campaign, eventually fighting at Cold Harbor and participating in the long siege around Petersburg. But it was in the Wilderness where David first encountered the sheer destructiveness of

Grant's campaign strategy—a war of attrition fought in conditions that shredded traditional military doctrine. His role in delivering swift and deadly artillery support during one of the Civil War's most savage engagements speaks to the determination and resolve that defined both McGregor's Battery and the young men who served within it.

* * *

2nd Lieutenant Joel Richard Cardwell – *Company H, 13th North Carolina Infantry (CSA)*

Joel Richard Cardwell entered Confederate service on 03 May 1861, enlisting as a Private in Company H of the 13th North Carolina Infantry. At just eighteen years old, his quick rise through the ranks—from Private to 2nd Lieutenant within a year—reflected both his leadership potential and the urgency of the Confederate cause in the war's early days. By the time of the Battle of the Wilderness in May 1864, Joel was a seasoned officer in a regiment that had seen some of the Civil War's fiercest combat, including Second Manassas, Fredericksburg, and Gettysburg.

As part of the Army of Northern Virginia, the 13th North Carolina Infantry served under General Robert E. Lee and was integrated into the Third Corps by 1864. During the Overland Campaign, which marked the beginning of General Ulysses S. Grant's relentless push toward Richmond, Joel's regiment was called into action in the tangled wilderness of Spotsylvania County. The Battle of the Wilderness, fought from 05 May to 07 May 1864, was a brutal clash of armies in a dense forest where smoke from gunfire mingled with the choking haze of burning leaves and brush. Traditional tactics collapsed amid the terrain, and soldiers often fired blindly into the woods, unable to see friend or foe.

In this disorienting and savage environment, Joel Cardwell led his men in some of the most harrowing combat of the war. The 13th North Carolina was positioned to meet the initial Union thrusts and was drawn into sustained engagements along key corridors such as the Orange Plank Road and Brock Road. These positions became scenes of chaotic, close-range combat, as both Union and Confederate soldiers collided in fire-swept thickets and pine groves that offered little protection or visibility.

For junior officers like Lieutenant Cardwell, the battle demanded constant movement, quick decisions, and visible leadership. Communication was nearly impossible in the din of combat, and many officers fell while trying to rally their companies in the field. That Joel survived the battle without being killed or captured is a testament to his discipline and situational awareness under fire. He had already withstood the devastating losses of Gettysburg —including the carnage of Pickett's Charge—and now faced a new kind of trial in the feral terrain of the Wilderness.

Although no specific record confirms a wound at the Wilderness, Joel's continued service throughout the Overland Campaign and into the war's final year speaks to his endurance. The fact that he lived only two years after the war's end and died at the age of twenty-four suggests that his health may have been permanently affected by his wartime service.

The Battle of the Wilderness tested every soldier's will and every officer's capacity for leadership. For Lieutenant Joel Richard Cardwell, it was another chapter in a relentless succession of battles that ultimately shaped—and perhaps shortened—his life. His service in the 13th North Carolina Infantry during that grim campaign exemplified the resolve of Confederate junior officers who bore the burden of command amid smoke, confusion, and carnage.

* * *

Sergeant Pleasant Dalton Cardwell – *Company D, 45th North Carolina Infantry (CSA)*

By the time of the Battle of the Wilderness in May 1864, Pleasant Dalton Cardwell had already earned the rank of Sergeant in Company D of the 45th North Carolina Infantry, CSA. Enlisting on 29 April 1862 at Camp Magnum, North Carolina, Pleasant was only nineteen years old when he entered Confederate service. Over the next two years, he became a seasoned noncommissioned officer, enduring some of the bloodiest campaigns in the Eastern Theater—from Malvern Hill to Gettysburg. By early 1864, as General Ulysses S. Grant launched his Overland Campaign, Pleasant and his regiment were once again called to the front lines to face the renewed might of the Union Army.

The 45th North Carolina Infantry was part of General Robert E. Lee's Army of Northern Virginia, operating under the Third Corps commanded by A. P. Hill. As the Union forces crossed the Rapidan River and advanced into the tangled thickets of the Wilderness in early May, Confederate troops moved swiftly to intercept. The Wilderness was a dismal, foreboding place for a battle—dense with underbrush, pine, and oak, it severely limited visibility, making traditional battlefield coordination nearly impossible. It was a setting that turned orderly formations into chaotic melees and allowed fires sparked by gunfire to consume the wounded where they lay.

Pleasant's regiment was among those positioned to meet the initial surge of Federal forces on May 05 and 06, 1864. Fighting along the Orange Plank Road, the 45th North Carolina was heavily engaged in the brutal and confused skirmishing that defined the battle. For Pleasant, this meant directing his men under fire in close quarters, navigating the choking woods, and reacting swiftly to rapidly shifting threats. The danger was constant; the terrain left little room for retreat, and units could easily be cut off or overrun.

As a sergeant, Pleasant carried the burden of leadership during this grim engagement—relaying orders, keeping ranks steady, and doing his part to prevent collapse under pressure. The 45th held its ground through multiple Union assaults, but at a terrible cost. The battle devolved into near-mindless violence, with many men fighting hand-to-hand or through smoke and fire they could barely see through. Though casualty lists for individual companies at the Wilderness are often incomplete, Pleasant was among those who survived the ordeal and pressed forward with the regiment into the next phase of the Overland Campaign.

Just weeks later, at the Battle of Cold Harbor, Pleasant's luck ran out. On 31 May 1864, during Confederate counterattacks against Union cavalry who had seized the strategic crossroads at Old Cold Harbor, he was shot in the hip —listed as a "V.S. of hip," meaning a gunshot wound. He was taken to Moore Hospital Number 24 in Richmond, but despite medical efforts, died from his wounds on 06 June 1864.

Though his life ended before the war's conclusion, Pleasant's actions during the Battle of the Wilderness remain part of his legacy. He fought bravely in one of the Civil War's most chaotic and brutal battles, leading his men through flame-choked woods and smoke-filled hollows. His endurance through Gettysburg and the Wilderness, and his sacrifice at Cold Harbor, stand as lasting testimony to the grit and resolve of the 45th North Carolina Infantry.

* * *

Private Robert Dibrel Cardwell - *Company I, 2nd Regiment, Virginia Cavalry (CSA)*

At just seventeen years old, Robert Dibrel Cardwell entered Confederate service in August 1863, joining Company I of the 2nd Virginia Cavalry—one of the most seasoned mounted regiments in the Army of Northern Virginia. As a member of Fitzhugh Lee's Division under Brigadier General Thomas L. Rosser, Cardwell was thrust into the chaos and urgency of 1864's Overland Campaign, a brutal series of engagements that included the infamous Battle of the Wilderness.

When Union General Ulysses S. Grant launched his spring offensive in May 1864, Confederate cavalry played a vital role in delaying and shadowing the advancing Union army through the tangled forests of Spotsylvania and Orange Counties. The 2nd Virginia Cavalry, operating ahead of Lee's main force, was among the first to confront Union cavalry and scouts in the dense thickets of the Wilderness. Their early skirmishes helped define the lines and timing of the main engagement that erupted on 05 May 1864.

During the opening hours of the battle, Confederate cavalry under Fitzhugh Lee clashed with Union horsemen in a series of brutal, close-quarters fights along the Orange Turnpike and Plank Road. Though the thick undergrowth rendered traditional cavalry charges ineffective, men like Robert Cardwell dismounted and fought with carbines and pistols, holding ground until Longstreet's and Ewell's infantry columns arrived to strengthen the lines.

Throughout the two-day battle, the 2nd Virginia Cavalry continuously harassed Union flanks, gathered intelligence, and protected supply lines, all while enduring the punishing terrain, thick smoke, and spontaneous wildfires that became the hallmark of the Wilderness fighting. Though not part of the main infantry assault, the regiment's actions were essential in maintaining Confederate mobility and disrupting Federal coordination.

While Robert would not be wounded until the Battle of Cold Harbor a month later, his service at the Wilderness marked the beginning of a relentless period of combat and hardship. His endurance through this grueling campaign, followed by later injuries and illness, speaks to the physical and mental toll faced by cavalrymen on continuous operations. At the Wilderness, Robert Cardwell witnessed firsthand the unpredictable, savage nature of war in the Virginia wilderness, where command structure often collapsed, visibility vanished, and victory was measured by inches of ground held.

As the Overland Campaign ground on into Spotsylvania and beyond, Robert continued to serve despite the mounting strain, demonstrating the resolve that would carry him to Appomattox Court House in 1865. His experience in the Wilderness foreshadowed the bitter, unyielding struggle that defined the final year of the war for Lee's Army.

* * *

Corporal Wade Hampton Cardwell - *Company D, 12th Regiment, Alabama Infantry (CSA)*

By the spring of 1864, Wade Hampton Cardwell had already endured nearly three years of relentless campaigning with the 12th Alabama Infantry. A veteran of some of the Civil War's bloodiest battles—from the Sunken Road at Antietam to the shattered ranks at Gettysburg—Wade entered the Wilderness Campaign as a seasoned soldier and rising noncommissioned officer. When General Ulysses S. Grant launched his Overland Campaign in early May, the 12th Alabama was drawn into the tangled forests of central Virginia to face the opening onslaught in the Battle of the Wilderness.

The Wilderness, fought from 05 to 07 May 1864, was a chaotic and brutal clash fought in deep woods and underbrush so thick that traditional lines of battle dissolved into isolated firefights. Visibility was nearly nonexistent, and men fought at close range with little sense of larger strategy. Wade's unit, part of Rodes' Division within Ewell's Second Corps, was thrust into the heart of the Confederate right on the Orange Turnpike. On the morning of 05 May, the 12th Alabama helped spearhead the initial Confederate attacks, advancing aggressively through the dense undergrowth and catching Union forces off guard.

The regiment's momentum stalled as it encountered stiff resistance, but the Alabamians held their ground in the face of repeated assaults. Trees exploded from artillery fire, smoke and fire hung in the air, and in many areas the forest floor became a charred graveyard. By nightfall, neither army had achieved a decisive breakthrough. On 06 May, Union reinforcements struck again, this time along the Confederate left, and fierce fighting resumed. Rodes' Division, including the 12th Alabama, shifted position to help reinforce vulnerable sectors and prevent a total collapse.

While Wade Hampton Cardwell's individual actions during those days are not recorded in surviving service documents, he was present with

Company D throughout the campaign and later promoted to Corporal—an indication of his reliability and leadership in the field. Surviving the Wilderness was no small feat. The battle claimed more than 29,000 casualties and left lasting scars on those who fought it. For Wade, it was yet another trial in a war that had already demanded years of hardship, sacrifice, and perseverance.

Following the Wilderness, Wade continued with the 12th Alabama through the Overland Campaign, enduring further combat at Spotsylvania, Cold Harbor, and eventually Petersburg. He remained with the regiment until the very end, surrendering with the Army of Northern Virginia at Appomattox Court House on 09 April 1865. His capture on the same day as General Lee's surrender marked the final chapter of his Confederate military service.

* * *

Private Wyatt Cardwell – *Company K, 22nd North Carolina Infantry (CSA)* - **Wounded in Action**

Although Wyatt Cardwell entered the Confederate Army late in the war, his timing placed him directly in the path of one of its most grueling and savage battles—the Battle of the Wilderness. At nearly forty years of age, Wyatt was older than most new recruits and was likely drafted rather than volunteering. He formally enlisted as a Private in Company K of the 22nd North Carolina Infantry, CSA, on 06 February 1864 in Stokes County. The 22nd had already established a reputation as a hard-fighting regiment in the Army of Northern Virginia, having seen heavy action in every major engagement from Seven Pines to Gettysburg. By early 1864, the regiment was struggling to maintain its ranks, and Wyatt's enlistment was part of the larger Confederate effort to replenish depleted units.

Just weeks before the Wilderness Campaign began, Wyatt was hospitalized with rubeola—measles—a common illness in Civil War camps that could debilitate even healthy young men. He was listed as sick on 18 April 1864, but recovered in time to rejoin his regiment for the start of Grant's Overland Campaign. The Battle of the Wilderness began on 05 May 1864 in Orange County, Virginia. The terrain—dense, tangled forest undergrowth—turned the confrontation into a chaotic and terrifying fight. Visibility was poor, formations broke down quickly, and the thick woods often caught fire from muzzle flashes and exploding shells, trapping the wounded in burning brush.

On the very first day of battle, Wyatt was among the twenty-one men of the 22nd North Carolina Infantry wounded during the initial engagement. His wound was not fatal, but serious enough to necessitate evacuation. He was transported to Wayside Hospital in Richmond on 09 May 1864, one of hundreds of injured Confederate soldiers removed from the field in the days after the battle. Like many of the wounded, Wyatt's time in the hospital was not well documented. It is unclear whether he fully recovered or was formally discharged, but he never returned to his regiment. By late 1864 or early 1865, he was marked as "Absent Without Leave," a common designation for wounded or sick soldiers who failed to report back during the Confederacy's final chaotic months.

A year after the battle, in May 1865, the Confederate Bureau of Conscription noted Wyatt's presence in Stokes County and ordered his arrest if he was found without official leave. But the war was over, and no further action appears to have been taken. For Wyatt, the Battle of the Wilderness marked the beginning and end of his active military service—a brief but violent encounter in a forest soaked with fire, blood, and confusion.

Though his time as a Confederate soldier was short, Wyatt Cardwell's experience at the Wilderness reflected the broader desperation and suffering of the Southern war effort in its final phase. A middle-aged farmer conscripted into a crumbling army, he marched into one of the war's most horrific battles and emerged wounded, likely never to serve again. After the war, Wyatt resumed his quiet life in Stokes County. He died in 1894 and was buried in a family cemetery that still bears his name.

* * *

Conclusion

The Battle of the Wilderness did not end in triumph or clear resolution. It was not a glorious charge nor a celebrated victory. Instead, it was a brutal stalemate that set the tone for the long, attritional campaigns that followed. Yet for the eight Cardwell men who fought there, the Wilderness was a defining moment. It tested their courage, exposed them to the full horrors of war, and in some cases, claimed their health or their lives.

For Union soldiers William Henry Cardwell and William John Cardwell, both Irish-born and Pennsylvania-raised, the Wilderness represented their part in a cause they believed would preserve the Union and end slavery. For their Southern counterparts—Robert Dibrel Cardwell in the cavalry, David Adams Cardwell Jr. in the horse artillery, and Joel, Pleasant, Wyatt, and Wade in the ranks of Confederate infantry—the same woods bore witness to their resistance, their hardship, and in Pleasant's case, their mortal sacrifice.

Together, these men shared in a battle that was less about victory and more about endurance. Their paths may have diverged in loyalty, but they converged in the suffering and resilience required of every soldier who fought in that inferno of tangled limbs, gunpowder smoke, and fire. Today, their names endure as part of the greater story of the Wilderness—a battle that exemplifies the Civil War's capacity to bring out both the brutality of armed conflict and the quiet strength of those caught in its grasp.

RESEARCH

Sources

This project utilized the following sources.

***

Ancestry.com is a leading online genealogy platform that offers tools and resources to help individuals explore their family history. Its core services include access to billions of historical records—such as census data, military records, immigration documents, and birth, marriage, and death certificates—which users can search to build family trees. **NOTE: Ancestry.com's DNA testing does not provide Y-DNA results, which are essential for lineage-specific projects such as the Cardwell Family DNA Project. For that service, we utilize FamilyTreeDNA.com, which offers detailed Y-DNA testing suitable for tracing direct paternal lines.** I have created five comprehensive Cardwell family databases on Ancestry.com, all accessible to anyone with a membership. These trees are titled **Cardwell Line I**, **Cardwell Line II**, **Cardwell Line III**, **Cardwell Line IV**, and **Cardwell – Unlinked Lines**. To the best of my knowledge, they represent the most complete and thoroughly researched Cardwell family trees in America to date. Their development has been the result of over thirty-five years of dedicated genealogical research. Please note that many family trees related to the Cardwell family on this platform contain incomplete or poorly sourced research. Be careful when building your own tree! So, when you see the note at the end of a veterans's biography (example: Cardwell Line I - Predicted) you have a place of reference.

* * *

Fold3.com provides convenient access to military records, including the stories, photos, and personal documents of the men and women who served in the military. Its records include Revolutionary, Civil War, World War I, World War II, and numerous other conflicts. They are part of the Ances try.com family of research websites.

I used this service to help develop an Index of Cardwell men that served during the Civil War. Afterwards, the real work began. I accessed individual service records and painstakingly pieced this story together - one man at a time. By reviewing the service records, it usually allowed me to find the date and location of their enlistment or commission, in some cases it provided a physical description of the individual, and the all important muster rolls that showed if the individual was present at given time intervals. They often include information if they were captured, wounded, hospitalized, or deserted.

* * *

Newspapers.com is a subscription-based research platform that provides access to one of the largest online archives of historical newspapers in the world. It is especially valuable to genealogists, historians, and family researchers seeking to uncover personal stories, obituaries, marriage announcements, military service reports, and community events tied to individuals and places. The site features millions of digitized pages from thousands of newspapers, with coverage spanning from the 1700s to the present day. Its powerful search tools allow users to locate names, dates, or keywords quickly, and view high-quality scans of original newspaper pages that preserve the look and feel of the time. Users can clip articles, save them to personal folders, and even attach them to family trees if they also use Ancestry.com, which owns the platform. Newspapers.com provides unique insights into local history that often can't be found in official records, making it an essential tool for bringing ancestors and historical events to life with contemporary detail.

Sources

* * *

Find-A-Grave.com is a valuable online resource for genealogical and historical research, offering access to millions of cemetery records from around the world. The site allows users to search for and view individual memorial pages that typically include the name, birth and death dates, burial location, and often a photograph of the gravestone. Many memorials also feature biographical information, obituaries, links to relatives' memorials, and user-contributed photographs. Researchers can use the platform to trace family connections, verify burial sites, and locate ancestors in specific cemeteries. Additionally, users can create and manage memorials, request photographs, and contribute information to enhance the accuracy and depth of existing entries, making it a collaborative and ever-growing archive of burial records. I have been very successful in requesting a photograph of a particular grave-stone using the volunteer network.

* * *

The National Archives website (archives.gov) offers a wide range of resources for those researching genealogy and military records. Through its online portals, researchers can access digitized federal census records, immigration and naturalization documents, pension files, land grants, and service records from various U.S. conflicts, including the Revolutionary War, Civil War, World Wars I and II, and beyond. The site provides searchable databases, downloadable forms for requesting copies of original documents, and guidance on how to interpret historical records. For military research in particular, it offers enlistment and discharge records, draft registration cards, and prisoner of war data. While not all records are available online, the National Archives serves as a key gateway to locating and ordering physical documents housed at its locations across the country, making it an essential starting point for those tracing ancestral and military histories.

* * *

Wikipedia.org is a free, user-edited online encyclopedia that offers a broad range of information useful to researchers across many disciplines, including genealogy and historical studies. While it does not provide primary source records, Wikipedia serves as a valuable starting point for research by offering concise summaries of people, events, places, and topics. Many entries include bibliographies, references, and external links to authoritative sources, helping users locate more detailed information or original documents. For genealogists and military historians, Wikipedia can provide background on historical figures, military units, battles, and geographic locations, offering essential context to supplement other primary records. However, because content can be edited by anyone, users are encouraged to verify facts through cited references or trusted secondary sources.

* * *

FamilyTreeDNA.com is a specialized genetic testing service that focuses on using DNA to uncover family ancestry and lineage connections. It is particularly valuable for genealogists because it offers **Y-DNA testing (tracing the direct paternal line)**, mitochondrial DNA testing (tracing the direct maternal line), and autosomal DNA testing (which examines broader genetic relationships across all family lines). The site supports surname-based projects, like the Cardwell Family DNA Project, allowing researchers to group individuals by shared genetic markers and identify ancestral lines with greater accuracy. FamilyTreeDNA provides tools for comparing DNA results, viewing genetic matches, and analyzing haplogroups, which can help confirm traditional paper-trail genealogy or resolve questions about unknown parentage and historical family relationships. I served as Administrator of the Cardwell Family DNA Project for twenty years. To gain an understanding of how the paternal lines are connected it is of the utmost importance to get the Y-DNA testing. This needs to be with a living male descendant in the line, either a father, uncle, brother, cousin, or self. Even though I am no longer Administrator of the project, I can be contacted at cardwellhistory@yahoo.com and will assist in analyzing your test results.

* * *

East Tennessee Historical Society (easttnhistory.org), located in downtown Knoxville, Tennessee, offers an exceptional in-person experience for those researching regional genealogy and history. Visitors can access the

Sources

Calvin M. McClung Historical Collection, one of the premier genealogical and historical research libraries in the Southeast, housed within the East Tennessee History Center. On-site, researchers will find a wealth of materials including census records, family histories, rare books, Civil War documents, and local newspapers on microfilm. The center also features exhibits, rotating displays, and staff who are available to assist with research inquiries. Genealogists and historians alike benefit from direct access to primary source documents and expertly curated collections that are often not available online. A visit to the ETHS is a valuable step for anyone looking to uncover the rich past of East Tennessee families and communities. I have countless hours in their archives and appreciative of all the assistance from its staff.

Understanding DNA Testing for Genealogy: How It Works and What It Reveals

Understanding DNA Testing for Genealogy: How It Works and What It Reveals

Over the past two decades, DNA testing has transformed the way people research their family histories. With a simple cheek swab or saliva sample, people can now uncover long-lost relatives, learn about their ancestral origins, confirm family connections, and even solve mysteries that have remained unsolved for generations. But how does DNA testing for genealogy actually work? What kinds of tests are available, and what can they really tell us? This paper will explain the basics of DNA testing for genealogical purposes in clear and simple language, covering how the tests are done, the different types of tests, how results are interpreted, and what they mean for understanding family history.

1. What Is DNA and Why Is It Useful for Genealogy?

DNA (short for deoxyribonucleic acid) is the genetic code that exists in nearly every cell of the human body. It acts like an instruction manual for how our bodies develop and function. More importantly for genealogists, DNA also carries information that is passed down from our parents, grandparents, and ancestors many generations back.

Every person inherits half of their DNA from their mother and half from their father. This means that your DNA is a mix of the people who came before you. Over time, small changes—called mutations—happen in DNA and are passed along through generations. These changes can act like finger-prints, helping us track where someone came from and how they are related to others.

In genealogy, DNA can do things that traditional records cannot. It can confirm or deny suspected relationships, link people to distant relatives they never knew existed, and even suggest ancestral locations when paper records are missing or incomplete.

2. The Three Main Types of DNA Tests for Genealogy

There are three major types of DNA tests used in genealogy: autosomal DNA, **Y-DNA**, and mitochondrial DNA (mtDNA). Each test focuses on a different part of your DNA and provides different kinds of information.

a. Autosomal DNA (atDNA)

Autosomal DNA testing is the most common type and is offered by popular companies like AncestryDNA, 23andMe, and MyHeritage. This test looks at your 22 pairs of non-sex chromosomes—called autosomes—which you inherit equally from both parents.

What it tells you:

• Ethnicity estimates (your ancestral origins by region)
• Close and distant cousin matches (from both sides of the family)
• Possible connections within about five to seven generations

Autosomal DNA is useful for building family trees and confirming relationships with cousins, siblings, parents, grandparents, and more. However, because autosomal DNA gets "diluted" over time, it is less accurate for finding relatives more than 6–7 generations back.

b. Y-DNA

Y-DNA testing focuses on the Y chromosome, which is passed down only from father to son. Since only males have a Y chromosome, this test can only be taken by men. However, women can still benefit by asking a close male relative (like a brother, father, or paternal cousin) to take the test.

What it tells you:

• Direct paternal lineage (father's father's father, and so on)
• Surname studies and ancient male ancestors
• Haplogroup (deep ancestral branch showing where your paternal line originated thousands of years ago)

Y-DNA is especially valuable in surname projects or when trying to confirm whether two men with the same last name are related. Because the Y chromosome changes very slowly over time, it can trace a male line back for hundreds or even thousands of years.

NOTE: The Y-DNA method is what we used in the Cardwell DNA Project, which is with FamilyTreeDNA.com. You will notice that at the end of each biography of a Cardwell Civil War veteran there is a statement that states the specific line identified and if it is Confirmed or Predicted. (Example: Cardwell Line II - Confirmed.) That means that a living, direct-line descendant of that man has taken part in the Cardwell DNA Project and their results confirm them being a member of that specific line.

c. Mitochondrial DNA (mtDNA)

Mitochondrial DNA is passed down from mothers to all their children, but only daughters continue to pass it along. mtDNA testing examines this unique DNA found outside the nucleus of a cell.

What it tells you:
- Direct maternal lineage (mother's mother's mother, and so on)
- Ancient maternal origins and migration patterns
- Maternal haplogroup

Like Y-DNA, mtDNA changes slowly, so it can trace deep maternal ancestry far back in time. However, it's not very helpful for identifying recent relatives unless there is a specific question about the maternal line.

3. How the DNA Testing Process Works

DNA testing is very simple from the user's perspective. After you order a test kit from a company, they send you a package with easy instructions.

Step-by-step process:

1 Collect your DNA sample. This usually involves spitting into a tube or swabbing the inside of your cheek with a cotton swab.

2 Mail the sample back. You send the sample to the lab in a prepaid envelope.

3 Wait for results. It usually takes 3–8 weeks for processing, depending on the company.

4 Access your results online. You'll receive an email when your results are ready. You can log into a private account and explore them on a website or app.

The lab extracts the DNA from your sample and analyzes it by looking at specific markers in your genetic code. These markers are compared to databases of other people's DNA to identify matches and provide ancestry insights.

4. Interpreting Your DNA Test Results

Once your results are in, there are several things you can explore like ethnicity estimates or DNA matches for relatives. For our project, we are concerned with Y-DNA that shows groupings called Haplogroups and direct Y-DNA lineages.

5. What DNA Can Confirm or Disprove

DNA testing is a powerful tool for confirming relationships:

• Is this man really my biological grandfather? → Y-DNA can help.

• Do we descend from the same ancestor? → Y_DNA shared matches can answer this.

• Are two branches of the family related? → Y-DNA comparison can prove or disprove it.

• Was there a break in the male line (a Non-Paternal Event)? → Y-DNA often reveals this.

It's also used to **disprove** assumptions. Sometimes, records are wrong or incomplete. DNA can show that someone listed on paper as your ancestor may not be biologically related. This is especially true in cases of adoptions, name changes, or undocumented family events.

6. Common Uses of Genealogical DNA Testing
a. Confirming Family Trees

Many people use DNA to double-check their family tree. When you find DNA matches who trace their ancestry to the same family line, it confirms your research. This adds another layer of confidence to your genealogy.

b. Breaking Through Brick Walls

A "brick wall" in genealogy is a dead end—like not knowing who your great-grandmother's parents were. DNA can help by identifying genetic cousins who may have records or clues about that ancestor.

c. Finding Biological Relatives

Some people use DNA testing to find birth parents or siblings, especially if they were adopted or separated at birth. The growing size of testing databases makes this more successful every year.

d. Surname and Lineage Projects

Groups of people with the same last name sometimes start Y-DNA projects to explore how they're related. These projects can uncover shared ancestors, migration paths, and even ancient surname origins.

e. Deep Ancestry and Migration

While not always the primary goal, many people enjoy learning about their ancient ancestors and how their family may have migrated across continents over thousands of years.

7. Privacy and Ethical Considerations

While DNA testing is exciting, it also comes with responsibilities and potential concerns.

• **Privacy:** Your DNA contains personal information. Most companies allow you to opt out of public databases or sharing features if you prefer.

• **Unexpected Results:** You might discover things like unknown siblings, family secrets, or non-parental events. It's important to be prepared for surprises.

• **Data Use:** Read the company's terms about how your DNA data will be used. Some allow law enforcement access under certain circumstances.

Being informed and thoughtful before testing is wise, especially if you're inviting other family members to participate.

8. Choosing a DNA Testing Company

Several companies offer DNA tests, each with different strengths, but our project uses the following:

• **FamilyTreeDNA (FTDNA)** – Offers all three types of tests, especially strong for Y-DNA and mtDNA.

For deep paternal or maternal lineage, use FamilyTreeDNA's Y-DNA or mtDNA tests.

Conclusion

DNA testing for genealogy is a powerful, accessible tool that has revolutionized family history research. Whether you're curious about your ethnic roots, want to confirm family tree connections, or hope to uncover lost relatives, DNA offers a window into the past that paper records alone cannot match.

With just a simple sample and a few weeks' wait, you can open doors to a better understanding of where you come from. The science behind DNA is complex, but its application to genealogy has been made easy for everyday people. As the databases grow and technology improves, the potential to discover and connect continues to expand—one test, one match, and one story at a time.

Notes

Delaware

1. https://www.ancestry.com/family-tree/person/tree/182939085/person/212489990449//facts

2. United States Census - The National Archives in Washington, DC; Record Group: *Records of the Bureau of the Census*; Record Group Number: 29; Series Number: *M432*; Residence Date: *1850*; Home in 1850: *Southwark Ward 6, Philadelphia, Pennsylvania*; Roll: 822; Page: *426b*

3. United States Census - Year: 1860; Census Place: Wilmington Ward 5, New Castle, Delaware; Roll: M653_98; Page: 169; Image: 486.

4. United States Census - Year: 1870; Census Place: Wilmington Division 25, New Castle, Delaware; Roll: M593_121; Page: 197; Image: 403.

5. United States Census - Year: 1880; Census Place: Wilmington, New Castle, Delaware; Roll: 119; Page: 317A; Enumeration District: 013

6. United States Census - Year: 1900; Census Place: Wilmington Ward 5, New Castle, Delaware; Roll: ; Page: ; Enumeration District: .

7. United States Census - Year: 1910; Census Place: Wilmington Ward 5, New Castle, Delaware; Roll: T624_146; Page: 4A; Enumeration District: 33; Image: 1307.

8. *Find a Grave*, database and images (https://www.findagrave.com/memorial/129807071/thomas-cardwell: accessed February 20, 2025), memorial page for Thomas Cardwell (30 Aug 1831–21 Feb 1912), Find a Grave Memorial ID 129807071, citing Wilmington and Brandywine Cemetery, Wilmington, New Castle County, Delaware, USA; Maintained by DNealeDE (contributor 47447815).

9. This represents the first confirmed branch of Cardwell Line III traced directly to Lancashire, England. Based on geographic distribution models and the high concentration of Cardwell families in that region, Lancashire appears to have been the ancestral home of the Cardwell family. Other identified branches include: (1) Thomas Cardwell (1744/52–1799) of Granville County, North Carolina, whose descendants migrated across Tennessee, Kentucky, and Alabama; (2) William Cardwell of Philadelphia, Pennsylvania, believed to be Thomas's brother; and (3) Thomas Cardwell (1739–1782) of Dinwiddie County, Virginia.

10. Photo 1.1: Photograph used as originally posted on FindAGrave.com (Memorial ID: 129807071). Original added by DNealeDE on 14 May 2014. Photograph resized, cropped, enhanced, and/or repaired by the author.

Illinois

1. United States Census - Year: 1850; Census Place: District 13, McNairy, Tennessee; Roll: M432_888; Page: 26; Image: 54.

2. Illinois, U.S., Marriage Index, 1860-1920. Ancestry.com

3. United States Census - Year: 1860; Census Place: Township 7 S Range 4 E, Franklin, Illinois; Roll: M653_177; Page: 508; Image: 509.

4. United States Census - Year: 1850; Census Place: Richmond, Philadelphia, Pennsylvania; Roll: M432_820; Page: 203B; Image: .

5. Historical Society of Pennsylvania - Ancestry.com. *Pennsylvania and New Jersey, U.S., Church and Town Records, 1669-2013* [database on-line]. Lehi, UT, USA: Ancestry.com Operations, Inc., 2011.

6. United States Census - Year: 1860; Census Place: Reading, South East Ward, Berks, Pennsylvania; Roll: ; Page: ; Image: .

7. United States Census - Year: 1870; Census Place: Chicago Ward 3, Cook, Illinois; Roll: M593_; Page: ; Image:

8. *Find a Grave*, database and images (https://www.findagrave.com/memorial/272042000/arthur_wellington-cardwell: accessed February 22, 2025), memorial page for Arthur Wellington Cardwell (1818–5 Jan 1887), Find a Grave Memorial ID 272042000, citing Graceland Cemetery, Chicago, Cook County, Illinois, USA; Maintained by Billie (Morris) Barushak (contributor 46923336).

9. United States Census - Year: 1830; Census Place: , Putnam, Indiana; Roll: ; Page: .

10. Ancestry.com. *Illinois, U.S., Compiled Marriages, 1791-1850* [database on-line]. Provo, UT, USA: Ancestry.com Operations Inc, 1997. Original data: Dodd, Jordan, Comp.. Electronic transcription of marriage records held by the individual counties in Illinois.

11. United States Census - Year: 1860; Census Place: Township 8 Range 4, Montgomery, Illinois; Roll: ; Page: 38; Image: 38.

12. Ancestry.com. *Illinois, U.S., County Marriage Records, 1800-1940* [database on-line]. Lehi, UT, USA: Ancestry.com Operations, Inc., 2016. Original data: *Marriage Records. Illinois Marriages*. Various Illinois County collections.

13. United States Census - Year: 1900; Census Place: Otter Creek, Vigo, Indiana; Roll: T623_410; Page: 8A; Enumeration District: 130; FHL microfilm: 1240410.

14. United States Census - Year: 1880; Census Place: North Litchfield, Montgomery, Illinois; Roll: 237; Family History Film: 1254237; Page: 333D; Enumeration District: 152; Image: 0667.

15. *Find a Grave*, database and images (https://www.findagrave.com/memorial/269748470/hezekiah-cardwell: accessed February 22, 2025), memorial page for Hezekiah Cardwell (17 Aug 1829–2 Jul 1910), Find a Grave Memorial ID 269748470, citing Markle Cemetery, North Terre Haute, Vigo County, Indiana, USA; Maintained by J. D. VanDerMark (contributor 46978439).

16. Photo 2.1: Photograph used as originally posted on Ancestry.com. MarieThomersonBarrett originally shared this on 19 Apr 2014. Photograph resized, cropped, enhanced, and/or repaired by the author.

17. United States Census - Year: 1910; Census Place: Taylor Ward 3, Lackawanna, Pennsylvania; Roll: T624_1358; Page: 3A; Enumeration District: 0140; FHL microfilm: 1375371

18. *Find a Grave*, database and images (https://www.findagrave.com/memorial/80495290/james-cardwell: accessed February 21, 2025), memorial page for James Cardwell (4 May 1845–25 Jun 1916), Find a Grave Memorial ID 80495290, citing Hollenback Cemetery, Wilkes-Barre, Luzerne County, Pennsylvania, USA; Maintained by CRB (contributor 47161387).

19. Photo 2.2: Photograph used as originally posted on FindAGrave.com (Memorial ID: 80495290). Original added by Joan Cavanaugh on 06 Feb 2019. Photograph resized, cropped, enhanced, and/or repaired by the author.

Notes

Indiana

1. Ancestry.com. *Indiana, U.S., Marriages, 1810-2001* [database on-line]. Provo, UT, USA: Ancestry.com Operations, Inc., 2014. Original data: *Indiana, Marriages, 1810-2001*. Salt Lake City, Utah: FamilySearch, 2013.

2. Indiana Archives and Records Administration - Ancestry.com. *Indiana, U.S., Marriage Certificates, 1960-2012* [database on-line]. Lehi, UT, USA: Ancestry.com Operations, Inc., 2016. Original data: Indiana State Board of Health. Marriage Certificates, 1958–2012. Microfilm. Indiana Archives and Records Administration, Indianapolis, Indiana.

3. *Find a Grave*, database and images (https://www.findagrave.com/memorial/463199/james_e-cardwell: accessed February 22, 2025), memorial page for James E Cardwell (1836–30 Oct 1876), Find a Grave Memorial ID 463199, citing Dayton National Cemetery, Dayton, Montgomery County, Ohio, USA; Maintained by Sons of Union Veterans of the Civil War (contributor 48353502).

4. Photo 3.1: Photograph used as originally posted on FindAGrave.com (Memorial ID: 463199). Original added by Jim Glidewell on 19 Feb 2018. Photograph resized, cropped, enhanced, and/or repaired by the author.

5. Ancestry.com. *Indiana, U.S., Marriages, 1810-2001* [database on-line]. Provo, UT, USA: Ancestry.com Operations, Inc., 2014. Original data: *Indiana, Marriages, 1810-2001*. Salt Lake City, Utah: FamilySearch, 2013.

6. United States Census - Year: 1860; Census Place: Washington, Hamilton, Indiana; Roll: M653_263; Page: 314; Image: 315.

7. United States Census - Year: 1870; Census Place: Washington, Hamilton, Indiana; Roll: M593

8. United States Census - Year: 1880; Census Place: Washington, Hamilton, Indiana; Roll: T9_281; Family History Film: 1254281; Page: 404.4000; Enumeration District: 38; Image: 0457.

9. United States Census - Year: 1900; Census Place: Denver, Arapahoe, Colorado; Roll: T623 120; Page: 8B; Enumeration District: 125.

10. *Find a Grave*, database and images (https://www.findagrave.com/memorial/53922077/peter-cardwell: accessed February 21, 2025), memorial page for Peter Cardwell (20 Dec 1825–12 Dec 1904), Find a Grave Memorial ID 53922077, citing Fairmount Cemetery, Denver, City and County of Denver, Colorado, USA; Maintained by VDR (contributor 47292775).

11. Photo 3.2: Photograph used as originally posted on FindAGrave.com (Memorial ID: 53922077). Original added by Joyce Escue Culver on 20 Jun 2010. Photograph resized, cropped, enhanced, and/or repaired by the author.

Iowa

1. United States Census - Year: 1850; Census Place: Monroe, Johnson, Iowa; Roll: M432_185; Page: 178; Image: 358.

2. United States Census - Year: 1860; Census Place: Monroe, Johnson, Iowa; Roll: M653_327; Page: 453; Image: 453.

3. United States Census - Year: 1870; Census Place: Monroe, Johnson, Iowa; Roll: M593

4. United States Census - Year: 1880; Census Place: Monroe, Johnson, Iowa; Roll: T9_347; Family History Film: 1254347; Page: 4.3000; Enumeration District: 215; Image: 0386.

5. Photo 4.1: Photograph used as originally posted on Ancestry.com. rcardwell189 originally shared this on 1 Nov 2012. Photograph resized, cropped, enhanced, and/or repaired by the author.

6. Photo 4.2: Photograph used as originally posted on FindAGrave.com (Memorial ID: 101603742). Original added by R Passmore on 02 Dec 2012. Photograph resized, cropped, enhanced, and/or repaired by the author.

Kansas

1. New York Daily Herald, New York, New York. Friday, August 23, 1861, Page 8.

2. United States Census - Year: 1850; Census Place: Hamblen, Brown, Indiana; Roll: M432_137; Page: 224; Image: 71.

3. United States Census - Year: 1860; Census Place: Lecompton, Douglas, Kansas Territory; Roll: ; Page: ; Image: .

4. https://en.wikipedia.org/wiki/Battle_of_Baxter_Springs

5. *Find a Grave*, database and images (https://www.findagrave.com/memorial/29300334/john_t-cardwell: accessed April 8, 2025), memorial page for John T. Cardwell (1845–6 Oct 1863), Find a Grave Memorial ID 29300334, citing Baxter Springs City Cemetery Soldiers' Lot, Baxter Springs, Cherokee County, Kansas, USA; Maintained by Connecting ⍤ Families (contributor 47715879).

6. Photo 5.1: Photograph used as originally posted on FindAGrave.com (Memorial ID: 29300334). Original added by Laura Charles on 18 May 2012. Photograph resized, cropped, enhanced, and/or repaired by the author.

Kentucky

1. United States Census - Year: 1850; Census Place: Division 2, Oldham, Kentucky; Roll: M432_216; Page: 118; Image: 29.

2. United States Census - Year: 1860; Census Place: , Oldham, Kentucky; Roll: ; Page: 817; Image: 300.

3. Ancestry.com. *Kentucky, U.S., County Marriage Records, 1783-1965* [database on-line]. Lehi, UT, USA: Ancestry.com Operations, Inc., 2016. Original data: *Marriage Records. Kentucky Marriages.* Madison County Courthouse, Richmond, Kentucky.

4. United States Census - Year: 1870; Census Place: Spring Dale, Jefferson, Kentucky; Roll: M593

5. Untied States Census - Year: 1880; Census Place: Middletown, Jefferson, Kentucky; Roll: T9_421; Family History Film: 1254421; Page: 74.2000; Enumeration District: 90; Image: 0346.

6. United States Census - Year: 1850; Census Place: Division 2, Oldham, Kentucky; Roll: M432_216; Page: 118; Image: 29.

7. United States Census - Year: 1850; Census Place: District 1, Breathitt, Kentucky; Roll: M432_193; Page: 18; Image: 230.

8. Kentucky Marriage Records, 1852-1914. Online publication - Ancestry.com, Provo, UT, USA: The Generations Network, Inc., 2007.

9. United States Census - Year: 1860; Census Place: Booneville, Owsley, Kentucky; Roll: M653_391; Page: 0; Image: 342.

10. Ancestry.com. *Kentucky, U.S., Marriage Records, 1852-1914* [database on-line]. Lehi, UT, USA: Ancestry.com Operations Inc, 2007.

Notes

11. United States Census - Year: 1870; Census Place: Irvine, Estill, Kentucky; Roll: M593

12. United States Census - Year: 1880; Census Place: Irvine and Forks, Estill, Kentucky; Roll: T9_412; Family History Film: 1254412; Page: 34.4000; Enumeration District: 37; Image: 0259.

13. *Find a Grave*, database and images (https://www.findagrave.com/memorial/75393087/isaac_newton-cardwell: accessed June 1, 2025), memorial page for Maj Isaac Newton Cardwell (27 Sep 1827–Jun 1899), Find a Grave Memorial ID 75393087, citing Frankfort Cemetery, Frankfort, Franklin County, Kentucky, USA; Maintained by Roger Adams (contributor 46562712).

14. Photo 6.1: Photograph used as originally posted on FindAGrave.com (Memorial ID: 75393087). Original added by Roger Adams on 23 Aug 2011. Photograph resized, cropped, enhanced, and/or repaired by the author.

15. Photo 6.2: Photograph used as originally posted on FindAGrave.com (Memorial ID: 75393087). Original added by Tina Toles Wingate on 28 Sep 2011. Photograph resized, cropped, enhanced, and/or repaired by the author.

16. United States Census - Year: 1850; Census Place: Division 2, Oldham, Kentucky; Roll: M432_216; Page: 118; Image: 29.

17. https://www.newspapers.com/article/the-louisville-daily-courier-tolbert-car/124690278/

18. Carroll County, Kentucky Marriages, 1838-1920. Online publication - Ancestry.com, Provo, UT, USA: The Generations Network, Inc., 2000.

19. United States Census - Year: 1860; Census Place: , Oldham, Kentucky; Roll: M653_390; Page: 0; Image: 304.

20. United States Census - Year: 1870; Census Place: Middletown, Jefferson, Kentucky; Roll: M593

21. United States Census - Year: 1880; Census Place: Beat 2, Amite, Mississippi; Roll: T9_640; Family History Film: 1254640; Page: 444.1000; Enumeration District: 44; Image: 0584.

22. An extensive search in the Cardwell family database, examination of census records, marriage records, family histories, death records, etc., both in print and online have not established a connection to any of the known Cardwell families in the Mercer and Anderson Counties of Kentucky. More research is needed.

23. United States Census - The National Archives in Washington, DC; Record Group: *Records of the Bureau of the Census*; Record Group Number: 29; Series Number: *M432*; Residence Date: *1850*; Home in 1850: *District 2, Mercer, Kentucky*; Roll: *213*; Page: *318a*

24. Ancestry.com. *Kentucky, U.S., County Marriage Records, 1783-1965* [database on-line]. Lehi, UT, USA: Ancestry.com Operations, Inc., 2016. Original data: *Marriage Records. Kentucky Marriages.* Madison County Courthouse, Richmond, Kentucky.

25. United States Census - The National Archives in Washington D.C.; Record Group: *Records of the Bureau of the Census*; Record Group Number: 29; Series Number: *M653*; Residence Date: *1860*; Home in 1860: *Jessamine, Kentucky*; Roll: *M653_378*; Page: *61*; Family History Library Film: *803378*

26. United States Census - Year: 1870; Census Place: *District 2, Jessamine, Kentucky*; Roll: *M593_477*; Page: *46A*

27. United States Census - Year: 1880; Census Place: *Plaquemine, Jessamine, Kentucky*; Roll: *425*; Page: *111c*; Enumeration District: *112*

28. United States Census - Year: 1900; Census Place: *Nicholasville, Jessamine, Kentucky*; Roll: *534*; Page: *13*; Enumeration District: *0024*

29. United States Census - Year: 1910; Census Place: *Nicholasville Ward 3, Jessamine, Kentucky*; Roll: *T624_482*; Page: *9a*; Enumeration District: *0037*; FHL microfilm: *1374495*

30. Dodd, Jordan, comp. *Kentucky, U.S., Compiled Marriages, 1851-1900* [database on-line]. Provo, UT, USA: Ancestry.com Operations Inc, 2001. Original data: Dodd, Jordan, comp. *Kentucky Marriages, 1851-1900.* See extended description for original data sources listed by county.

31. *Find a Grave*, database and images (https://www.findagrave.com/memorial/146241437/thomas_w-cardwell: accessed February 21, 2025), memorial page for Thomas W Cardwell (1845–11 Mar 1925), Find a Grave Memorial ID 146241437, citing Maple Grove Cemetery, Nicholasville, Jessamine County, Kentucky, USA; Maintained by Anonymous (contributor 48595604).

32. United States Census - Year: 1850; Census Place: District 2, Hopkins, Kentucky; Roll: M432_205; Page: 153; Image: 307.

33.

34. Photo 6.3: Photograph used as originally posted on FindAGrave.com (Memorial ID: 3183258). Original added by Elizabeth M. on 23 Oct 2016. Photograph resized, cropped, enhanced, and/or repaired by the author.

35.

36. Dodd, Jordan, comp. *Kentucky, U.S., Compiled Marriages, 1851-1900* [database on-line]. Provo, UT, USA: Ancestry.com Operations Inc, 2001. Original data: Dodd, Jordan, comp. *Kentucky Marriages, 1851-1900.* See extended description for original data sources listed by county.

37. United States Census - Year: 1870; Census Place: Precinct 5, Butler, Kentucky; Roll: M593_451; Page: 299A; Image: 41; Family History Library Film: 545950

38. United States Census - Year: 1880; Census Place: Burdens, Butler, Kentucky; Roll: T9_406; Family History Film: 1254406; Page: 377.3000; Enumeration District: 109; Image: 0276.

39. United States Census - Year: 1900; Census Place: Fleenerville, Butler, Kentucky; Roll: ; Page: ; Enumeration District: .

40. United States Census - Year: 1910; Census Place: Magisterial District 5, Butler, Kentucky; Roll: T624_468; Page: 11B; Enumeration District: 39; Image: 1174.

41. *Find a Grave*, database and images (https://www.findagrave.com/memorial/191541013/william_benjamin-cardwell: accessed February 22, 2025), memorial page for William Benjamin Cardwell (20 Jul 1841–1 May 1926), Find a Grave Memorial ID 191541013, citing Morgan-Smith Cemetery, Butler County, Kentucky, USA; Maintained by nathandebora (contributor 49095834).

42. Photo 6.4: Photograph used as originally posted on Ancestry.com. Julyette originally shared this on 5 Aug 2010. Photograph resized, cropped, enhanced, and/or repaired by the author.

43. Photo 6.5: Photograph used as originally posted on Ancestry.com. Eugene Embry originally shared this on 9 Nov 2015. Photograph resized, cropped, enhanced, and/or repaired by the author.

44. Photo 6.6: Photograph used as originally posted on FindAGrave.com (Memorial ID: 191541013). Original added by nathandebora on 21 Jul 2018. Photograph resized, cropped, enhanced, and/or repaired by the author.

45. United States Census - Year: 1850; Census Place: District 1, Breathitt, Kentucky; Roll: M432_193; Page: 33; Image: 259.

46. United States Census - Year: 1860; Census Place: District 1, Breathitt, Kentucky; Roll: M653_357; Page: 0; Image: 390.

47. United States Census - Year: 1870; Census Place: Jackson, Breathitt, Kentucky; Roll: M593

48. United States Census - Year: 1880; Census Place: Jackson, Breathitt, Kentucky; Roll:

Notes

T9_405; Family History Film: 1254405; Page: 604.2000; Enumeration District: 15; Image: 0010.

49. United States Census - Year: 1860; Census Place: Covington Ward 3, Kenton, Kentucky; Roll: ; Page: 627; Image: 343.

50. United States Census - Year: 1860; Census Place: Madisonville, Hopkins, Kentucky; Roll: M653_374; Page: 0; Image: 391.

51. United States Census - Year: 1870; Census Place: Madisonville, Hopkins, Kentucky ; Roll: M593

52. United States Census - Year: 1880; Census Place: Madisonville, Hopkins, Kentucky; Roll: T9_420; Family History Film: 1254420; Page: 289.4000; Enumeration District: 191; Image: 0583.

53. *Find a Grave*, database and images (https://www.findagrave.com/memorial/66862292/w_w-cardwell: accessed February 21, 2025), memorial page for W. W. Cardwell (31 May 1822–26 May 1885), Find a Grave Memorial ID 66862292, citing Grapevine Cemetery #1, Madisonville, Hopkins County, Kentucky, USA; Maintained by Carl Lansden (contributor 46968416).

54. Photo 6.7: Photograph used as originally posted on FindAGrave.com (Memorial ID: 66862292). Original added by Lorna on 06 Nov 2013. Photograph resized, cropped, enhanced, and/or repaired by the author.

Missouri

1. United States Census - Year: 1850; Census Place: Benton, Greene, Missouri; Roll: M432_400; Page: 339; Image: 191.

2. Missouri, Marriage Records, 1805-2002

3. United States Census - Year: 1860; Census Place: Finley, Webster, Missouri; Roll: M653_660; Page: 0; Image: 275.

4. Missouri State Archives; Jefferson City, MO, USA; Missouri Marriage Records [Microfilm]

5. *Find a Grave*, database and images (https://www.findagrave.com/memorial/14235952/alexander_gaines-cardwell: accessed March 1, 2025), memorial page for Alexander Gaines Cardwell (14 Dec 1837–15 Apr 1914), Find a Grave Memorial ID 14235952, citing Cardwell Family Cemetery, Webster County, Missouri, USA; Maintained by Mary Lambert (contributor 46623093).

6. Photo 7.1: Photograph used as originally posted on FindAGrave.com (Memorial ID: 14235952). Original added by Anonamouse on 20 Apr 2011. Photograph resized, cropped, enhanced, and/or repaired by the author.

7. United States Census - Year: 1850; Census Place: Subdivision 7, Claiborne, Tennessee; Roll: M432_874; Page: 293; Image: 118.

8. Missouri Marriage Records, 1805-2002. Online publication - Provo, UT, USA: The Generations Network, Inc., 2007. Original data - Missouri Marriage Records. Jefferson City, MO, USA: Missouri State Archives. Microfilm.

9. United States Census - Year: 1860; Census Place: Big River, Jefferson, Missouri; Roll: M653_626; Page: 0; Image: 212.

10. United States Census - Year: 1880; Census Place: Upton, Texas, Missouri; Roll: T9_739; Family History Film: 1254739; Page: 336.4000; Enumeration District: 127; Image: 0175.

11. United States Census - Year: 1900; Census Place: Upton, Texas, Missouri; Roll: T623 906; Page: 6A; Enumeration District: 148.

12. *Find a Grave*, database and images (https://www.findagrave.com/memorial/26857287/anderson_huffman-cardwell: accessed February 28, 2025), memorial page for Sgt Anderson Huffman Cardwell (15 Mar 1837–18 Nov 1905), Find a Grave Memorial ID 26857287, citing Mincy Cemetery, Mincy, Taney County, Missouri, USA; Maintained by Stone County Skillet (Stone County, Mo) (contributor 49348772).

13. *Find a Grave*, database and images (https://www.findagrave.com/memorial/70836884/john_wesley-cardwell: accessed February 28, 2025), memorial page for John Wesley Cardwell (1822–1900), Find a Grave Memorial ID 70836884, citing Elmwood Church Cemetery, Lonedell, Franklin County, Missouri, USA; Maintained by Diane (contributor 47064130).

14. *Find a Grave*, database and images (https://www.findagrave.com/memorial/69897160/reuben-cardwell: accessed February 28, 2025), memorial page for Reuben Cardwell (1821–16 Aug 1862), Find a Grave Memorial ID 69897160, citing Elmwood Church Cemetery, Lonedell, Franklin County, Missouri, USA; Maintained by Diane (contributor 47064130).

15. *Find a Grave*, database and images (https://www.findagrave.com/memorial/70836832/rial_dow-cardwell: accessed February 28, 2025), memorial page for Rial Dow Cardwell (18 Apr 1824–20 Sep 1862), Find a Grave Memorial ID 70836832, citing Elmwood Church Cemetery, Lonedell, Franklin County, Missouri, USA; Maintained by Diane (contributor 47064130).

16. *Find a Grave*, database and images (https://www.findagrave.com/memorial/26857287/anderson_huffman-cardwell: accessed February 28, 2025), memorial page for Sgt Anderson Huffman Cardwell (15 Mar 1837–18 Nov 1905), Find a Grave Memorial ID 26857287, citing Mincy Cemetery, Mincy, Taney County, Missouri, USA; Maintained by Stone County Skillet (Stone County, Mo) (contributor 49348772).

17. *Find a Grave*, database and images (https://www.findagrave.com/memorial/54708700/james_n-cardwell: accessed February 28, 2025), memorial page for James N Cardwell (7 Dec 1835–25 Feb 1907), Find a Grave Memorial ID 54708700, citing Prospect Church Cemetery, Lonedell, Franklin County, Missouri, USA; Maintained by Nancy (contributor 47082844).

18. Photo 7.2: Photograph used as originally posted on FindAGrave.com (Memorial ID: 26857287). Original added by Gerry Grummons on 01 Jan 2014. Photograph resized, cropped, enhanced, and/or repaired by the author.

19. United States Census - National Archives and Records Administration, 1850.M432, 1,009 rolls. , Hancock, Illinois, roll M432_109, page 423, image 311.

20. Ancestry.com. Missouri Marriage Records, 1805-2002 [database on-line]. Provo, UT, USA: The Generations Network, Inc., 2007.Original data - Missouri Marriage Records. Jefferson City, MO, USA: Missouri State Archives, Microfilm.

21. *Find a Grave*, database and images (https://www.findagrave.com/memorial/62243936/arrelius_l-cardwell: accessed March 1, 2025), memorial page for Arrelius L. Cardwell (4 May 1833–4 Jul 1890), Find a Grave Memorial ID 62243936, citing Combs Cemetery, Luray, Clark County, Missouri, USA; **Maintained by:** Find a Grave.

22. Photo 7.3: Photograph used as originally posted on FindAGrave.com (Memorial ID: 62243936). Original added by Peggy Dochterman on 28 Nov 2010. Photograph resized, cropped, enhanced, and/or repaired by the author.

23. United States Census - Year: 1850; Census Place: Subdivision 7, Claiborne, Tennessee; Roll: M432_874; Page: 293; Image: 118.

24. United States Census - Year: 1860; Census Place: Richwoods, Washington, Missouri; Roll: M653_659; Page: 0; Image: 433.

25. United States Census - Year: 1880; Census Place: Prairie, Franklin, Missouri; Roll: T9_686; Family History Film: 1254686; Page: 206.3000; Enumeration District: 75; Image: 0414.

26. United States Census -

27. *Find a Grave*, database and images (https://www.findagrave.com/memorial/54708700/james_n-cardwell: accessed February 28, 2025), memorial page for James N Cardwell (7 Dec 1835–25 Feb 1907), Find a Grave Memorial ID 54708700, citing Prospect Church Cemetery, Lonedell, Franklin County, Missouri, USA; Maintained by Nancy (contributor 47082844).

28. Photo 7.4: Photograph used as originally posted on FindAGrave.com (Memorial ID: 54708700). Original added by Diane on 26 Jul 2010. Photograph resized, cropped, enhanced, and/or repaired by the author.

29. United States Census - Year: 1850; Census Place: Round Grove, Marion, Missouri; Roll: M432_406; Page: 365; Image: 215.

30. United States Census - Year: 1860; Census Place: Bethel, Shelby, Missouri; Roll: M653_657; Page: 0; Image: 208.

31. United States Census - Year: 1880; Census Place: Mullally, Harlan, Nebraska; Roll: T9_750; Family History Film: 1254750; Page: 440.1000; Enumeration District: 33; Image: 0322.

32. *Find a Grave*, database and images (https://www.findagrave.com/memorial/59466317/john_anthony-cardwell: accessed March 1, 2025), memorial page for John Anthony Cardwell (26 Oct 1834–18 Nov 1898), Find a Grave Memorial ID 59466317, citing Minden Cemetery, Minden, Kearney County, Nebraska, USA; Maintained by T&C Lloyd (contributor 47320243).

33. Photo 7.5: Photograph used as originally posted on FindAGrave.com (Memorial ID: 59466317). Original added by Coffeehouse 3 on 23 May 2011. Photograph resized, cropped, enhanced, and/or repaired by the author.

34. United States Census - Year: 1850; Census Place: Benton, Greene, Missouri; Roll: M432_400; Page: 339; Image: 191.

35. United States Census - Year: 1860; Census Place: Scott, Taney, Missouri; Roll: M653_658; Page: 0; Image: 353.

36. United States Census - Year: 1870; Census Place: Scott, Taney, Missouri; Roll: M593

37. United States Census - Year: 1880; Census Place: Scott, Taney, Missouri; Roll: T9_738; Family History Film: 1254738; Page: 227.1000; Enumeration District: 123; Image: 0570.

38. United States Census - Year: 1900; Census Place: Cedar Creek, Taney, Missouri; Roll: T623 905; Page: 8B; Enumeration District: 129.

39. United States Census - Year: 1910; Census Place: Cedar Creek, Taney, Missouri; Roll: T624_827; Page: 5B; Enumeration District: 0204; Image: 89; FHL microfilm: 1374840.

40. United States Census - Year: 1910; Census Place: Cedar Creek, Taney, Missouri; Roll: T624_827; Page: 5B; Enumeration District: 0204; Image: 89; FHL microfilm: 1374840.

41. Fold3, *US, Organization Index to Pension Files of Veterans Who Served Between 1861 and 1900.* (https://www.fold3.com/publication/57/us-civil-war-pensions-index-1861-1900

42. *Find a Grave*, database and images (https://www.findagrave.com/memorial/24705831/john_hugh_curtis-cardwell: accessed February 28, 2025), memorial page for John Hugh Curtis Cardwell (10 Dec 1829–24 Jan 1922), Find a Grave Memorial ID 24705831, citing Cardwell Cemetery, Diggins, Webster County, Missouri, USA; Maintained by shirley warren (contributor 46961375).

43. Photo 7.6: Photograph used as originally posted on FindAGrave.com (Memorial ID: 24705831). Original added by Anonamouse on 11 May 2011. Photograph resized, cropped, enhanced, and/or repaired by the author.

44. United States Census - Year: 1850; Census Place: District 26, Keokuk, Iowa; Roll: M432_185; Page: 252; Image: 503.

45. United States Census - Year: 1860; Census Place: , Cass, Nebraska Territory; Roll: M653_665; Page: 0; Image: 78.

46. https://archives.byui.edu/family-history/wsmri

47. United States Census - Year: 1880; Census Place: Lewis, Lander, Nevada; Roll: T9_758; Family History Film: 1254758; Page: 319.1000; Enumeration District: 25; Image: 0646.

48. *Find a Grave*, database and images (https://www.findagrave.com/memorial/122665872/ john_t-cardwell: accessed February 28, 2025), memorial page for John T. Cardwell (Jan 1838–6 Apr 1903), Find a Grave Memorial ID 122665872, citing Fir Grove Cemetery, Cottage Grove, Lane County, Oregon, USA; Maintained by Martin Burrell (contributor 46932334).

49. Photo 7.7: Photograph used as originally posted on FindAGrave.com (Memorial ID: 122665872). Original added by Cheryl Cooper on 27 Jun 2015. Photograph resized, cropped, enhanced, and/or repaired by the author.

50. United States Census - Year: 1850; Census Place: Subdivision 7, Claiborne, Tennessee; Roll: M432_874; Page: 293; Image: 118.

51. Ancestry.com: Tennessee State Marriages, 1780-2002

52. United States Census - Year: 1860; Census Place: Richwoods, Washington, Missouri; Roll: M653_659; Page: 0; Image: 433.

53. *Find a Grave*, database and images (https://www.findagrave.com/memorial/70836884/ john_wesley-cardwell: accessed May 31, 2025), memorial page for John Wesley Cardwell (1822–1900), Find a Grave Memorial ID 70836884, citing Elmwood Church Cemetery, Lonedell, Franklin County, Missouri, USA; Maintained by Diane (contributor 47064130).

54. Photo 7.8: Photograph used as originally posted on FindAGrave.com (Memorial ID: 70836884). Original added by Diane on 04 Jun 2011. Photograph resized, cropped, enhanced, and/or repaired by the author.

55. United States Census - Year: 1850; Census Place: Subdivision 7, Claiborne, Tennessee; Roll: M432_874; Page: 292; Image: 117.

56. United States Census - Year: 1860; Census Place: Big River, Jefferson, Missouri; Roll: M653_626; Page: 0; Image: 211.

57. Missouri State Archives; Jefferson City, MO, USA; Missouri Marriage Records [Microfilm] 1805-2002

58. United States Census - Year: 1870; Census Place: Richwoods, Washington, Missouri; Roll: M593

59. United States Census - Year: 1880; Census Place: Prairie, Franklin, Missouri; Roll: T9_686; Family History Film: 1254686; Page: 202.4000; Enumeration District: 75; Image: 0407.

60. *Find a Grave*, database and images (https://www.findagrave.com/memorial/70836161/ melville-cardwell: accessed February 28, 2025), memorial page for Melville Cardwell (30 Dec 1846–24 Mar 1891), Find a Grave Memorial ID 70836161, citing Elmwood Church Cemetery, Lonedell, Franklin County, Missouri, USA; Maintained by Diane (contributor 47064130).

61. Photo 7.9: Photograph used as originally posted on FindAGrave.com (Memorial ID: 70836161). Original added by Diane on 04 Jun 2011. Photograph resized, cropped, enhanced, and/or repaired by the author.

62. United States Census - Year: 1850; Census Place: Subdivision 7, Claiborne, Tennessee; Roll: M432_874; Page: 292; Image: 117.

63. United States Census - Year: 1860; Census Place: Big River, Jefferson, Missouri; Roll: M653_626; Page: 0; Image: 211.

Notes

64. *Find a Grave*, database and images (https://www.findagrave.com/memorial/69897160/reuben-cardwell: accessed February 28, 2025), memorial page for Reuben Cardwell (1821–16 Aug 1862), Find a Grave Memorial ID 69897160, citing Elmwood Church Cemetery, Lonedell, Franklin County, Missouri, USA; Maintained by Diane (contributor 47064130).

65. Photo 7.10: Photograph used as originally posted on FindAGrave.com (Memorial ID: 69897160). Original added by Diane on 15 May 2011. Photograph resized, cropped, enhanced, and/or repaired by the author.

66. United States Census - Year: 1840; Census Place: Greene, Arkansas; Page: 138

67. United States Census - Year: 1860; Census Place: Cache, Lawrence, Arkansas; Roll: M653_45; Page: 138; Image: 139.

68. United States Census - Year: 1870; Census Place: Big Creek, Craighead, Arkansas; Roll: M593

69. United States Census - Year: 1850; Census Place: Round Grove, Marion, Missouri; Roll: M432_406; Page: 365; Image: 215.

70. United States Census - Year: 1860; Census Place: Bethel, Shelby, Missouri; Roll: M653_657; Page: 0; Image: 208.

71. Missouri State Archives; Jefferson City, MO, USA; Missouri Marriage Records [Microfilm] - Title: Missouri, Marriage Records, 1805-2002

72. United States Census - Year: 1900; Census Place: Fresno Ward 1, Fresno, California; Roll: T623 86; Page: 3A; Enumeration District: 10.

73. United States Census - Year: 1910; Census Place: Fresno Ward 1, Fresno, California; Roll: T624_76; Page: 19A; Enumeration District: 35; Image: 52.

74. United States Census - Year: 1920; Census Place: Fresno, Fresno, California; Roll: T625_97; Page: 7B; Enumeration District: 42; Image: 366.

75. Obituary of William McAfee Cardwell. Source: The Fresno Morning Republican, Fresno, California • Sat, Nov 27, 1920, Page 13, Column 2.

76. *Find a Grave*, database and images (https://www.findagrave.com/memorial/263025670/william_m-cardwell: accessed February 27, 2025), memorial page for William M. Cardwell (23 Nov 1837–26 Nov 1920), Find a Grave Memorial ID 263025670, citing Mountain View Cemetery, Fresno, Fresno County, California, USA; Maintained by Pam Witherow (contributor 47364463).

77. Photo 7.11: Photograph used as originally posted on FindAGrave.com (Memorial ID: 263025670). Original added by Pam Witherow on 13 Jan 2024. Photograph resized, cropped, enhanced, and/or repaired by the author.

78. Photo 7.12: Photograph used as originally posted on FindAGrave.com (Memorial ID: 263025670). Original added by Elle Dee on 03 May 2025. Photograph resized, cropped, enhanced, and/or repaired by the author.

79. United States Census - Year: 1850; Census Place: District 1, Calloway, Kentucky; Roll: M432_194; Page: 467B; Image: 513

80. United States Census - Year: 1860; Census Place: Township 39 Range 22, Benton, Missouri; Roll: M653_607; Page: 266; Family History Library Film: 803607

81. Missouri State Archives; Jefferson City, MO, USA; Missouri Marriage Records [Microfilm] - Title: Missouri, Marriage Records, 1805-2002

82. United States Census - Year: 1870; Census Place: Union, Benton, Missouri; Roll: M593

83. United States Census - Year: 1880; Census Place: Precinct 1, Fannin, Texas; Roll: T9_1302; Family History Film: 1255302; Page: 337.2000; Enumeration District: 23; Image:

84. Geneanet - https://gw.geneanet.org/robbie77?n=cardwell&oc=&p=william+nimrod

Nebraska Territory

1. United States Census - Year: 1850; Census Place: District 26, Keokuk, Iowa; Roll: M432_185; Page: 252; Image: 504.
2. United States Census - Year: 1860; Census Place: , Cass, Nebraska Territory; Roll: M653_665; Page: 0; Image: 78.
3. United States Census - Year: 1870; Census Place: Lincoln, Andrew, Missouri; Roll: M593
4. United States Census - Year: 1880; Census Place: Carbon, Carbon, Wyoming; Roll: T9_1454; Family History Film: 1255454; Page: 108.4000; Enumeration District: 16; Image: .
5. United States Census - Year: 1850; Census Place: District 26, Keokuk, Iowa; Roll: M432_185; Page: 252; Image: 503.
6. United States Census - Year: 1860; Census Place: , Cass, Nebraska Territory; Roll: M653_665; Page: 0; Image: 80.
7. United States Census - Year: 1870; Census Place: Sherman and On Rr, Albany, Wyoming Territory; Roll: M593
8. United States Census - Year: 1880; Census Place: Miles City, Custer, Montana; Roll: T9_742; Family History Film: 1254742; Page: 91.3000; Enumeration District: 6; Image: 0186.
9. 1890 Veterans Schedule - Year: 1890; Census Place: Cottage Grove, Lane, Oregon; Roll: 77; Page: 1; Enumeration District: 83
10. *Find a Grave*, database and images (https://www.findagrave.com/memorial/122666024/george_washington-cardwell: accessed May 19, 2025), memorial page for George Washington Cardwell (1836–26 Apr 1891), Find a Grave Memorial ID 122666024, citing Fir Grove Cemetery, Cottage Grove, Lane County, Oregon, USA; Maintained by Martin Burrell (contributor 46932334).
11. Photo 8.1: Photograph used as originally posted on FindAGrave.com (Memorial ID: 122666024). Original added by Cheryl Cooper on 27 Jun 2015. Photograph resized, cropped, enhanced, and/or repaired by the author.
12. United States Census - Year: 1850; Census Place: District 26, Keokuk, Iowa; Roll: M432_185; Page: 252; Image: 504.
13. United States Census - Year: 1860; Census Place: , Cass, Nebraska Territory; Roll: M653_665; Page: 0; Image: 78.
14. Missouri, Marriage Records, 1805-2002. Ancestry.com. Provo, UT, USA. 2007.
15. United States Census - Year: 1870; Census Place: Center, Atchison, Kansas; Roll: M593
16. United States Census - Year: 1880; Census Place: Jackson, Andrew, Missouri; Roll: T9_671; Family History Film: 1254671; Page: 218.3000; Enumeration District: 37; Image: 0441.
17. United States Census - Year: 1900; Census Place: Delaware, Leavenworth, Kansas; Roll: T623_485; Page: 18B; Enumeration District: 85.
18. United States Census - Year: 1910; Census Place: Mill Creek, Polk, Arkansas; Roll: T624_61; Page: 5B; Enumeration District: 99; Image: 618.
19. United States Census - Year: 1920; Census Place: Talihina, Le Flore, Oklahoma; Roll: T625_1468; Page: 6A; Enumeration District: 121; Image: 826.

New York

1. United States Census - The National Archives in Washington D.C.; Record Group: Records of the Bureau of the Census; Record Group Number: 29; Series Number: M653; Residence Date: 1860; Home in 1860: Urbana, Steuben, New York; Roll: M653_863; Page: 440; Family History Library Film

2. United States Census - Year: 1870; Census Place: Bath, Steuben, New York; Roll: M593_1094; Page: 412A

3. United States Census - Year: 1880; Census Place: Bath, Steuben, New York; Roll: 932; Page: 424c; Enumeration District: 158

4. United States Census - Year: 1900; Census Place: Bath, Steuben, New York; Roll: 1163; Page: 18; Enumeration District: 0062

5. United States Census - Year: 1910; Census Place: Constantia, Oswego, New York; Roll: T624_1062; Page: 5a; Enumeration District: 0107; FHL microfilm: 1375075

6. *Find a Grave*, database and images (https://www.findagrave.com/memorial/107451655/lucius_d-cardwell: accessed February 23, 2025), memorial page for Lucius D. Cardwell (1830–11 Sep 1911), Find a Grave Memorial ID 107451655, citing Grove Cemetery, Bath, Steuben County, New York, USA; Maintained by Jean Doherty (contributor 47349305).

7. Photo 9.1: Photograph used as originally posted on FindAGrave.com (Memorial ID: 107451655). Original added by Jean Doherty on 28 Mar 2013. Photograph resized, cropped, enhanced, and/or repaired by the author.

8. United States Census - Year: 1840; Census Place: Rockingham, North Carolina; Roll: 369; Page: 171; Image: 348; Family History Library Film: 0018097

9. United States Census - Year: 1850; Census Place: Snow Creek, Stokes, North Carolina; Roll: M432_645; Page: 137; Image: 276.

10. United States Census - Year: 1860; Census Place: District 2, Polk, Tennessee; Roll: M653_1268; Page: 428; Image: 279.

11. Ancestry.com. *North Carolina, U.S., Marriage Records, 1741-2011* [database on-line]. Provo, UT, USA: Ancestry.com Operations, Inc., 2015.

    Original data: North Carolina County Registers of Deeds. Microfilm. Record Group 048. North Carolina State Archives, Raleigh, NC.

12. United States Census - Year: 1870; Census Place: Mayo, Rockingham, North Carolina; Roll: M593

13. United States Census - Year: 1880; Census Place: Madison, Rockingham, North Carolina; Roll: T9_980; Family History Film: 1254980; Page: 64.1000; Enumeration District: 229; Image: 0130.

14. United States Census - Year: 1900; Census Place: Madison, Rockingham, North Carolina; Roll: T623 1215; Page: 19A; Enumeration District: 74.

15. *Find a Grave*, database and images (https://www.findagrave.com/memorial/54855880/walker_c-cardwell: accessed February 24, 2025), memorial page for Walker C. "Dock" Cardwell (Mar 1833–14 Feb 1905), Find a Grave Memorial ID 54855880, citing Cardwell Family Cemetery, Ayersville, Rockingham County, North Carolina, USA; Maintained by Barbara Spears Pipek (contributor 46800452).

16. Photo 9.2: Photograph used as originally posted on FindAGrave.com (Memorial ID: 54855880). Original added by Jan Bellard on 17 Mar 2011. Photograph resized, cropped, enhanced, and/or repaired by the author.

17. William Newton Cardwell's father is listed as a Printer in the 1850 census in Philadelphia, Philadelphia County, Pennsylvania census. This was a major clue that helped to place his

particular "William" with the correct family. Printer was an uncommon profession for the Cardwell family in that period.

18. *Find a Grave*, database and images (https://www.findagrave.com/memorial/165883974/ william_n-cardwell: accessed February 25, 2025), memorial page for William N. Cardwell (1841–6 Jul 1880), Find a Grave Memorial ID 165883974, citing Mount Moriah Cemetery, Philadelphia, Philadelphia County, Pennsylvania, USA; Maintained by John Cahill (contributor 48323555).

19. Photo 9.3: Photograph used as originally posted on FindAGrave.com (Memorial ID: 165883974). Original added by John Cahill on 22 Jun 2016. Photograph resized, cropped, enhanced, and/or repaired by the author.

Oregon Territory

1. United States Census - Year: 1850; Census Place: District 13, Wapello, Iowa; Roll: M432_189; Page: 423; Image: 361.

2. United States Census - Year: 1860; Census Place: Canyonville, Douglas, Oregon; Roll: M653_1055; Page: 115; Image: 232.

3. California State Library. Ancestry.com. *California, U.S., Voter Registers, 1866-1898* [database on-line]. Provo, UT, USA: Ancestry.com Operations, Inc., 2011.

4. United States Census - Year: 1870; Census Place: Canyonville, Douglas, Oregon; Roll: M593

5. *Find a Grave*, database and images (https://www.findagrave.com/memorial/12624883/ julius_c-cardwell: accessed March 1, 2025), memorial page for Julius C Cardwell (31 Mar 1838–18 Nov 1915), Find a Grave Memorial ID 12624883, citing Oakland Masonic and Old Town Oakland Cemeteries, Oakland, Douglas County, Oregon, USA; Maintained by Merry Watkins Barrett (contributor 48977641).

6. Photo 10.1: Photograph used as originally posted on FindAGrave.com (Memorial ID: 12624883). Original added by Cross-Philpott on 31 May 2013. Photograph resized, cropped, enhanced, and/or repaired by the author.

7. United States Census - Year: 1850; Census Place: District 13, Wapello, Iowa; Roll: M432_189; Page: 423; Image: 361.

8. United States Census - Year: 1860; Census Place: Roseburg, Douglas, Oregon; Roll: M653_1055; Page: 141; Image: 285.

9. United States Census - Year: 1880; Census Place: Myrtle Creek, Douglas, Oregon; Roll: T9_1081; Family History Film: 1255081; Page: 502.2000; Enumeration District: 42; Image: 0143.

10. United States Census - Year: 1900; Census Place: Myrtle Creek, Douglas, Oregon; Roll: T623 1346; Page: 5A; Enumeration District: 57.

11. *Find a Grave*, database and images (https://www.findagrave.com/memorial/9457107/ zachariah-cardwell: accessed March 1, 2025), memorial page for Zachariah Cardwell (5 Apr 1832–25 Dec 1909), Find a Grave Memorial ID 9457107, citing Stephens Cemetery, Myrtle Creek, Douglas County, Oregon, USA; Maintained by Merry Watkins Barrett (contributor 48977641).

12.

13. 9457107
    Merry Watkins Barrett on 13 Sep 2004

Notes

Pennsylvania

1. United States Census - Year: 1850; Census Place: Middletown, Delaware, Pennsylvania; Roll: M432_776; Page: 199B; Image: .

2. United States Census - Year: 1860; Census Place: Chester, Delaware, Pennsylvania; Roll: ; Page: ; Image: .

3. United States Census - Year: 1870; Census Place: Upland, Delaware, Pennsylvania; Roll: M593_; Page: ; Image: .

4. United States Census - Year: 1880; Census Place: Upland, Delaware, Pennsylvania; Roll: T9_1126; Family History Film: 1255126; Page: 259.1000; Enumeration District: 15; Image: 0125.

5. The National Archives at Washington, D.C.; Washington, D.C.; Special Schedules of the Eleventh Census (1890) Enumerating Union Veterans and Widows of Union Veterans of the Civil War; Series Number: M123.

6. *Find a Grave*, database and images (https://www.findagrave.com/memorial/63321666/ calvert-cardwell: accessed February 22, 2025), memorial page for Calvert Cardwell (1820– 11 Feb 1895), Find a Grave Memorial ID 63321666, citing Upland Baptist Church Cemetery, Upland, Delaware County, Pennsylvania, USA; Maintained by Kelly Crane (contributor 49315568).

7. Photo 11.1: Photograph used as originally posted on FindAGrave.com (Memorial ID: 63321666). Original added by Kimberly on 26 Dec 2010. Photograph resized, cropped, enhanced, and/or repaired by the author.

8. United States Census - Year: 1870; Census Place: *Coal, Northumberland, Pennsylvania*; Roll: *M593_1384*; Page: *71A*

9. United States Census - Year: 1880; Census Place: *Bear Valley, Northumberland, Pennsylvania*; Roll: *1163*; Page: *38d*; Enumeration District: *144*

10. *Find a Grave*, database and images (https://www.findagrave.com/memorial/42796532/ john-cardwell: accessed February 22, 2025), memorial page for John Cardwell (29 Oct 1829–31 Jul 1897), Find a Grave Memorial ID 42796532, citing Shamokin Cemetery, Shamokin, Northumberland County, Pennsylvania, USA; Maintained by Grave Hunters (contributor 46978735).

11. Photo 11.2: Photograph used as originally posted on FindAGrave.com (Memorial ID: 42796532). Original added by Carrie on 22 Jan 2012. Photograph resized, cropped, enhanced, and/or repaired by the author.

12. https://gw.geneanet.org/gwpedlow?n=cardwell&oc=&p=john+jacob

13. United States Census - Year: 1840; Census Place: , Delaware, Pennsylvania; Roll: 457; Page: 16.

14. United States Census - Year: 1850; Census Place: Middletown, Delaware, Pennsylvania; Roll: M432_776; Page: 197A; Image: .

15. United States Census - Year: 1860; Census Place: Middletown, Delaware, Pennsylvania; Roll: ; Page: ; Image:

16. United States Census - Year: 1870; Census Place: Hyde Park, Wabasha, Minnesota; Roll: M593_; Page: ; Image: .

17. United States Census - Year: 1850; Census Place: Middletown, Delaware, Pennsylvania; Roll: M432_776; Page: 197A; Image: .

18. United States Census - Year: 1860; Census Place: Middletown, Delaware, Pennsylvania; Roll: ; Page: ; Image: .

19. United States Census -

20. United States Census -

21. United States Census -

22. United States Census -

23. The Philadelphia Inquirer, Philadelphia, Pennsylvania, Sat, Oct 18, 1919, Page 17

24. *Find a Grave*, database and images (https://www.findagrave.com/memorial/190599564/john-cardwell: accessed February 22, 2025), memorial page for John Cardwell (28 Oct 1842–14 Oct 1919), Find a Grave Memorial ID 190599564, citing Westminster Cemetery, Bala Cynwyd, Montgomery County, Pennsylvania, USA; Maintained by Crypt Tonight (contributor 48494116).

25. Photo 11.2: Photograph used as originally posted on FindAGrave.com (Memorial ID: 190599564). Original added by JEC on 30 Mar 2021. Photograph resized, cropped, enhanced, and/or repaired by the author.

26. United States Census - Year: 1850; Census Place: Middletown, Delaware, Pennsylvania; Roll: M432_776; Page: 197A; Image: .

27. United States Census - Year: 1860; Census Place: Chester, Delaware, Pennsylvania; Roll: ; Page: ; Image: .

28. *Find a Grave*, database and images (https://www.findagrave.com/memorial/192347448/robert_e-cardwell: accessed March 27, 2025), memorial page for Robert E. Cardwell (unknown–unknown), Find a Grave Memorial ID 192347448, citing Chester Rural Cemetery, Chester, Delaware County, Pennsylvania, USA; Maintained by Crypt Tonight (contributor 48494116).

29. United States Census - The National Archives in Washington D.C.; Record Group: *Records of the Bureau of the Census*; Record Group Number: 29; Series Number: *M653*; Residence Date: *1860*; Home in 1860: *Philadelphia Ward 19, Philadelphia, Pennsylvania*; Roll: *M653_1169*; Page: *158*; Family History Library Film: *805169*

30. United States Census - Year: 1870; Census Place: *Philadelphia Ward 24 District 81, Philadelphia, Pennsylvania*; Roll: *M593_1411*; Page: *639A*

31. *Find a Grave*, database and images (https://www.findagrave.com/memorial/283516378/william-cardwell: accessed June 13, 2025), memorial page for William Cardwell (1818–Mar 1890), Find a Grave Memorial ID 283516378, citing Cathedral Cemetery, Philadelphia, Philadelphia County, Pennsylvania, USA; Maintained by Crypt Tonight (contributor 48494116).

32. Canada Census - Year: 1851; Census Place: Addington, Canada West (Ontario); Schedule: A; Roll: C-11712; Page: 17; Line: 44

33. United States Census - Year: 1870; Census Place: Whitpain, Montgomery, Pennsylvania; Roll: M593_1379; Page: 459B; Family History Library Film: 552878

34. United States Census - Year: 1880; Census Place: Philadelphia, Philadelphia, Pennsylvania; Roll: 1181; Page: 350A; Enumeration District: 445

35. *Find a Grave*, database and images (https://www.findagrave.com/memorial/67448096/william_h-cardwell: accessed June 13, 2025), memorial page for William H. Cardwell (1819–9 Jul 1887), Find a Grave Memorial ID 67448096, citing Ivy Hill Cemetery, Philadelphia, Philadelphia County, Pennsylvania, USA; Maintained by Crypt Tonight (contributor 48494116).

36. *Find a Grave*, database and images (https://www.findagrave.com/memorial/67448096/william_h-cardwell: accessed June 13, 2025), memorial page for William H. Cardwell (1819–9 Jul 1887), Find a Grave Memorial ID 67448096, citing Ivy Hill Cemetery, Philadelphia, Philadelphia County, Pennsylvania, USA; Maintained by Crypt Tonight (contributor 48494116).

37. United States Census - Year: 1860; Census Place: Philadelphia Ward 19, Philadelphia, Pennsylvania; Roll: ; Page: ; Image: .

38. The Philadelphia Inquirer, Wednesday, May 08, 1867 ·Page 5. Newspapers.com

39. Ancestry.com. *U.S., Headstones Provided for Deceased Union Civil War Veterans, 1861-1904* [database on-line]. Lehi, UT, USA: Ancestry.com Operations Inc, 2007.

   Original data: Card Records of Headstones Provided for Deceased Union Civil War Veterans, ca. 1879-ca. 1903; (National Archives Microfilm Publication M1845, 22 rolls); Records of the Office of the Quartermaster General, Record Group 92; National Archives, Washington, D.C.

Tennessee

1. United States Census - Year: 1850; Census Place: District 14, Grainger, Tennessee; Roll: M432_880; Page: 124; Image: 252.

2. United States Census - Year: 1860; Census Place: District 4, Union, Tennessee; Roll: M653_1276; Page: 443; Image: 206.

3. Ancestry.com. *Tennessee, U.S., Marriage Records, 1780-2002* [database on-line]. Lehi, UT, USA: Ancestry.com Operations Inc, 2008. Original data: *Tennessee State Marriages, 1780-2002.* Nashville, TN, USA: Tennessee State Library and Archives. Microfilm.

4. United States Census - Year: 1870; Census Place: District 14, Grainger, Tennessee; Roll: M593

5. United States Census - Year: 1880; Census Place: District 4, Union, Tennessee; Roll: T9_1283; Family History Film: 1255283; Page: 160.1000; Enumeration District: 113; Image: .

6. United States Census - Year: 1900; Census Place: Civil District 4, Knox, Tennessee; Roll: T623 1582; Page: 21A; Enumeration District: 74.

7. United States Census - Year: 1910; Census Place: Corryton, Knox, Tennessee; Roll: T624_1508; Page: 9A; Enumeration District: 0113; FHL microfilm: 1375521

8. *Find a Grave*, database and images (https://www.findagrave.com/memorial/51089320/alfred-cardwell: accessed May 8, 2025), memorial page for Alfred Cardwell (1 Dec 1843–22 Jul 1913), Find a Grave Memorial ID 51089320, citing Little Flat Creek Cemetery, Corryton, Knox County, Tennessee, USA; Maintained by Paula Via (contributor 47266648).

9. Photo 12.1: Photograph used as originally posted on FindAGrave.com (Memorial ID: 51089320). Original added by Rand Cardwell on 05 Aug 2010. Photograph resized, cropped, enhanced, and/or repaired by the author.

10. Ancestry.com. *Tennessee, U.S., Marriage Records, 1780-2002* [database on-line]. Lehi, UT, USA: Ancestry.com Operations Inc, 2008. Original data: *Tennessee State Marriages, 1780-2002.* Nashville, TN, USA: Tennessee State Library and Archives. Microfilm.

11. United States Census - Year: 1860; Census Place: District 2, Roane, Tennessee; Roll: M653_1269; Page: 124; Image: 254.

12. United States Census - Year: 1870; Census Place: District 2, Roane, Tennessee; Roll: M593

13. United States Census - Year: 1880; Census Place: Eatons Cross Roads, Loudon, Tennessee; Roll: T9_1267; Family History Film: 1255267; Page: 444.3000; Enumeration District: 220; Image: .

14. 1890 Veterans Schedules - The National Archives at Washington, D.C.; Washington, D.C.; Special Schedules of the Eleventh Census (1890) Enumerating Union Veterans and Widows of Union Veterans of the Civil War; Series Number: M123.

15. United States Census - Year: 1900; Census Place: Civil District 2, Roane, Tennessee; Roll: T623 1593; Page: 2B; Enumeration District: 114.

16. *Find a Grave*, database and images (https://www.findagrave.com/memorial/10609217/anthony_warren-cardwell: accessed May 8, 2025), memorial page for Anthony Warren Cardwell (20 Nov 1836–24 Jan 1904), Find a Grave Memorial ID 10609217, citing Oral Cemetery, Oral, Roane County, Tennessee, USA; Maintained by Mary Everett (contributor 49425960).

17. Photo 12.2: Photograph used as originally posted on FindAGrave.com (Memorial ID: 10609217). Original added by Rand Cardwell on 01 May 2008. Photograph resized, cropped, enhanced, and/or repaired by the author.

18. Photo 12.3: Photograph used as originally posted on Ancestry.com. Fred Hecox originally shared this on 13 Sep 2018.

19. Photo 12.4: Photograph used as originally posted on FindAGrave.com (Memorial ID: 10609217). Original added by Hughston Burnheimer on 17 Dec 2024. Photograph resized, cropped, enhanced, and/or repaired by the author.

20. United States Census - Year: 1850; Census Place: District 2, Grainger, Tennessee; Roll: M432_880; Page: 15; Image: 31.

21. United States Census - Year: 1860; Census Place: District 2, Grainger, Tennessee; Roll: M653_1250; Page: 417; Image: 447.

22. Ancestry.com. *Tennessee, U.S., Marriage Records, 1780-2002* [database on-line]. Lehi, UT, USA: Ancestry.com Operations Inc, 2008. Original data: *Tennessee State Marriages, 1780-2002.* Nashville, TN, USA: Tennessee State Library and Archives. Microfilm.

23. United States Census - Year: 1870; Census Place: District 11, Sevier, Tennessee; Roll: M593

24. United States Census - Year: 1880; Census Place: Unitia, Loudon, Tennessee; Roll: T9_1267; Family History Film: 1255267; Page: 415.1000; Enumeration District: 218; Image: .

25. United States Census - Year: 1900; Census Place: Civil District 11, Sevier, Tennessee; Roll: T623 1596; Page: 9B; Enumeration District: 146.

26. *Find a Grave*, database and images (https://www.findagrave.com/memorial/46594213/clisby-cardwell: accessed May 8, 2025), memorial page for Clisby Cardwell (1843–1905), Find a Grave Memorial ID 46594213, citing PA Proffitt Glades-Lebanon Baptist Church Cemetery, The Glades, Sevier County, Tennessee, USA; Maintained by Deanna (Mrs. Virgil G) Cooley (contributor 36950484).

27. Photo 12.5: Photograph used as originally posted on FindAGrave.com (Memorial ID: 46594213). Original added by Richard Jordan on 21 Sep 2011. Photograph resized, cropped, enhanced, and/or repaired by the author.

28. United States Census - Year: 1880; Census Place: *District 15, Davidson, Tennessee*; Roll: *1251*; Page: *261b*; Enumeration District: *075*

29. United States Census - Year: 1850; Census Place: District 8, Grainger, Tennessee; Roll: M432_880; Page: 61; Image: 124.

30. United States Census - Year: 1860; Census Place: District 8, Grainger, Tennessee; Roll: M653_1250; Page: 460; Image: 534.

31. Ancestry.com. *Tennessee, U.S., Marriage Records, 1780-2002* [database on-line]. Lehi, UT, USA: Ancestry.com Operations Inc, 2008. Original data: *Tennessee State Marriages, 1780-2002.* Nashville, TN, USA: Tennessee State Library and Archives. Microfilm.

32. United States Census - Year: 1870; Census Place: District 7, Grainger, Tennessee; Roll: M593

33. United States Census - Year: 1880; Census Place: District 7, Grainger, Tennessee; Roll: T9_1257; Family History Film: 1255257; Page: 456.4000; Enumeration District: 98; Image: .

34. 1890 Veterans Schedules. The National Archives at Washington, D.C.; Washington, D.C.; Special Schedules of the Eleventh Census (1890) Enumerating Union Veterans and Widows of Union Veterans of the Civil War; Series Number: M123.

35. United States Census - Year: 1900; Census Place: Boone, Greene, Missouri; Roll: T623 855; Page: 12B; Enumeration District: 34.

36. United States Census - Year: 1910; Census Place: Boone, Greene, Missouri; Roll: T624_781; Page: 9A; Enumeration District: 17; Image: 986.

37. *Find a Grave*, database and images (https://www.findagrave.com/memorial/50444889/henry_h-cardwell: accessed May 9, 2025), memorial page for Henry H Cardwell (2 Nov 1836–3 Dec 1923), Find a Grave Memorial ID 50444889, citing Kelley Cemetery, Ash Grove, Greene County, Missouri, USA; Maintained by Travis Cott (contributor 47324817).

38. Photo 12.6: Photograph used as originally posted on FindAGrave.com (Memorial ID: 50444889). Original added by OzarkGraves_Cat on 04 Sep 2019. Photograph resized, cropped, enhanced, and/or repaired by the author.

39. United States Census - Year: 1850; Census Place: District 5, Grainger, Tennessee; Roll: M432_880; Page: 38; Image: 77.

40. United States Census - Year: 1860; Census Place: District 2, Sevier, Tennessee; Roll: M653_1270; Page: 391; Image: 278.

41. Ancestry.com. *Tennessee, U.S., Marriage Records, 1780-2002* [database on-line]. Lehi, UT, USA: Ancestry.com Operations Inc, 2008. Original data: *Tennessee State Marriages, 1780-2002*. Nashville, TN, USA: Tennessee State Library and Archives. Microfilm.

42. United States Census - Year: 1870; Census Place: District 2, Sevier, Tennessee; Roll: M593

43. United States Census - Year: 1880; Census Place: Emerts Cove, Sevier, Tennessee; Roll: T9_1277; Family History Film: 1255277; Page: 319.2000; Enumeration District: 179; Image: .

44. *Find a Grave*, database and images (https://www.findagrave.com/memorial/36093627/john_preston-cardwell: accessed May 9, 2025), memorial page for John Preston Cardwell (16 Feb 1846–30 Oct 1891), Find a Grave Memorial ID 36093627, citing Emerts Cove Cemetery, Pittman Center, Sevier County, Tennessee, USA; Maintained by Kathie L. Webb Blair (contributor 47399339).

45. Photo 12.7: Photograph used as originally posted on FindAGrave.com (Memorial ID: 36093627). Original added by S Sill on 20 Apr 2009. Photograph resized, cropped, enhanced, and/or repaired by the author.

46. United States Census - Year: 1850; Census Place: District 14, Grainger, Tennessee; Roll: M432_880; Page: 119; Image: 242.

47. Tennessee State Marriages, 1780-2002. Ancestry.com. Online publication - Provo, UT, USA: The Generations Network, Inc., 2008.Original data - Tennessee State Marriages, 1780-2002. Nashville, TN, USA: Tennessee State Library and Archives. Microfilm.Original data: Tennessee State Marriages, 1780-2002.

48. Tennessee State Marriages, 1780-2002. Ancestry.com. Online publication - Provo, UT, USA: The Generations Network, Inc., 2008.Original data - Tennessee State Marriages, 1780-2002. Nashville, TN, USA: Tennessee State Library and Archives. Microfilm.Original data: Tennessee State Marriages, 1780-2002.

49. United States Census - Year: 1870; Census Place: District 4, Union, Tennessee; Roll: M593

50. United States Census - Year: 1880; Census Place: District 3, Union, Tennessee; Roll:

T9_1283; Family History Film: 1255283; Page: 139.1000; Enumeration District: 112; Image: .

51. United States Census - Year: 1900; Census Place: Civil District 14, Union, Tennessee; Roll: T623 1602; Page: 14B; Enumeration District: 155.

52. United States Census - Year: 1910; Census Place: Civil District 8, Obion, Tennessee; Roll: T624_1514; Page: 17B; Enumeration District: 121; Image: 1022.

53. *Find a Grave*, database and images (https://www.findagrave.com/memorial/81805930/ richard-cardwell: accessed February 25, 2025), memorial page for Richard Cardwell (17 Dec 1845–15 May 1916), Find a Grave Memorial ID 81805930; Cremated, Other; Maintained by Yesteryear (contributor 46575690).

54. United States Census - Year: 1850; Census Place: North of Cumberland and East of Caney Fork Rivers, Smith, Tennessee; Roll: M432_896; Page: 214; Image: 11.

55. United States Census - Year: 1860; Census Place: District 2, Smith, Tennessee; Roll: M653_1272; Page: 276; Image: 25.

56. Ancestry.com. *Tennessee, U.S., Marriage Records, 1780-2002* [database on-line]. Lehi, UT, USA: Ancestry.com Operations Inc, 2008. Original data: *Tennessee State Marriages, 1780-2002.* Nashville, TN, USA: Tennessee State Library and Archives. Microfilm.

57. United States Census - Year: 1880; Census Place: District 8, Smith, Tennessee; Roll: 1280; Family History Film: 1255280; Page: 95D; Enumeration District: 119; Image: .

58. United States Census - Year: 1900; Census Place: Civil District 8, Smith, Tennessee; Roll: T623 1600; Page: 5A; Enumeration District: 97.

59. *Find a Grave*, database and images (https://www.findagrave.com/memorial/122988530/ samuel_s-cardwell: accessed February 26, 2025), memorial page for Samuel S Cardwell (18 Dec 1841–27 Sep 1906), Find a Grave Memorial ID 122988530, citing Cardwell Family Cemetery, Chestnut Mound, Smith County, Tennessee, USA; **Maintained by:** Find a Grave.

60. Photo 12.8: Photograph used as originally posted on FindAGrave.com (Memorial ID: 122988530). Original added by Roy G Spurlock on 01 Mar 2016. Photograph resized, cropped, enhanced, and/or repaired by the author.

61. Photo 12.9: Photograph used as originally posted on FindAGrave.com (Memorial ID: 122988530). Original added by Roy G Spurlock on 27 Feb 2016. Photograph resized, cropped, enhanced, and/or repaired by the author.

62. NOTE: The author has developed an extensive database on the Cardwell family for over four decades, which was throughly checked for a match. Likewise, examination of census, marriage, death, newspaper accounts, etc., have all not provided any additional information of this William. It has to be considered that his birth year or birth county is incorrect on his enlistment records. The possibility exists that his last name could have been recorded incorrectly, as well. Research is ongoing to determine the identity of this Civil War veteran.

63. United States Census - Year: 1850; Census Place: District 2, Grainger, Tennessee; Roll: M432_880; Page: 14; Image: 30.

64. United States Census - Year: 1860; Census Place: District 2, Grainger, Tennessee; Roll: M653_1250; Page: 417; Image: 447.

65. *Find a Grave*, database and images (https://www.findagrave.com/memorial/51152372/ william_c-cardwill: accessed February 26, 2025), memorial page for William C Cardwill (unknown–27 Mar 1864), Find a Grave Memorial ID 51152372, citing Andersonville National Cemetery, Andersonville National Historic Site, Macon County, Georgia, USA; Maintained by John C. Anderson (contributor 47208015).

66. Photo 12.10: Photograph used as originally posted on FindAGrave.com (Memorial ID:

51152373). Original added by Kevin Frye Andersonville Historian on 19 Jan 2017. Photograph resized, cropped, enhanced, and/or repaired by the author.

67. United States Census - Year: 1850; Census Place: District 8, Grainger, Tennessee; Roll: M432_880; Page: 61; Image: 124.

68. United States Census - Year: 1860; Census Place: District 8, Grainger, Tennessee; Roll: M653_1250; Page: 460; Image: 534.

69. *Find a Grave*, database and images (https://www.findagrave.com/memorial/3183018/william-cardwell: accessed February 27, 2025), memorial page for PVT William Cardwell (unknown–22 Jun 1863), Find a Grave Memorial ID 3183018, citing Nashville National Cemetery, Madison, Davidson County, Tennessee, USA; Maintained by Sons of Union Veterans of the Civil War (contributor 48353502).

   NOTE: There is documentation in William J. Cardwell's Civil War records that mentions his name was incorrectly spelled as "Caldwell" on his headstone. The photo of his headstone shows the incorrect spelling, but the Grave number (L.15725) matches records for William J. Cardwell.

70. Photo 12.11: Photograph used as originally posted on FindAGrave.com (Memorial ID: 3183018). Original added by Graveyard Granny on 31 Mar 2019. Photograph resized, cropped, enhanced, and/or repaired by the author.

West Virginia

1. United States Census - Year: 1850; Census Place: District 10, Cabell, Virginia; Roll: M432_938; Page: 62; Image: 125.

2. United States Census - Year: 1870; Census Place: Guyandotte, Cabell, West Virginia; Roll: M593

3. United States Census - Year: 1880; Census Place: Guyandotte, Cabell, West Virginia; Roll: T9_1401; Family History Film: 1255401; Page: 178.1000; Enumeration District: 18; Image:

U.S. Colored Troops

1. Ancestry.com. *1860 U.S. Federal Census - Slave Schedules* [database on-line]. Lehi, UT, USA: Ancestry.com Operations Inc, 2010. Original data: United States of America, Bureau of the Census. *Eighth Census of the United States, 1860.* Washington, D.C.: National Archives and Records Administration, 1860. M653, 1,438 rolls.

2. Ancestry.com. *1860 U.S. Federal Census - Slave Schedules* [database on-line]. Lehi, UT, USA: Ancestry.com Operations Inc, 2010. Original data: United States of America, Bureau of the Census. *Eighth Census of the United States, 1860.* Washington, D.C.: National Archives and Records Administration, 1860. M653, 1,438 rolls.

3. Ancestry.com. *1860 U.S. Federal Census - Slave Schedules* [database on-line]. Lehi, UT, USA: Ancestry.com Operations Inc, 2010. Original data: United States of America, Bureau of the Census. *Eighth Census of the United States, 1860.* Washington, D.C.: National Archives and Records Administration, 1860. M653, 1,438 rolls.

4. *Find a Grave*, database and images (https://www.findagrave.com/memorial/463232/william_p-cardwell: accessed February 22, 2025), memorial page for PVT William P. Cardwell (unknown–20 Mar 1865), Find a Grave Memorial ID 463232, citing Camp Nelson National Cemetery, Nicholasville, Jessamine County, Kentucky, USA; Maintained by Sons of Union Veterans of the Civil War (contributor 48353502).

5. Photo 13.1: Photograph used as originally posted on FindAGrave.com (Memorial ID: 463232). Original added by L.E. on 07 May 2020. Photograph resized, cropped, enhanced, and/or repaired by the author.

Miscellaneous

1. United States Census - Year: 1850; Census Place: , James City, Virginia; Roll: M432_953; Page: 280A; Image: .

2. United States Census - Year: 1860; Census Place: Eastern Division, Henrico, Virginia; Page: 706

3. United States Census - Year: 1870; Census Place: Bruton, York, Virginia; Roll: M593_1682; Page: 526B

4. United States Census - Year: 1880; Census Place: Stone House, James City, Virginia; Roll: 1374; Page: 369B; Enumeration District: 035

5. *Find a Grave*, database and images (https://www.findagrave.com/memorial/14135057/patrick_h-cardwell: accessed March 1, 2025), memorial page for Patrick H. Cardwell (unknown–19 Apr 1908), Find a Grave Memorial ID 14135057, citing Greenlawn Memorial Park, Newport News, Newport News City, Virginia, USA; Maintained by Dawn Bilik (contributor 46839075).

6. Photo 14.1: Photograph used as originally posted on FindAGrave.com (Memorial ID: 463232). Original added by L.E. on 07 May 2020. Photograph resized, cropped, enhanced, and/or repaired by the author.

7. *New York, New York, U.S., Vital Records, Births 1847-1897, Marriages 1847-1903, Deaths 1798-1900* [database on-line]. Lehi, UT, USA: Ancestry.com Operations, Inc., 2023. Original data: *New York City Vital Records, 1798-1903*. Municipal Archives, City of New York, New York City Department of Records and Information Services.

8. United States Census - The National Archives in Washington D.C.; Record Group: *Records of the Bureau of the Census*; Record Group Number: 29; Series Number: M653; Residence Date: 1860; Home in 1860: *Hartford District 3, Hartford, Connecticut*; Roll: M653_78; Page: 202; Family History Library Film: 803078

9. Victoria, Australia, Assisted and Unassisted Passenger Lists, 1839-1923. Ancestry.com. Ancestry.com Operations Inc. Provo, UT, USA, 2009. Series: VPRS 7667; Series Title: Inward Overseas Passenger Lists (Foreign Ports) [Microfiche Copy of VPRS 947]

10. *Find a Grave*, database and images (https://www.findagrave.com/memorial/19458969/william-cardwell: accessed June 9, 2025), memorial page for William Cardwell (1837–7 Jul 1874), Find a Grave Memorial ID 19458969, citing Mitta Mitta Cemetery, Mitta Mitta, Towong Shire, Victoria, Australia; Maintained by woowoo (contributor 49949980).

11. Australia, Death Index, 1787-1985. Ancestry.com Operations, Inc., Provo, UT, USA, 2010.

12. Photo 14.2: Photograph used as originally posted on Ancestry.com. Robert Till originally shared this on 17 Apr 2018.

13. Photo 14.3: Photograph used as originally posted on FindAGrave.com (Memorial ID: 19458969). Original added by shazcardy on 05 Dec 2015. Photograph resized, cropped, enhanced, and/or repaired by the author.

Alton Military Prison

1. Photo UPA.1: Source: https://www.altonjaegerguards.org/confederate-prison-in-alton.html

2. Photo UPA.2: Photograph used as originally posted on FindAGrave.com (Memorial ID: 15857367). Original added by Brian D. McKinney on 13 May 2011. Photograph resized, cropped, enhanced, and/or repaired by the author.

3. Photo UPA.3: Photograph used as originally posted on FindAGrave.com (Memorial ID: 204526604). Original added by CemeteryRegistry.US on 13 May 2011. Photograph resized, cropped, enhanced, and/or repaired by the author.

Camp Butler Military Prison

1. Photo UPB.1: Camp Butler in Action: Original Source: *Photographic History of the Civil War in Ten Volumes*, 1911. Courtesy of Sangamon County Historical Society.

Camp Chase Military Prison

1. By The original uploader was Georgeccampbell at English Wikipedia. - Transferred from en.wikipedia to Commons by Kurpfalzbilder.de using CommonsHelper., Public Domain, https://commons.wikimedia.org/w/index.php?curid=5864894

Camp Douglas Military Prison

1. Photo UPD.1: Digital Library of University of Illinois. https://digital.library.illinois.edu. Original source: *Bygone days in Chicago;* Cook, Frederick Francis; 1910.

2. Photo UPD.2: Photograph used as originally posted on FindAGrave.com (Memorial ID: 7093666). Original added by HallowedGround on 11 Sep 2012. Photograph resized, cropped, enhanced, and/or repaired by the author. NOTE: The memorial sits on a slight incline of grass, is 46′ tall and is a bronze figure of a Confederate infantry soldier, arms folded across his chest, hat in hand, and kit hanging at his side, standing atop a square Georgia granite column. The monument is surrounded by cannons, cannon balls, and a flag pole. The Confederate Mound was dedicated on Memorial Day on May 30, 1895 with President Grover Cleveland and his cabinet in attendance.

Elmira Prison Camp

1. Photo UPE.1: New York State Archives (State). Department of Education. Division of Visual Instruction. Instructional later slides, ca. 1856-1939. Series A3045-78, No. A10004.

2. Photo UPE.2: Photograph used as originally posted on FindAGrave.com (Woodlawn National Cemetery). Original added by Paul E. Newell on 14 Nov 2016. Photograph resized, cropped, enhanced, and/or repaired by the author.

Camp Morton Military Prison

1. Photo UPM.1: By Unknown author - Digital copy posted by the Indiana State Archives: https://www.reddit.com/r/indianapolis/comments/a1t0s3/prisoners_at_camp_morton_c_1863/, Public Domain, https://commons.wikimedia.org/w/index.php?curid=76415501

Point Lookout POW Camp

1. Photo UPL.1: By Sachse E., & Co. - Library of Congress, Public Domain, https://commons.wikimedia.org/w/index.php?curid=46537716

Andersonville Prison

1. Photo CA.1: Wikipedia. Public Domain. https://dlg.usg.edu/record/nps-ande_odea_8d8b9a1b-1dd8-b71c-072d9db5d13cc202
2. Photo CA.2: Wikipedia. Public Domain. http://memory.loc.gov/service/pnp/cph/3c20000/3c22000/3c22600/3c22695v.jpg

INDEX

A

B

INDEX

. . .

CONFEDERATE UNITS

CONFEDERATE VETERANS - See companion book Brothers in Grey

D

G

J

K

KENTUCKY UNION VETERANS

L

M

MISCELLANEOUS UNION UNITS

MISCELLANEOUS UNION VETERANS

MISSOURI UNION UNITS

MISSOURI UNION VETERANS

N

O

OREGON TERRITORY UNION UNITS

OREGON TERRITORY UNION VETERANS

P

PENNSYLVANIA UNION UNITS

. . .

PRISONER OF WAR CAMPS

Alton Military Prison - Union, 195–200

Andersonville Prison - Confederate, 237–241. See also Camp Sumter, Georgia

Camp Butler Military Prison - Union, 201–204

Camp Chase Military Prison - Union, 205–208

Camp Douglas Military Prison - Union, 209–214

Confederate Mound Memorial, 210, 341

Camp Morton Military Prison - Union, 219–222

Elmira Prison Camp - Union, 215–218

Point Lookout POW Camp, 223–228

Prouty, N.D., 14

Provost Marshal, 32, 48

Putnam County, Indiana, 14

Q

Quantrill, William - CSA, 29, 75

R

Rachel Paine, 86, 105, 107

Rains, James - CSA General, 263

Rapidan River, 292, 294, 297

Rash, Stephen D., 47

Reconstruction, 13, 20, 45, 82, 88, 119, 131, 155, 162, 231–232, 243–244, 285

Red Springs, Tennessee, 137

Reese, John J. - U.S. Army Captain Mexican War, 36

Reese, Sarah, 19

Republic County, Kansas, 24–25

Revolutionary War, 36, 100, 309

Rheumatism, 37, 119

Richardson, William P., 207

T

TENNESSEE UNION UNITS

TENNESSEE UNION VETERANS

INDEX

U

U.S. COLORED TROOP UNITS

U.S. COLORED TROOPS VETERANS

V

W

WEST VIRGINIA UNION UNITS

WEST VIRGINIA UNION VETERANS

Y

About the Author

Rand Cardwell has dedicated more than forty years to the meticulous research of his family's American roots, with a particular focus on those bearing the Cardwell surname. He is the former publisher of the *Cardwell Family* website and served as the original administrator of the *Cardwell Family DNA Project*, a role through which he helped uncover vital connections between family branches and deepened the understanding of Cardwell lineage across generations.

Known for his generous spirit, Cardwell has long assisted fellow researchers and distant relatives with their own family history efforts, always eager to share records, insight, and guidance. His reputation in genealogical circles is grounded not only in his extensive knowledge but in his collaborative approach to the often solitary pursuit of ancestry.

This book is the culmination of decades of work—painstaking documentation, archival digging, and personal correspondence—all united by a single purpose: to preserve the stories of Cardwell men who served in the American Civil War and to honor their legacy for future generations.

Though genealogy has long been his central passion, Cardwell is also a writer and thinker of diverse interests. He is the author of the *Becoming Stoic* series, a multi-volume exploration of Stoic philosophy drawn from his own lived experience and more than twenty-five years of study. His published works also include titles on martial arts history and poetic reflection, most notably *Unhurried: and other poems*.

He resides in East Tennessee, where he balances his time between historical research, writing, trout fishing, and enjoying life's simple pleasures.

f

Also by Rand Cardwell

The Western Bubishi

The 36 Deadly Bubishi Points

Unhurried: and other poems

The Becoming Stoic Series:

Becoming Stoic: Lessons on Perception

Becoming Stoic: Lessons on Action

Becoming Stoic: Lessons on Will

* * *

New titles will be announced at:

www.randcardwell.com

www.ingramcontent.com/pod-product-compliance
Lightning Source LLC
Chambersburg PA
CBHW080803120626
46556CB00009B/3206